TART

TART

Misadventures of an Anonymous Chef

Slutty Cheff

MARYSUE
RUCCI
BOOKS

New York   Amsterdam/Antwerp   London
Toronto   Sydney/Melbourne   New Delhi

An Imprint of Simon & Schuster, LLC
1230 Avenue of the Americas
New York, NY 10020

For more than 100 years, Simon & Schuster has championed authors and the stories they create. By respecting the copyright of an author's intellectual property, you enable Simon & Schuster and the author to continue publishing exceptional books for years to come. We thank you for supporting the author's copyright by purchasing an authorized edition of this book.

No amount of this book may be reproduced or stored in any format, nor may it be uploaded to any website, database, language-learning model, or other repository, retrieval, or artificial intelligence system without express permission. All rights reserved. Inquiries may be directed to Simon & Schuster, 1230 Avenue of the Americas, New York, NY 10020 or permissions@simonandschuster.com.

Copyright © 2025 by Slutty Cheff

Originally published in Great Britain in 2025 by Bloomsbury Publishing

All rights reserved, including the right to reproduce this book or portions thereof in any form whatsoever. For information, address Simon Element Subsidiary Rights Department, 1230 Avenue of the Americas, New York, NY 10020.

First Marysue Rucci Books hardcover edition August 2025

MARYSUE RUCCI BOOKS and colophon are trademarks of Simon & Schuster, LLC

Simon & Schuster strongly believes in freedom of expression and stands against censorship in all its forms. For more information, visit BooksBelong.com.

For information about special discounts for bulk purchases, please contact Simon & Schuster Special Sales at 1-866-506-1949 or business@simonandschuster.com.

The Simon & Schuster Speakers Bureau can bring authors to your live event. For more information or to book an event, contact the Simon & Schuster Speakers Bureau at 1-866-248-3049 or visit our website at www.simonspeakers.com.

Manufactured in the United States of America

1 3 5 7 9 10 8 6 4 2

Library of Congress Cataloging-in-Publication Data has been applied for.

ISBN 978-1-6680-7022-2
ISBN 978-1-6680-7025-3 (ebook)

For Monica and her wicked ways

Ignorance is like a delicate exotic fruit; touch it and the bloom is gone.

—Oscar Wilde

CONTENTS

	Preface: Too Much	xi
1	The Civilians Don't Know I'm a Chef	1
2	An In-Denial Dalliance	39
3	Massive Attack	73
4	Michelin Star Pussy Juice	77
5	Eating Kebabs in London	107
6	Going Down	145
7	In Love with Andrew Edmunds	169
8	Ready Steady Cock	191
9	Achy Breaky Artichoke Hearts	213
10	Hot Soapy Daydreams	237
11	Empty Tables	261
12	Tart	283
	Acknowledgments	311

Preface
Too Much

I'm in the kitchen. I'm scared.

How did I get here? This is too much.

The last time I felt like this I was at school. A teacher told me off in the playground. My body was eaten up by fear until, suddenly, it happened: I pissed my pants.

I'm scared it's going to happen again. I doubt my Head Chef would express the same guilt and sorrow that Mrs. Morris did.

"You've really fucked up!" my Head Chef shouts at me.

I swallow and tighten my stomach muscles to secure the floodgates. This is too much.

"Yes, sorry, Chef." I muster these words from the bottom of my throat, the tiny space buried beneath the solid rock of tears wedged in my esophagus.

The fear is leaving my body but here comes the bloody emotion. This is too much. My eyelids are filling up with teardrops but I am blinking them away. I'm not going to let myself cry, not a chance. Mrs. Morris might've defeated me, but I was a kid then and I'm a woman now. I'm stronger; I'm a chef.

"Don't do that again," he says while grimacing at me as if I am the shit on his shoe.

Okay, he's walking away, thank God. Fucking hell. This is too much.

I look down at my workbench and make my hands move to distract me from my dread. I can't think, so I just start cleaning my knives to look busy. My heart is still beating fast. I'm embarrassed. The other chefs are silent; they don't know how I—the only Woman in the kitchen—am going to react to my first big bollocking from our Head Chef.

I can't handle this. It's too much. I need to leave the kitchen. I'm going to subtly excuse myself and go and have a cigarette. That's what I'll do.

I descend the spiraling kitchen stairs with nervous knees; they feel wobbly like jellied stock. I might trip and fall down. Maybe that would be a good thing: a couple of broken legs would be a valid enough excuse to leave early, right?

I perch outside on the pavement in my chef whites, roll a cigarette with shaky hands, and light it. I inhale and take a deep breath.

This job is too fucking much. How did I get here? I think about my old life.

I used to be an office worker wearing tight arse-hugging jumpsuits, not baggy chef trousers designed specifically for men, tailored so there is ample space for my nonexistent balls and little to no space for my child-bearing hips and plump arse. My hair used to be long and flowing, not tied up and greasy. I used to have an hour-long lunch break, not four minutes to smoke a cigarette during a ten-hour shift. My gut used to be filled with cardboard-boxed snacks from expensive eateries; now my gut is filled with so much tension that I can barely breathe. It's too much.

I take another inhale of my cigarette and my breathing calms down a little. Under my breath, with my head in my hands, I mutter, "Fucking hell," and the corners of my lips turn upward. You have to laugh. I giggle for a moment, thinking about my dire state of affairs.

I take another drag on my roll-up. Lovely. That's better.

My body is coming down from the adrenaline and I am feeling giddy. I made it out alive. I didn't cry. And I didn't do the other dreaded thing (piss my pants). What a result! The relief that my Head Chef is no longer hurling insults in my ear feels so good that it was almost worth the bollocking. What a thrill. The cigarette smoke is filling my head with delirious pleasure. This is too much.

As I sit on the pavement smoking, commuters walk by. Would I rather be in their shiny shoes instead of my mangled Crocs? Would I rather have a normal job and a normal life? Is being a chef too much for me?

Yes, it is. But the thing is, I like too much and I always have. Not just in my work, but in my personal life too. It is the lack of things that I cannot stand. I don't want my job to be a means to an end; I want it to be a pilgrimage of passion. I don't want my sex life to be active; I want it to be award-winning. I don't want my love to be lackluster; I want it to be life-changing. I don't want my oyster to be the size of a little snot rocket; I want it to be a fleshy bulbous pearl swimming in an iridescent sea of salty juice.

I am a greedy person at my core. I don't want to eat; I want to devour. I don't want to have dinner; I want to dine. To me, food is not for nourishment or survival but for pleasure. My appetite exceeds that of the average Western woman. It is more like that of a starved pig, employed by Brick Top to crunch through human bones as if they're butter. And with love, I am not capable of crushes, only infatuation. I don't want him to kiss me; I want him to grip my jaw, glue his lips to mine, and inhale all the hot air that is trapped in my body. I don't want to copulate; I want to be consumed. I don't want an orgasm; I want a paroxysm of pleasure. I don't want to go on dates with polite perfumed men; I want my partner to be a wild boar, where I am a little scared of just how dangerous he could be. I want to risk it all for a slice of his wild boar sausage.

I take another drag of my cigarette and my heart fills with the satisfaction of survival. I am addicted to this feeling.

Even if working in a kitchen turns out to be too much, I suspect a life without restaurants would've always been too little. Being a chef is more than a job for me; it is a means to wrangle the angst in my body, to harness my desire for too much. Being shouted at was scary, but the feeling I have now is euphoric. If there is a storm on the horizon, I don't want it to arrive in the form of bleak rainfall; I want to be awoken by a monstrous thrash of thunder and a biblical bolt of lightning. Like a true masochist, there's a bit of me that enjoys a challenge; it consumes me like heartbreak or heartburn. Like a good stock, the longer I simmer in my struggle, the richer and more flavorful my story will be.

I take the last toke of my cigarette, stub it out, and stand up. I walk up the stairway and pass through the towering doors of my hell, or is it my heaven?

*A few years earlier,
at my first trial shift*

1

The Civilians Don't Know I'm a Chef

OCTOBER

Against the strict guidance of my teacher at cooking school, I have booked myself a trial shift in a restaurant tonight.

My teacher believes it is vital for us to postpone any proper restaurant work until we have graduated from her esteemed course; with her floral feminine aesthetic, she likes to present as Miss Honey, but in her soul, she is more like Miss Trunchbull. Her name is Helen.

She tells us that cooking at a restaurant will be too tiring, and it will disrupt our focus, distracting us from what's really important: her lessons. Helen reminds my class of this fact while she is performing a painstaking procedure on a shiny white Christmas cake. Her shaky hand grips a pair of tweezers, which she uses to lift up a naff, bright-green Christmas tree made of fondant, sticking it onto the white marzipan that is wrapped around the cake. Tomorrow we will attempt making this cake ourselves, but only once we have donned our culinary school costume: checked trousers, starchy chef whites, a silly little white hat, and a ridiculously pompous neckerchief. Perhaps part of the reason this course is so extortionately expensive is because of the merch that comes with it.

I am sitting behind a desk in a classroom full of adolescent adults, peeling my eyes open; it seems I have been in dreamland for a minute or two. But I love cooking—I *need* cooking—and I want to be a chef. When I quit my office job, this felt like the obvious, though expensive, next step. I thought about going straight into working for a restaurant, but I was too scared to make the drastic switch from my luxury lifestyle; to go from gazing out of skyscraper windows while eating nutritious cardboard snacks straight to a smoggy kitchen with raucous boys and big hunks of meat. It felt like too big a change, so I opted for the slower, less intimidating path that is cooking school, a great privilege which the majority of people can't afford.

In the classroom I try to be a good student. I write down all the notes from class and I turn up on time, but the truth is, I am one month into a three-month course and I am deeply bored. I expected to be doing a lot more actual cooking, and I expected to be doing the cooking with a group of hot, rugged aspiring chefs; but I'm not. It turns out hot, rugged aspiring chefs don't have a spare ten grand knocking about to learn how to perfect a mini quiche. It turns out they are rugged because they are tired and overworked, not enjoying a tea and biscuit break between cake-decorating classes. I was impulsive in my decision to sign up for cooking school; I paid the deposit in the midst of a depressive episode this summer just gone, and now here I am, spending my days with a group of teens fresh from their gap year. Many of them don't have any interest in being a restaurant chef; instead they have plans to do private catering for rich families on ski seasons, or dreams of putting on dairy-free spreads at all-white weddings. I am not totally clear on my aspirations; I just know I want to fill all my time with cooking good food, and working in restaurants sounds like the obvious way to do that. So, much to Helen's dismay, yesterday I organized a trial shift at a restaurant, and I will be heading there straight after school today. No time like the present, I suppose.

I was on the phone with my oldest friend and confidante, Ruby, when I pulled the trigger.

We browsed restaurants online, mainly on Instagram. Unlike with corporate job descriptions, there was no lengthy list of responsibilities or desired attitudes there; you just needed to want to cook, and many of the entry-level jobs actually specified that there was no experience required. I delved into the different restaurant pages, analyzing the curated pictures of the atmosphere, staring into the eyes of the Head Chefs and trying to determine if they would be nice to a lowly woman like me. I looked at pictures of the staff, carefully scanning the lineup of men to see if there were any hot chefs to be found, the ones I thought I'd meet at cooking school. Then I read the reviews online. I read Giles Coren's thoughts, and Tim Hayward's and Jay Rayner's, Jimi Famurewa's and Marina O'Loughlin's. I couldn't escape my craving for status; I wanted to work at a place that would make me feel like a proper chef.

Some places looked *too* modern and neat. I didn't want anything that sleek. I wanted a bit of the chaos and delinquency that Anthony Bourdain talked about.

Ruby and I focused for a bit on central London's glitz and glamour, then we turned northward. I didn't want anything too stale, either, where the custom has remained the same since the restaurant opened: old white guys in suits speaking too loudly about their second properties. Where is the thrill in cooking for them? Can they even taste anything with their chubby, Côtes-du-Rhône-and-cigar-soaked tongues?

Then I found it: a chic little restaurant in Islington with a handsome Head Chef at the helm. It had opened a year ago and was described in one headline as: "A thrilling menu of phenomenally cooked modern dishes, served with warmth and charm. The crab bottarga pasta is otherworldy." The menu was embellished with ingredients I had never heard of, like bottarga and bonito. It was just a Tube ride away from my parents' house, where I am living due to the fact that I used all my corporate savings on cooking school. So it would be easy to get to. The restaurant was celebrated by all the influential food people in London, and the customers in the pictures online looked fun and young and hot. The Head Chef had recently uploaded a post saying the restaurant was looking for a prep chef, so I messaged him asking if I could come for a trial shift. I ended the call with Ruby and put down my phone, not expecting to hear back from the restaurant until tomorrow, seeing as it was 9 p.m.

My phone buzzed within seconds. He'd replied. The job ad had stated that experience was preferred, but the Head Chef didn't ask me anything. He simply said:

Great, can you come in for a trial tomorrow evening? 5 p.m.?

I told Ruby. I deliberated for a while and gave excuses to Ruby as to why I might not be ready to do it.

"Five p.m.? I'll have to go there straight after cooking school. I won't have time for a shower."

"So?" she said. "I don't think chefs are famous for clean bodies."

"What if I'm shit? Or what if I'm too shy to speak?" I asked her.

In the past year I've struggled in ways my friends don't really know about, apart from Ruby. I started having panic attacks often, and was so depressed I couldn't really get out of bed. I guess that was part of the reason I moved home, too: to be doted on by my parents. I feel better now, much better, but I still have residual angst around certain things—like new challenges or new experiences.

Thoughts of inadequacy popped up in my mind and anxious feelings bred in my chest; am I really cut out for a job that famously demands so much of a person? Am I ready to speak to strangers? In cooking school the stakes are low, it's all make-believe, but this is the real world.

"You won't be. You're not depressed anymore. I don't think you realize how far you've come since summer. You're ready to do this," Ruby reassures me.

I found the same "fuck it" in my gut that I used when I put down the cooking school deposit in the midst of my depression. I replied to the Head Chef:

Yes, sounds good. Do I need to bring anything?

He typed back:

Just bring a black T-shirt and trousers. And your knives. See you then!

"Well done!" Ruby said to me. "I'm sure you're going to love it."

Lovely Ruby. What does she bloody know?

Helen's classroom, unlike her disposition, is warm and cozy. It's the perfect place to nap. Soon class is over and I am free to go. It's not all relief, though; now I must travel straight to the trial shift, and I'm shitting it. I pack up my bag with all my serious cooking-school equipment (a pencil case and a notepad) and I head out the school gates into the sharp winds of October.

I immediately call my dad. "I'm on my way to the trial," I say as I head to the Tube. This is the third time we've spoken today. I am far too reliant on my parents at the moment. I felt brave when we ate our breakfast together this morning before school, but now the nerves are back.

"You'll be fine. Just put one foot in front of the other. Call me when it's over. When will you finish?" he asks.

"No fucking idea," I say.

"You're going to be fine," he says.

"Yeah, yeah, alright, bye," I say.

"Bye, darling."

I hang up with my dad, then immediately text my family on WhatsApp.

Fuck this—I write.

You'll be fine!—my dad replies.

It will be fun—says my brother, who lives in America and is watching my quarter-life crisis from a distance.

You'll be fine. Remember, you can always leave if you want to—my mum says. My lovely mum, who rarely gets a word in at home due to the fact my dad and I love talking too much.

THE CIVILIANS DON'T KNOW I'M A CHEF

My dad and I are the same. We are soft and sentimental but, for the most part, squash our emotions by talking all the time. We are narcissistic loudmouths. My mum and brother are different; they are quiet and sweet in nature but when it comes to facing adversity, they are stoic and strong like oxen. My family is absurdly nuclear: a married couple with an elder son and a younger daughter. We are safe and happy and privileged—the luck I had in being spawned into such a secure world sometimes makes me feel embarrassed and greedy.

I exit Angel Station and make pace through the streets. The air is icy and sharp; as I walk under some scaffolding, I feel a momentary relief from the wind, but when I emerge, my body shivers with the cold. I am so cold that I am moving fast, but I wish for a second that I could walk backward, all the way home. I'm about to begin my new career: my first trial shift, my first time behind the scenes of a real restaurant. What if I want to leave the minute I get there? And I can't, so I have a panic attack?

When I arrive, I walk past the restaurant so I can peep in through the window: the dining room is small and candlelit. It looks warm and welcoming, but I know it's secretly cool and sceney; that's part of why I chose it. I am forever on a quest to be someone I am not, someone cooler and more confident. It's ten to five. I'm early, so I wander around the backstreets with my hands under my armpits. Part of me wants to get inside the restaurant for warmth but I'd rather savor these last few moments of solitude so I can gear myself up for what's to come.

I am about to enter a world that underpins the fabric of fun in London, a world where the sole purpose is to provide pleasure. How romantic. If only I wasn't on the brink of running away from it all.

Black cabs crawl past me and I feel like a tourist, my heart jumping at every beep of a car horn. My stomach is bubbling and my breath is short. I try to remind myself how far I have come. Six months ago, I was having daily panic attacks. What I'm feeling now is not anxiety, I tell myself. This is just simple, run-of-the-mill, totally normal nerves.

But the irrational side of my brain tells me that the next few hours could expose me as weak if I crack under the pressure; it could clarify that I am indeed not suited to be a chef. The trial shift becomes so big, so much bigger than it actually is: it feels like this trial shift will determine whether or not I can work in this industry.

I pull up the last few texts from my family and friends, whom I have messaged incessantly since I reached out to the Head Chef yesterday. They have all filled me with great levels of confidence, reminding me how far I have come, but now the confidence has blown away in the October wind. The one text that resonates is my mum's: *You can always leave if you want to.* I wish I took note of more of the sage things my mum says, instead of only listening to my dad.

Under my breath I repeat her words, "You can always leave if you want to." Three deep breaths and I'm off.

I open the door and walk inside the restaurant. It's warm. The space is small, with wooden tables arranged so they can squeeze in as many people as possible. I am met by a slightly lanky, immaculately dressed man. He looks me up and down.

"Hi, I'm here for a trial shift," I say, with about the

same level of confidence as a shy child trick-or-treating on Halloween.

"Hello, there! I am Axel, the General Manager," the lanky man says with a thick German accent.

"Nice to meet you," I say, standing still but feeling wobbly.

He looks at me with pity. "Is your trial in the kitchen?"

"Yes," I say, clutching my rucksack on my right shoulder.

"Okay, excellent. Come with me." He leads me through the dining room. I notice how he treats me like I'm a customer, and I am only now realizing how much skill it must take to be so professional and performative at all times.

We walk past a couple of staff members sitting at tables, clipboards, black laptops, and carafes of water before them. They look at me as I pass: I imagine they are wondering why a nervous girl like me is heading to the kitchen. "Just through here," Axel says.

"Cool," I say, swallowing a lump in my throat. He leads me toward a large swinging door, and as we pass through it, I realize I've taken an irreversible step into this world. No going back now.

Axel leads me down a hallway. I feel like I'm in the wings of a West End stage: there are muffled voices, as if the audience is about to be calmed so the show can begin. As we hurry on, I see a team of chefs in black T-shirts and trendy denim aprons with their heads down, preoccupied with the equipment in their hands. It looks like a grown-up version of cooking school. Less hormonal acne, less insecurity, and less women— in fact, seemingly none. There is no space for doubt in this room; everyone's posture is proud. They are getting paid to cook, instead of paying to learn how to cook. There is general chitchat, but my mind is too consumed by the set design and the props on stage to be able to decipher the actors' dialogue. There are shiny metallic bowls, the same colorful chopping boards we have at school, but industrial-sized, endless pots and pans and monstrous hobs. I can feel heat: thick, smoggy, oily. My eyes widen as I take it in: all the men going about their business with their sharp knives, their strong arms, their steamy bodies, and their dark determined eyes. Now I know why Helen didn't want me to come to this place; she didn't want me being seduced by just how erotic this whole thing appears to be.

Axel calls out at a volume I didn't expect from someone with his slim frame: "Marty, I have a chef here for you." A chef? Me? Don't think so, mate.

Marty, the Head Chef, the guy who responded to my incredibly informal job application, is standing at the front of the kitchen, leaning against a wall with a pen in his mouth and squinting at a clipboard.

Marty looks completely different from his pictures on the restaurant website. Online, he looks tall, dark, and handsome, with a clean, chiseled jaw and impassioned focus in his eyes. But in front of me now, there stands a short, stooped man with a receding hairline and a furrowed brow. He looks exhausted. His trousers are tight and his apron clings to his gut. He speaks with a thick South African accent.

"Hey, great to meet you," he says. Marty reaches out his hand to shake mine and I note how warm his clammy palm feels as I take it. "Let me show you to the changing room." Axel smiles at me and walks away; I didn't realize how emotionally attached I'd become to him in the three and a half minutes I'd known him. I miss him now. I follow Marty down some narrow stairs and, as we descend, we enter darkness. Bloody hell.

Marty pushes the door open to what appears to be the changing room. He gives me a quick briefing, speaking at double speed as he clearly has places to go, chefs to manage, food to cook. "Okay, so get changed into your black T-shirt and leave your stuff in a locker, if you can find an empty one. Bring your knives. You'll find aprons and a torchon on the way back up. See you up there." He averts his eyes from my body before exiting, and I wonder if he is worried that I might just start stripping while he's still in the room. I appreciate this awkward moment, his signaling to me that he is not a predator as if he suspects that I, a middle-class girl, might have heard the rumors about the delinquent nature of professional kitchens and the men who dominate them.

He leaves. I'm alone in the dark basement. What the fuck is a torchon? I get my phone out and google it. Ah, okay, it's a tea towel, a cloth. Great. Easy. I turn to lock the changing-room door, but I see there isn't a lock. That's okay. I have braced myself for bigger obstacles, like setting the restaurant on fire and then getting banned from the world I am so eager to join. I glance around. If there were ever any women in here, they've left no evidence.

The changing room is cluttered with rucksacks, dirty aprons, phone chargers, deodorant, beer cans, lighters, empty drug baggies, filters, Rizlas, and rancid Birkenstock Bostons. I perch my own rucksack on a nearby bench. The contrast of this space versus the dining room is mighty. I lift my top reluctantly, not knowing if someone is about to barge in on me. I resent my earlier self for choosing to wear my ugliest sports bra, then I resent my current self for caring about my sex appeal at this moment. I need to care less about what men think of me. That is imperative if I am to thrive in an industry which is dominated by men, or even, live in a *world* that is dominated by men.

I put on my plain black T-shirt. There is a toilet in the corner of the changing room, and above it graffiti in Sharpie that reads "IF UR GONNA TAKE A SHIT, THEN FUCKING FLUSH." I suppress my desire to pee. I have no idea how long my trial shift will last, but I'm not pissing with the door unlocked.

I remove my knife-wrap from my rucksack. There are no empty lockers so I shove my rucksack and coat under the bench on the floor. I don't use a coat hook for myself; someone more important might need it. I take a deep breath and dig up some grit from the pit of my stomach.

You can always leave if you want to, I tell myself. God bless my lovely mum; I must be nicer to her.

I head up the stairs to find the pile of clean aprons and torchons Marty mentioned. As I tie my apron strings, I feel like a phony, like I'm wearing a chef costume from Amazon. It's somehow worse than my cooking-school costume, because now I look like I know what I'm doing, but I don't. I walk toward the kitchen, knife-wrap and a torchon in my hand, and phone in my pocket in case of emergencies, in case I need to look on Google Maps to find the nearest patch of grass so I can have a panic attack there and not in the kitchen.

I hear the chefs before I see them: "If you're going to borrow my scissors, don't give them to the fucking KP to wash." In cooking school, we have a Kitchen Porter; I suppose KP is the abbreviation. But in cooking school, the KP is a white middle-aged mum, not a barely eighteen-year-old guy. "My scissors cost more than any of your fucking knives," the chef says with a thick Midlands accent. My insides seize at the sound of his rage but I try not to react. I stand up as straight as possible.

I have been in the kitchen for two seconds and I have already heard a swear word. This is fine: I come from a family who is fluent in fuck. It is not the swear word that startles me but the volume of his voice. The thunderous slandering came from a very young chef with thick glasses who is using a chinois, a cone-shaped sieve, to strain some sort of crunchy orange matter; I can see crab legs, tomatoes, fennel, and onion in the sieve, and a silky-smooth iridescent orange liquid is pouring out the other side. Helen told us just yesterday that the term is not technical but racist. It's French for "Chinese," because the cone shape is similar to that of a Chinese rice farmer's hat. I note this chinois is a lot more weathered and misshapen than the ones at school, perhaps from being slammed with ladles in the way this young chef is doing right now. He notes my presence and says nothing. He's a proper chef, I think, the angry brute type from TV. Opposite the young chef who just ignored me is a taller, muscular Black chef whose eyes are glued to the biggest monkfish I've ever seen; it is monstrous and slimy, like a decapitated alien. In one motion, he pulls back the skin with his hands and unveils the pinky-white flesh. I gaze around the rest of the kitchen, and yes, as I suspected, no women. That's fine, I tell myself. I know lots of nice men, like my dad, for example. Axel was nice enough. Marty seems fine.

If the worst that happens is the chef with thick glasses

and Midlands accent ignores me, I can deal with that. Another deep breath and I walk across the stage.

I am struck by the stark light beaming through the kitchen. The lamps reflect off the stainless-steel work surfaces, as well as other shiny things—knives, and little silver containers of butter or chives or chopped parsley. There are no windows, no signs of the outside world. Time stands still under these lamps—the space looks make-believe, artificially created for the performance.

Marty quickly spots me hovering at the entrance of the kitchen. "Hey," he shouts in the general vicinity of the chefs. Everyone goes silent and turns to look up at him. I am impressed by the power his voice holds. "We've got a trial shift today." He's clearly forgotten my name. "Everyone, say hi."

How incredibly vague. Am I to introduce myself? Or will they introduce themselves to me? I lift my hand. "Hello," I say, while waving my soft hand like the Queen of England. Like a group of cavemen, they mumble back to me. An excellent start.

Marty charges through the awkward silence by pointing at each of the chefs while listing job titles that don't mean much to me. All I know is that Sous Chef is below Head Chef. "Emil. Sous Chef." He points at the monkfish-prepping chef. Emil lifts his head and nods to me with an almost willing smile. "Zack. Chef de Partie and punk." Marty signals at the young chef with the glasses. The boy says "Oh, fuck off" to Marty and once again avoids my eyes. "And Nathan, our Commis, will be in there making pasta." Marty turns his head to a little cupboard room from which Nathan smiles and waves. He looks alright—sweet, I suppose.

None of them are hot, which I am both relieved and

disappointed by. I have been out of the game for a while, and although I would quite like to engage in a romantic affair soon, I'm not sure one set in the workplace is the best place to start. I know hot chefs are out there. I'll find them at the pub, not here; I don't need anything else amping up my nerves. The kitchen is small, now that I look around; it looks like a garden shed with an en suite fridge. I can't quite believe that these five men can cook for the whole restaurant out of this tiny space.

Each chef has carved out their own corner to get things done. There is not much room for Marty and me. I worry about where I'm going to stand. Surely it would be easier if I just went home?

"Backs," Marty shouts as he bends down by a chef's crotch and grabs a brown chopping board from beneath the workbench. From school, I know Backs is what you say when you let someone know you are behind them, and I know, too, that brown chopping boards are used for vegetables. It's exciting to see the things we are taught in cooking school come to life; it makes me feel less regretful for investing every penny I had in the whole damn charade.

"Right," Marty says, "come with me." Together, like a match made in hell—me, a delicate woman, and him a brute, a chef—we walk down the aisle to the front of the kitchen. He slams the chopping board on a narrow steel surface. "This is called the Pass," Marty tells me. "It's where we put the finished plates of food, which the runners collect and take to tables." I nod.

"Right," Marty says as he neatly folds blue paper towels into two rectangles and arranges them beneath the chopping board. I guess that's to keep it secure, like a DIY version of the rubber mats we use at cooking school. "We're going to have you do a couple of jobs that will really help out the guys during service, when orders are coming in from the dining room. Probably best if you start with brunoising chilies. You know how to brunoise?" Coincidentally we were tasked with brunoising chilies at school last week; it's destiny. I'm ready to finally do some work and leave behind the God-awful small talk.

"Yeah, it's when you dice it into small cubes, right?" I am hyperaware of the words I use. I don't want to sound like a clueless idiot or a swotty know-it-all.

"Exactly," he says with over-the-top enthusiasm, clearly picking up on my nerves and wanting to boost my confidence. He dumps a plastic box of about a hundred red chilies next to the green cutting board and picks one up. He then takes my knife directly from my hand to demonstrate.

His physicality with my knife is so natural; the blade looks as if it's an extension of his hand. He quickly slices through that chili, and several more, creating perfectly uniform, thin strips. He then rotates the strips horizontally and dices small cubes with such precision that they look machine-made. "Cool?" he says. I smile with tight lips, and he walks away. "Yep, thanks."

My friends and family kept telling me I would feel fine once the shift had started, but I don't. I feel worse. With my back facing the kitchen, I feel like the other chefs can see through my skin, that they can see the nerves jolting around in my body, the twists in my stomach and the curve of my hips. I feel hyperaware of my apron hugging my waist, of how it fits me differently from how it fits the men. Their strings hang loosely beneath their stomachs, whereas mine stretch across my middle and accent my figure. Despite me not fancying them, I don't want them to think I'm ugly or unattractive; perhaps it's because I have no real cooking skill to bring to the table, I feel like I should at least bring beauty and grace, or whatever feminine qualities these men might want from me. But moments pass, and I begin to chop, and then it happens: my mind wanders off and I remember why I'm here. I love cooking. I love the satisfying serenity of a task. It is so good for my brain; the sound of the chopping blocks out the noise, the sight of all the chilies piled on top of one another makes me see things clearer, and the feeling of heat beneath my fingertips from the chili seeds warms my mood. How lovely.

It's just after 5 p.m. I believe the dinner service starts at 6 p.m. Girls in matching oversize navy-blue jackets and black trousers start traipsing through the kitchen. They must be waitresses, I think. They giggle as they collect glasses and cutlery from a rack of shelves next to the kitchen in slow motion. Or maybe they're moving at normal speed and it just looks off in comparison to the manic pace in the kitchen. The waitresses walk up and down the pass and one of them steps into the kitchen to steal some milk with very little concern that she might be in the way. Impressive.

I feel the sexual tension between the waitresses and the chefs. They flirt openly like animals, unashamed of being watched. In my office job it was more secretive.

"Zack! Stop it! Oh my God! When did your arms get so muscly?" one waitress shrieks. The name Zack suits the young boy perfectly; it sounds a bit like yuck.

He laughs. "Must be all my wanking!"

"You are so fucking gross," she says with a smirk,

longing perhaps for his meat-marinating hands to marinate her. I wonder why he gives her attention and not me.

Another waitress creeps into the little room where the tall boy with dark hair is rolling pasta. I wonder if that might be the pasta for the crab bottarga dish, the one they are famous for. I hear fumbling and giggles, and I can see through the gap in the door that she's hugging him from behind. As they laugh and fawn, I wonder where I would fit into this zoo if I worked here. Who would I mate with? It seems all the chefs prey on the pretty waitresses, but I'm a pretty chef so where does that leave me? Am I to mate with a pretty waitress too? Will none of the chefs fancy me because I'm one of their own? It might be incestuous? Maybe I'm overthinking this. Maybe I don't *need* to mate with a chef. I consider mating with Axel for a second.

In this moment, I miss the dynamic of my old office job, where the roles were so clearly defined for me and my former lover, Declan. I was the marketing intern wearing an arse-hugging jumpsuit and he was the tall, senior Irish copywriter who couldn't resist me. Before I knew it, we were fucking on the photocopier like we were in a mainstream porn category. The first time Declan came back to my flat, I worried that out of the office the dynamic would change, but the sex was still phenomenal. It was forbidden and ferocious. No one in the office could ever find out. He was the first proper adult man I slept with; first he taught me where to eat good food, then he showed me how to fuck well. We'd spend an hour lunch break in Bao and then an evening after work fumbling each other's suited crotches in the streets. He'd wrap each lengthy limb around mine until my frame was swallowed by his. He was a soldier in seduction, stomping through no-man's-land to fight for each of my orgasms. With Declan, I wanted nothing but pleasure, just fun and games. And he gave it to me. We would snog on the streets of Southwark, and fumble at the edges of each other's underwear while the commuters passed us by. Then the next morning we would go to Black Sheep for a coffee and barely touch; but we knew that a few hours later, when the nine-to-five finished, we would disregard our professional pleasantries. We would guzzle Guinness and find a place, any place, to fuck. A sparkling jolt shoots up my body, between my thighs, as I think back on Declan, but I know I'll likely never see him again. That was my old life, before my brain started breaking, when my confidence was unwavering, when my hair flowed freely across my shoulders; now it's tied away from my face, leaving me nowhere to hide.

Marty walks through the kitchen. The waitresses creep away and the chefs return to their tasks.

One of the waitresses asks, "Any counts tonight, Marty?" I'm not sure what this means but I listen.

"Nope. As long as Nathan hasn't been a fucking idiot and forgot to order crab legs again. Actually, we need a count on the squid; we only have seven left." I guess that a count is a way to signal to the waitresses how many portions of something are left. I feel like I've moved abroad, like I'm a foreign exchange student, and instead of learning the language by reading books, I am immersing myself in the culture. In my mind, I add counts to the list of kitchen colloquialisms.

The boy from the little dungeon room appears. He has swishy, mousy hair and a hunched posture. He looks cheeky but nervous. I can tell he is the most junior one here.

"Did someone just say my name?" he says. He must be Nathan.

"Yeah, your girlfriend. She wants you to get a bigger dick," Zack says. All the men giggle. I smile awkwardly, looking down at my chopping board.

Marty turns and a big grin stretches all the way across his round face. He pokes the boy in the stomach several times. "Don't be sad, Nathan, sweetie. You are the best, cleverest Commis Chef I've ever worked with. We love you dearly," he says, clearly taking the piss. I smile again, still looking down at my cutting board. Marty notes my grin and I see a little flicker in his eyes that feels like he is inviting me in. But I know I am a long way from being poked in my stomach and called sweetie. Maybe one day.

I continue chopping my chilies on the pass, where most of the waitresses have gathered to gossip. I keep my eyes down on the chilies and wonder: How long is this task supposed to take me? It's half five now, and half an hour chopping chilies seems like an awfully long time. It feels like I shouldn't be taking this long but I'm not even close to halfway through; there are a *lot* of chilies. I am going as quick as I can but every now and again, I can see Marty side-eyeing me and it's making me feel like I'm somehow fucking up.

At this moment, I miss the regimented format of cooking school, where I am given exact instructions with exact timings, where I am in a room with other students doing the exact same thing, so I can compare myself to them. But here I'm all by myself, chopping chilies alone. Maybe Helen was right; maybe I'm not ready.

THE CIVILIANS DON'T KNOW I'M A CHEF

One of the waitresses, the one who asked Marty about counts, leans her elbow on the pass and looks up at me. "Hey! I'm Ella. Are you here on trial?"

She is beautiful and slender with shoulder-length dirty-blonde hair. I don't trust her. Maybe it's because I've never seen a woman so at ease with herself among so many men. She looks as though she feels the direct opposite of how I'm feeling, like she belongs here. She swans around the kitchen, basking in attention from the chefs; she has Marty's stamp of approval too, which seems like it might be hard to get. I feel a knot in my chest, and I realize it is envy. I want to feel confident around loud, scary men; I want Marty's seal of approval. Despite my envy, I like that she is talking to me. It is making me feel more important. Maybe I can learn how to be a woman at ease from her.

"Yeah, I'm just here on trial," I say, knowing I should've asked her something in return, that is how human beings are supposed to converse. But she just looks around, busying herself. Surely her head is full of nothing: no self-loathing, no self-doubt. She is made for hospitality, I think; she is at ease and made to make others feel the same.

She gives me another chance. "So, how long have you been working in kitchens?"

I don't like this question. It means that I have to come clean about the fact that I'm in cooking school. A retired chef from a Michelin-starred restaurant gave a talk to our class and he made it clear that cooking school is more like an expensive after-school club rather than the first step in a career path; this was later disputed by a bitter Helen, who had no real restaurant experience.

I confess. "I'm actually in cooking school at the

moment," I say quietly, not wanting the chefs to hear. "So, I'm looking for a part-time restaurant job."

"Oh, nice." She breezes past my admission with zero judgment. She probably feels no need to scrutinize people the way I do.

She tells me that she is training to be a sommelier. Of course. It makes sense. She seems like a quintessential Wine Girl. I've seen them out and about, when Declan used to take me out for secret work lunches at modern small-plate restaurants. A Wine Girl is a female sommelier who waits on tables in trendy restaurants with distressed walls and aesthetic Instagram pages. They always sound like they grew up in either West London or the "countryside" (any of the shires), and they ooze androgynous swag. They have short hair and very elegant hands, and they look like the love child of Princess Diana and Noel Gallagher.

"How long have you worked here?" I ask.

"About a year. I studied fashion but to be honest, I prefer hospitality." Of course you do, I think.

"What about you, do you want to be a full-time chef?"

"Yeah, I do," I say, still not convinced that my career as a chef is likely.

"Nice, well this is a great place to start. A little intense, but you'll learn a lot," she says.

I like that she just assumes I can do it. She has the confidence that I have craved my whole life. Just being around her makes me feel empowered.

I return to the chilies. There's still a lot more to chop but I want to impress Marty so I pick up the pace a little.

Ella starts to fold napkins. I note the chefs behind me begin to sound a little more tense; there is less frivolous banter and more directives. I look at the clock and it's nearly six. Service will begin soon. "You got enough butter churned?" Zack calls out, his Midlands accent thick and heavy.

"Yep," Nathan says, looking up beneath swishy hair which is turning greasier by the minute. He is clearly a man of few words, but I get the feeling he is quite funny.

"Yes, *Chef*," Zack bellows, teasing Nathan for not addressing him formally. I suppose that means they don't *seriously* say Chef here, but I'm not totally sure. I am the foreign exchange student learning the adolescent colloquialisms of this strange language from teenage boys; they will show me what's cool and what's not, they'll teach me all the swear words.

Suddenly, there is a loud robotic humming sound from a small black machine:

ZZZZ *zzzz* ZZZZ *zzzz*.

The boys stand to attention, appearing to be waiting for something. Marty snaps a piece of paper from the machine and shouts, "Okay!" *This* feels like the start of something. He continues: "Check on. One bread, one pickles, one ox cheek. To follow, one squid, one bavette and chips."

The chefs respond in unison: "Oui, Chef!" Ah, so they do say Chef. The teenage boys are suddenly taking themselves quite seriously, but the whole French thing is very camp.

I smile, then try to hide it. Ella catches me, and then she smiles too. The female camaraderie is like a hug; she knows I'm out in the trenches with the boys, and she is sending me support from afar. Before service, when I arrived, the chefs were making crude jokes, now they are suddenly a vision of formality and respect. I am shocked at the performance; I didn't realize just how the actors would transform when they took to the stage.

Soon Marty starts to bring the plates of food up to the pass, alongside where I am chopping chilies. He shouts, "Service!" and that's when the waitresses come and collect the plates. Marty confirms where each one is going.

"Okay, Table Three. One bread and one pickles. Ox cheek coming in a second," he says.

I peer at the plate; there are a few slices of warm bread stacked atop a white sheet of greaseproof paper. The bread is dark and crusty, and sliced generously. The plate of pickles is a piled-up heap of cauliflower, carrot, radish, and some other things I can't decipher. The warm sunset colors are vibrant beneath the bright lights on the pass. As Ella collects the bread and pickles, the ox cheek croquettes arrive. They are golden brown cubes with lengthy plump Cantabrian anchovies draped over the top.

Ella swoops up the croquettes and walks away with all three dishes. She knows what she's doing; she is the real deal.

ZZZ zzz ZZZZ.

"Check on. One bread, two oysters. To follow, pork secreto, monkfish, chips, and greens," Marty continues to shout as he reads the checks. And the chefs always respond in unison, each time, registering they have heard him and will do as he says. "Oui, Chef."

As more and more orders come through, I begin to make sense of the service. Marty says, "Check on," reads the check, and then tells the chefs what to cook. The chefs cook their dishes, talking to one another about how long they need, then they bring the plates to Marty, who inspects them, sometimes finishing their dishes by adding a few leaves or a drizzle of oil. Finally, he tells the waitress where to take each plate. My anxiety floats away as I realize no one around me gives a fuck what I'm doing; they're focused on cooking, on making everything look good and taste good, and vitally, on having fun. They're grinning and bouncing with a spring in their step; they're doing what the check monster tells them to, and they want more—give them more!

I am nearly finished with the chilies now, but I don't want to interrupt Marty while he's running service. It seems there is a constant onslaught of new dishes he is preparing on the pass. I suppose I can help Ella fold napkins when I'm done.

As time passes, the robotic sound of the check machine becomes familiar, as do the raised voices.

"I'm down already and we've only got a few tables in. Why is it always me?" says Emil at the back. I haven't heard him speak much yet, probably because he is standing behind a wall of fire, pots, and pans. He seems to be doing most of the cooking, and he's doing it *fast*, continuously chucking big hunks of meat and fish onto the angry embers.

"When are you not down, Emil?" Zack shouts.

"Mate, you've got fuck all on, pipe down, Larder boy," Emil shouts back, his voice rising over the clanging pots and pans. I like Emil more than Zack. He seems less obnoxious. They are both moving quickly on their stations, but with grace and elegance and big smiles on their faces.

Marty elbows me and whispers: "They're both down." We laugh together. What's happening? Was that Marty's seal of approval? Why does that feel so good? Maybe I don't want to leave this damn trial shift.

Now that I have been blessed by an approving smile from Marty, I indulge in a fun intrusive thought while working on my chilies: if I had to fuck one of the five men in this room, it would be Emil. Marty is too old and unattractive, Zack is seemingly a bit of a cunt, Nathan seems a little goofy, and while the KP is sweet, he is too short for me. I need to get laid soon, I think. I am grateful no one can see the thoughts in my head.

I finish my chilies. I clean down, wiping my board and giving it to the KP. "Gracias," he says with a happy-go-lucky grin.

I return to my station at the edge of the pass, and fold napkins with Ella as I watch the plates make their way to the dining room.

"Okay, that's squid and red mullet for Table Thirteen," Marty says. As Ella picks up the dishes, Marty stops her. "Wait, wait, you need the chips." Then he shouts, "Zack, hurry up on the chips, man, what the fuck's taking you so long?"

"Yes, Chef," Zack says.

I worry Marty is angry but he's not, he's fine, and he starts telling me about the dishes while we wait for the chips.

"Okay, so this is squid ink orzo." He points at a small bowl of jet-black matter; it almost looks like warm tarmac. He continues: "People love this one because of how it looks but it's actually super delicious. It's got black garlic in the sauce, so it has that kind of sweet tangy molasses flavor. And it has squid inside the sauce. The squid ink is more for aesthetic than taste, and we also grill some fresh squid. The whole dish is pretty intensely savory, hence why it's not a massive portion." My ears delight in everything he tells me. I want him to tell me everything he knows about every dish. It all makes sense when he talks about it. And he is clearly so passionate about it, even if he does look jaded.

"Mmmh, nice," I say. "Looks amazing," I hastily add, not wanting to sound illiterate. The chips arrive and Marty says, "Go, go, go," to the waitresses.

ZZZ zzz ZZZZZ zzz.

As we get even busier, and the checks keep coming, Marty hands me a tray of butterflied red mullet. "Okay," he says, "Emil's a bit busy and he's low on mullet, so I need you to bone these and I'll cook them for him." He has urgency in his voice. I know he needs these soon, for service. I feel confident with fish. When I was five, I ate the eyeball of a salmon. When I was ten, I cooked a tiny sandfish sourced from the beach near my granny's house in Cornwall. When I first made fish soup with my dad, I realized just how much I love food. When we made fish pie at school a few weeks ago, mine was the best.

Let's go. I get to work with some tweezers, very carefully plucking each bone from the butterflied mullet, thinking of the real paying customer who might choke and die if I miss one. I am moving slower than I should but I want to be precise. Marty motions for me to step to the side. "Watch," he says. He takes the tweezers from my hand. "Use hard pressure. Don't be hesitant because you'll mess up the flesh." He moves across the butterflied mullet incredibly quickly, not missing a bone. Just like that, he has finished in ten seconds. I know what to do, but it is in watching him and seeing how fast he moves that I can see just *how* to do it. I need to worry less and move quicker. "Here, your turn," he says. He hands me a new butterflied mullet. I try to copy him, less worried, quicker, and it works. I hand him over the boned mullet and move on to the next one. "Well done," he says. He heads over to Emil's section and lays the mullet on the plancha (a flat-top griddle), skin-side down. Then he returns to the pass to send some starters. I take a moment to let the "well done" sink in. Fuck me. It almost feels better than a hug from my mum.

"Okay, guys, get ready," Marty shouts to the waitresses. He still has to finish the plates. He spoons a sauce over a big slab of pink beef. He sees me watching.

"So, the côte de boeuf is a sharing dish and is served with our version of a Café de Paris sauce. Some things are best done simple. I like serving simple sauces with expensive meat. Beautiful people don't need lots of makeup." I wonder if he thinks I'm beautiful. Probably because I'm young and he's past it. I shut my intrusive thoughts up and then make a mental note to google Café de Paris later. He doesn't have time to explain it.

He continues to teach me, despite being manically busy. Marty returns and lifts the crispy mullet skin from the grill and lays the butterflied fillet on a hot plate beneath the lights on the pass. "The red mullet is just grilled skin-side down and then we let the flesh finish cooking under the hot lights," he says, pointing up at the big lamps hovering over the plates of food, keeping them warm.

"The mullet is finished with our take on Nam Jim, which is a Thai dressing with fish sauce, lime, garlic, chili, and other things. The chilies you're brunoising now will be used for Nam Jim, so you can see how precise and uniform prep makes the overall dish look better."

"Ah, I see," I say, trying to underplay my real delight. I can't believe the chilies I chopped will be used for real recipes, for real customers. I thought it was just a fake task to keep me busy, to keep me out of the way.

He calls for service. I look down at the mullet on the pass. That's my mullet, the one I boned.

That's my fish. That's my work. It's going to a customer. My feelings of inadequacy have vanished. Fuck. I'm learning how to cook better by being in a kitchen, not sitting in some stuffy classroom. I helped the Head Chef in service and I didn't mess up. I really think I could do this job. I think it might be my goddamn calling. I really think I could *love* this job, or that I could *love* life if this was my job.

I look back at the chefs. Moments ago, they were sweating and down in the dumps, but now it looks like their batteries have been replaced. They're like Energizer Bunnies: they're jumping all over the place, leaping through the checks. And they have started chatting again.

"What are you doing tonight, then?" Zack shouts over to Nathan, who is back in his pasta dungeon. It seems he is not really doing service, just occasionally helping by sending a few ice creams and chocolatey things to the pass. "Going to the pub, probably," Nathan says.

"Who with?" Zack shouts. He dumps another portion of chips in the fryer.

"Your mum," Nathan shouts back.

"Ha! Shut the fuck up, you loser," Zack says.

ZZZZ *zzzz* ZZZZZ.

They are grinning while violently insulting each other. It is almost like the chefs are happiest when their work becomes *too* difficult, when they are *too* busy. At the end of the day, it's just food. It's all fun and games. What the hell was I stressing out about? They are in their element, they have ten checks on and not enough hob space to cook their food, but they are delighting in the chaos. I am delighting in it too.

I don't know whether to ask Marty for another job. I glance over at him. He is plating six dishes at once, with sweat beading on his forehead. I decide to leave him alone and go back to the napkins. Right now, I feel it would be most helpful for me to stay out of the way instead of obstructing the narrow pass with my wide hips.

Marty continues to send plates of food out to the dining room. Next is the monkfish. It shimmers in places, the bright white flesh catching the light and turning iridescent like an oil spill on a hot road. "The monkfish comes with a curried pumpkin sauce. It's similar to a katsu but richer with cream."

Then a shimmering golden plate arrives on the pass. It's the crab pappardelle. Beneath the hot lights it's almost too shiny to see, but I recognize it straight away. Each silky ribbon of pasta is elegantly poised, with fleshy white chunks of crab disguised under a cloak of satin orange sauce. "And this is the crab dish, which I'm sure you've seen online. It's our most popular dish." As Marty grates bottarga on top he continues, "The reason it is so good is simple: a very rich shellfish stock and fuck loads of butter." It looks identical to the images from the review Ruby and I read last night. Seeing this dish put together in front of me is thrilling, like I'm being given a secret look at some crown jewels. The finished dish looks regal. Marty continues to multitask; he is reading out new checks, ordering the waitresses around, and orchestrating the chefs. I feel about as useful as an elephant ice-skating on hot grease, but I'm having fun.

That's when Zack, who has barely spoken to me, brings over a one-liter tub of peeled garlic cloves.

"You cool to mince this tub for me?"

"Yeah, sure!" I say, a little too enthusiastically.

The kitchen is still noisy but I get lost in my own world while mincing garlic; I finely chop a handful of cloves, then use the wide part of the blade of my knife to crush the garlic over and over until it forms a smooth paste. They taught us this at school, but we did one garlic at a time, not a kilo of the stuff. I think about what it would be like to work here full-time: the rush, the adrenaline, the excitement, the thrill. I want it all. I feel enticed by it.

Twenty or so minutes pass, and I'm about halfway through the tub of garlic when Marty dramatically plunges a check onto the check spike and shouts, "And that's our last table! Let's get the fuck out of here." Just like that, service is over. I guess Zack just gave me the tub of garlic to keep me busy. I like that he did that; it was like he wanted me to be a part of the show.

Marty is giddy. His boys have made him proud. He takes off his apron and then barges through the narrow kitchen to the workbench where Nathan is plating the final desserts under Zack's watchful eye. Marty reaches to switch on a Bose speaker, and as he does, his pale belly hangs below his T-shirt and knocks over an open tub of pear and brown-butter ice cream. He swipes at his gut with his thumb and sticks it in his mouth.

"Fucking gross!" Nathan says to him.

"You'll need to chuck that ice cream away now," Marty says, laughing. It's like he did it on purpose. "Leave it on the pass for the girls," he says. Marty clicks

Play on his phone and Mike Skinner shouts out from the speaker. The nerves that weighed me down at the start of my trial shift have gone. I feel as light as a feather and as fit as the girl in the song. My gosh do I know it. I could leave at any time, but I don't want to anymore. The dread has gone and now I'm loving it.

Marty switches the heat lamps off and the tension in the kitchen cools immediately.

The chefs methodically dump out the residual ingredients from service—herbs, butter, sauces, dressings—and tip them into new, shiny containers, covering them in cling film for the next day. They stack up used containers and push them to the side of their workbenches while mouthing lyrics. The waitresses float around the pass and lean on the counter on their limp wrists, gazing up at the chefs. They dip scraps of chips from a big metal tray into miso-butter ice cream. They all have their own crushes on the chefs, I'm sure of it. Oh, to have a work crush. I want one! I saw a hot delivery man walk through earlier, maybe he's there for the taking if Axel doesn't work out.

Beautiful Ella glances at sweaty Zack as he uses his damp T-shirt to wipe the lenses of his thick glasses. He looks younger without them, more innocent. I can tell they've fucked. I wonder why she fucked him? In the real world she'd be far too good for him, but I suppose here, in this space, in the kitchen, it makes sense; chefs have a special power. There is so much passion and so many thrills in service that it makes sense for people to be drawn to the chefs behind it. They are the main characters, the heroes, the leading actors on this stage; they're the ones reading the lines that make the audience stand on their feet and clap. I wonder if women chefs have the same appeal? Let's hope so.

Everyone in the kitchen is laughing. I start to feel like I have been a part of something quite magical. It doesn't feel like a job; it feels like a secret society. I help Marty clean down the pass. I watch the other chefs splash hot, soapy water over every inch of the kitchen. They wipe their sponges across each surface, and then the inside of their fridges too. They wipe away the foamy suds with a squeegee, sending splatters of hot, bubbly water flying to the floor. Then they refill their fridges with the new containers they packed, leaving no sign of service anywhere. I copy them. I have never seen men clean up with such gusto.

Ella brings over a tray of pints. "Here we go, boys and girls. Beer!" she beckons.

I note that she must've added the "girls" because I am here. I am part of it all. Everybody takes a beer.

As if thanking Ella for the pints, Nathan puts a mighty portion of chips fresh from the fryers onto the pass, and the waitresses and bartenders come fleeing to it like a flock of pigeons.

"Well done," Marty says, clinking his glass to mine.

"Cheers," I say.

My first sip is sensational. Cold, crisp golden bubbles pass down my throat and excite me. I want more and more. Never in my life has a beer tasted so good. Never in my life has one sip of alcohol traveled so rapidly to my head.

"You good?" Marty says with a wide grin.

I swallow, embarrassed. "Yeah, all good!"

"Shall we have a chat about how the shift went? Why

don't you go and get changed and meet me in the restaurant?" he says.

I do just that, and with haste.

The restaurant is brighter now than when I first arrived, like we're in a club when the music has stopped and the lights have come on. I walk, again, past the waitresses, who are now gathered around a table polishing cutlery and drinking wine out of tumblers. They all smile at me this time. Marty is sitting at a small table at the back, alone. His pint is before him, his phone in his hands. I wonder when he last took a break, a proper break. I pull up a chair.

"So, how have you found today?" he asks me, with this sensible, earnest look on his face that I hadn't seen before. I know that he has a lot of important things to do, but he is taking the time to chat with me and that makes me feel good.

I genuinely don't know how I found today. At the beginning I felt awful, but something happened when I was pin-boning that mullet. It was like the moment when you build up the courage to lean in for your first kiss, and only when you pull your lips away from the boy do you realize just how simple and human it all is, and you want to do it again. I want to do service again, but I'm not sure if the flutter in my heart is adrenaline or enjoyment—a bit like sex sometimes.

Despite my muddled head, obviously I am going to be English, lie, and say I enjoyed every second. I hear myself say it: "Yeah, it was really great. I would love to learn from a place like this."

Marty's face lights up, and I can tell I said the right

thing. "It's a really special place. I mean it's fast-paced and it can be intense, but I think you did great."

"Thank you." I suspect his definition of doing great must merely be that I did not slip over and chop someone's balls off.

"So, do you want to start next week? I know you have cooking school during the day, so you could do evenings. Say, Tuesday to Friday?" he says.

Just like that, I have the job? No second-round interview? No HR forms? Was he not at all concerned by the fact that I didn't actually cook during the trial shift? I buy some time by sipping my beer *real slow*.

I swallow. "Wow, yeah, great! Sounds great. Cool. Okay. Yeah."

I don't have time to think. Chefs aren't supposed to need time to think—they are supposed to just know, right? I'm so bored of being an overthinker, a worrier, a dweller. Maybe this job will rid me of that. Well, it's done now. I'm a chef. Fuck, that does sound cool.

I finish my beer as Marty talks shit about the waitresses, complaining about how they only work here to socialize and they're always messing up service, forgetting dishes or taking things to the wrong table. How is he trusting me with workplace gossip already? I put in years before a member of senior staff shared the good stuff with me at my old office job. It seems the rules of the restaurant game are just different. I like it.

"Right, I've got to head off but look forward to seeing you next week. Just text me if you have any questions," Marty says.

"Okay, great." I've probably said the word "great" seventeen times in the last five minutes. "Thank you so much!" I say. "This was really great." I stand up and make my way to the door.

I feel a surge of confidence as I leave the building. The swagger in my walk to the Tube is astounding. It's cold, even colder than this morning, but I can't feel the weather. I'm unstoppable. These people on the street, these civilians walking their dog late at night, these drunken dossers smoking fags, these teenagers on the platform, these Transport for London (TfL) workers rolling their eyes—none of them know it, but I'm a *chef*.

Cooking school tomorrow morning? How's that for a laugh? I'll go to class, of course. I paid a lot of money to attend, but that place seems like a silly little Pixar movie compared to the thriller blockbuster I just starred in. I'll finish the term, but after my trial shift, it's clear I will learn far more from working at a restaurant than sitting in a class, wearing a fucking neckerchief.

I slide open the window of the door between the train's conjoining carriages and let my hair blow in the gust of wind. Which other senses can I feel? I can smell the McDonald's from the lap of the drunk girl behind me, I can see the flash from the tracks, I can hear the rumbling of the carriage, and I can taste the post-shift beer on my tongue. But I don't really need to seek out these senses. I don't need the grounding because my anxiety has gone, it's rushing through the tunnels and I'm leaving it down here, in the London Underground, where it belongs.

I need to talk to someone about this and there's only one person who will be enthused to hear of my manic high after this morning's melodramatic lows: my dad. I can't wait to tell him how I did.

It's past midnight, but I call him anyway.

"Dad?" I say. As I march up the moving escalator to exit the Tube, I can start to feel the cold.

"Yes? How was it?" he asks, eagerly hoping to hear a success story rather than a tale of woe and self-pity.

"It was fucking excellent. I got the job. Starting next week," I say, rushing through my words.

"Bloody hell. That's great."

"Yeah, I know." I can barely grip the phone, my fingers are turning numb. "Can you and Mum stay up for a bit? Want to tell you about it," I say, knowing they will.

I look forward to describing every detail of the trial, partly because I'm high on adrenaline and I need to expel some energy in talking before I think about lying down horizontal and still in bed, but also because I want to let my parents know that I'm okay now, and I'm going to continue being okay. The past six months they have seen me quit my job, move home, and shrink into a shadow of myself as I faced depression in a way I never thought I would. I want to reassure them that I'll be back to myself soon because I've found what I want to do, and I'm pretty sure it's going to make me really happy—or at least keep me entertained.

2

An In-Denial Dalliance

JANUARY

I'm still in the tiny basement kitchen with all men, only they are no longer just men to me, they are my colleagues. My trial shift feels like years ago now, but it's only been three months since then.

I am, officially, a Commis Chef. I am right at the bottom. The way up the kitchen hierarchy generally goes like this:

Commis Chef to Chef de Partie, Chef de Partie to Sous Chef, Sous Chef to Head Chef, Head Chef to broken man with debilitating back issues and gout. The responsibilities that come with each job title vary but, broadly speaking, the higher up you get, the better you should be at cooking, and the less *bitch* work you do—painstaking, boring tasks like peeling, picking, and podding.

"Are you going to come out tonight? Come on!" asks Ella, while leaning over the pass. Today's lunch service was quiet, we've basically finished and it's only just past 3 p.m. It's January, so naturally the whole of London is staying home to recoup some of the prosperity and gut health they had before Christmas; now it's our time to celebrate. It's the hospitality industry's festive season, where we finally wind down, take time off, and get to do *our* excessive drinking.

"Hmm, I don't know," I reply, knowing I have drunk far too much this week already. But I suppose weekday drinking doesn't sound so bad when I consider there's no such thing as a weekend anymore. I haven't had one Saturday night off since I started working here.

"Come on! Everyone is coming. We'll be out of here at five-ish; it won't be a late one," she pleads. The whole entourage is going tonight: all the chefs, as well as the front of house: the general managers, the bar staff, the waitresses, the runners. Ella is a member of the front-of-house girl gang, a group made up of the prettiest and wildest waitresses; they are the Spice Girls and Ella is obviously Posh Spice. Instead of different hairstyles they have different dietary requirements: there's dairy-free Daisy, gluten-intolerant Georgia, and hash-brown Helina—it's the only thing she'll eat. Ella doesn't eat anything at the restaurant, she pops into Marks & Spencer on her lunch break and gets a wholemeal falafel wrap. It seems I have been invited into the band. Maybe they think I'm mysterious, when in reality I'm just shy. Or maybe they are merely using me to get intel on their lover boys, the chefs, whom I work with day in and day out. Either way, I have been invited on tour with them, where we will likely indulge in true hospitality hedonism; there will be sex, secrets, and Maldon salt. Hopefully they won't find out about my new lover; I fear I may be exiled if they do.

I hadn't had sex for a while due to last summer's spell of depression and whatnot, so being back in the game is excellent, regardless. I hadn't realized you could have such fantastic sex with someone you were, in part, turned off by. But there's something hot about no one else knowing. And my lack of infatuation or interest in this man is almost empowering: he is not taking over my life, like other men might; the kitchen is.

I'm glad to be officially out of cooking school. I'm no longer a student, I'm a grown woman having frequent sex and getting paid a monthly salary to cook. Finishing school was a relief in the end. I was exhausted from working evenings in the kitchen and then pretending to care in class the next day. I can safely say I will stay in touch with very few of my classmates.

Life will never be the same again, and nor will my skin. My arms are tainted by fresh burns from the deep-fat fryer spitting hot oil on me, while my hands are embellished with little red nicks in my fingers from too much chopping with too little time. I never really had to rush at cooking school, so I didn't have any visible proof of my new career then, but I do now. My minor injuries may be ever-growing, but my arse, on the other hand, is looking excellent; twenty thousand steps a day will do that to you.

"Yeah, alright, I'll come." I give in to Ella and agree to join her on tour. "I just need to hand over to Paul then I'll meet you guys out the front." Paul joined just before Christmas. He is an overqualified Chef de Partie who has the experience to be a Head Chef but has no interest in the responsibility that comes with it. He and I both work on my new section: Larder. He is older, late thirties maybe. He is stocky but handsome, and sometimes I fancy him. Whenever I hand over the section to him for dinner service, he always gives me shit, but I enjoy it. I go through the fridges, talking to him about what I have done in terms of mise en place and what is left for him to finish for dinner service. Mise en place in French means "to put in place," so in kitchens we refer to the ingredients we prepare—whether it be chopped parsley, portioned fish, cubed butter, a gallon of soup—as mise en place, or simply mise.

If I work hard, he has less mise to do on his shift, and if he works hard, I have less mise on mine.

It was working through the Christmas season that allowed me to bond with my new peers. In the lead-up to December, Marty warned me how busy the festive period is in the hospitality industry, but I didn't realize it would be so extreme. For a good three weeks we were completely run off our feet; everyone pulling extra double shifts and no one getting more than three or four hours of sleep a night. It was a true baptism of fire. It is easy to sit with anyone who has also worked a manically busy dinner service in December, chewing the fat effortlessly, bitching about customers, or laughing about our mistakes. When I was working part-time, I was too shy to stay for post-work drinks when I didn't really feel I deserved a seat at the table. And I was physically exhausted. I'd wake up each morning and my thighs would cramp, my arms would ache, and my face looked so pale it was almost translucent. I'd come home every night smelling like chip oil and barely make it to the shower. It was brand-new to me to use my body that much; I'd obsessively check my steps on my phone every night, then send screenshots to my family group chat and message my brother: *20,000 steps today, what did you do, you lazy bastard?* I felt proud but wrecked.

I was emotionally exhausted too. I wanted time out to

see my normal friends with normal jobs and to recharge my batteries in their normal company. Though whenever I did see them, they'd just say things like "It sounds so hard." They didn't, and still don't, understand. I realize no one can really understand working in hospitality unless they're in it. Still, I know that many chefs work harder than I do. I've heard Zack and Paul talk about how in their old jobs they'd do back-to-back doubles, fifteen- to sixteen-hour shifts, three or four days in a row. It motivates me to compete with the big boys.

Nowadays, getting home at 1 a.m. doesn't feel so strange. My thighs don't cramp in my sleep, and I'm getting used to not seeing my normal friends. I feel proud of myself for the first time in my life: proud of how hard I work, especially, and of how I'm getting better every day. I like the sense of accomplishment. And I like the romance and camaraderie of it. I am infatuated with the kitchen, the busy services, the stress, the going out late, the secret sex, and the hungover shifts the morning after.

I love the post-work drinks, too; they have become a sacred ritual, in fact.

After every shift there is beer and a cigarette with the chefs. It doesn't matter how many shifts you have worked in a row, it is vital for your sanity to sit down, drink, and laugh with the people who participate in this whole charade with you. You reflect on service, talk shit about customers, and chat about nonexistent weekend plans. The frosty beer slides down your throat as your body cools down, and your arse melds to a chair after hours of being on your feet. It's heaven; there is nothing else you could imagine consuming after a long day in a windowless basement, apart from maybe a line of coke or a pack of instant noodles.

Ella gleams when I confirm that I'll be joining her and the Spice Girls tonight.

"Okay, amazing!" she shrieks before asking me, in a quieter voice, "How was service, by the way? You're doing so well on the Larder section!"

I respond coyly. "It was good, thanks. Much prefer working on a proper section instead of being stuck round the back doing prep work."

When I first started, part-time, there was no real chance to prove myself as worthy of working on a section in service. Coming in solely in the evenings meant I headed straight to the back of the kitchen and completed a list of monotonous tasks that had been half-finished by the morning prep chef. These were tasks the other chefs would rather not do—organize the dry store by alphabetizing the herbs and spices, peel tomorrow's ten-kilogram sack of potatoes, clear the fridges of bad produce, then ensure that old produce was on top of new produce so it could be used first, pick herbs, vacuum-pack sauces, brunoise chilies, and sometimes, if it was a quiet day, organize the equipment.

That was fine; I understood it was necessary for me to start at the bottom. The kitchen is divided into sections where each cook prepares designated dishes from the menu. The most senior chefs usually cook with premium cuts of meat and fish and are in charge of stocks and sauces. The chefs on this section are always experienced, so as to avoid serving overcooked meat or ruining gallons of the stock which makes up the base of the most decadent dishes. This could be called the Mains section or the Pan section or the Sauce section. In bigger kitchens there might be a section dedicated solely to Sauce, where the Saucier works. And in some kitchens the Hot

AN IN-DENIAL DALLIANCE

Meat Mains and the Hot Fish Mains are divided. But it varies kitchen to kitchen. We're a small kitchen, so we just have Hot Mains.

Then there are the cold starters and appetizers—salads and smaller, simpler dishes like bread and butter, oysters, cured fish, terrines, and charcuterie; this is usually referred to as the Larder section. And, finally, the Pastry section, which is the desserts.

When I started full-time, though, I wanted to be out there, under the hot lights, cooking food for customers. And finally it happened: about a month ago, Head Chef Marty asked me to cover Paul on Larder service because he was sick. I kept up with Zack and Emil—I had my salads and snacks on the pass at the same time as they had their mains up; I proved myself. Ever since, I have been on the Larder section, day in, day out, and I love it. I do the mornings, and Paul does the evenings, because they tend to be busier. The only time I don't enjoy service is when the new chef, Omar, is running the pass. Omar is a Sous Chef who replaced Emil after he left in November. Emil wanted to work less in restaurants that demanded more of his time due to his girlfriend getting pregnant. He was a good guy, and I miss him. Omar is a big macho man who picks on me, perhaps in an attempt to flirt. It's a schoolboy trick, and unfortunately for him, I am a taken lady. Unfortunately for me, I am taken by a man I don't actually fancy. Perhaps I'm being too harsh; my secret lover has a *Men's Health* magazine body and a good face. It's what he does with the hair on top of his head that ruins it all. Yes, my new dalliance has quite the extraordinary hairstyle.

But I keep thinking about the sex: the tender touch, the generous groping, and the moments of intimacy after the climax. I like lying with him in bed; maybe it's just because he's a warm body, or maybe it's because that, despite my cruel judgment of his hairstyle, I actually have feelings for him. Whatever it is, I can't seem to put an end to it.

"How far is the pumpkin on Table Seven?" Zack asks me. Zack got promoted to Junior Sous Chef and he's been an even bigger arsehole since.

"I'm ready in one minute," I say.

We have just one more check to send.

I look down at my section, my workplace, my shiny steel office. It's like a desk, only instead of a pot of pens, I have pots and pans. Instead of stationery, I have knives and spoons. Instead of a mouse and keyboard, I have a long row of metal containers filled with roasted pumpkin seeds and nuts, black sesame seeds, chopped mint, chopped parsley, grilled pumpkin, and pans of dressings like guanciale oil, nori oil, and mustard vinaigrette. On my desk, instead of a framed picture of my wife and kids, I have a mise list, defaced in black Sharpie from crossing off tasks as I go. The ingredients on my workbench are my data: I take the shallots from the suppliers, I format them into cubes, and then I use a formula to make a pickling liquid. Now my pickled shallots sit in Column A, alongside my spoons in Column B.

"Louder! We need to hear you," Zack shouts back at me.

I move quickly and take a few slices of grilled pumpkin from a shallow container on my workbench. Paul told me not to put them in their fridge because the olive oil solidifies and becomes claggy. I pile the slices of pumpkin in a stainless-steel bowl and put it to the side. Next, I take a spoon, pull open the top drawer of my service fridge, and scoop out a big mound of labneh. I spread it onto a plate with conviction.

I get the bowl of the pumpkin and add a load of black sesame seeds and roasted and crushed peanuts, dress the mix with nori oil and a little salt, then toss it gently with a spoon in one hand and my fingers in the other. I deftly prop the pumpkin atop the labneh. And I drizzle more nori oil on top, which appears bright green against the white of the labneh. It looks lovely. I take it up and call, "Service," hoping it's loud enough that Zack won't bug me again.

Zack always nags me about being louder. It pisses me off because I am perfectly loud enough, but this guy wants me to be a dick-swinger like him. Despite being a run-of-the-mill-looking lad with thick-rimmed glasses, he has clearly stolen the heart of beautiful Ella. The thing that sets him apart from all the other run-of-the-mill-looking guys in the world is this thing he holds in his hand: a knife. He is a chef, and thus he has inherent sex appeal. Why, after all the strength and power womankind have obtained, do we still end up fancying the man with the loudest voice, the dirtiest sense of humor? The one who makes the biggest bang with the biggest weapon, using the unstoppable force of his masturbation arm to chop away at a hunk of meat? I *do* understand the appeal. The attributes of a chef overlap with two things: passion and pleasure. Passion is what they are fueled by, and they use it to create pleasure—whether it be in the kitchen or the bedroom. Or so I imagine. That's why chefs are innately hot.

It goes beyond the chefs. It's hospitality staff in general—everyone has sex-appeal stains on their uniforms. There's not much an HR team can do about coworker copulation; how are we supposed to find love outside of work when we spend our whole lives in the restaurant? Paul told me if a restaurant has an HR team, which is a rare offering in itself, it's likely to deal with issues most other industries do not encounter: not just sexual relationships but, for example, in his old restaurant they had to have a meeting about encouraging people to clear their drug baggies off the changing-room floor. I thought coke was passé, but I've learned it's still very much on trend. It feels like the restaurant world should've changed, but a strange bit of me is enthralled that it hasn't all that much, because it feels like I'm getting the real experience, and that no one is diluting their character for my tender, female sensibilities.

In another sense, the restaurant world feels beautifully modern: it encourages people to be who they are, to engage in authentic and personal conversation, and to pursue a passion, to cook! And there is very little evidence of unfair hierarchy here. There is no way you could schmooze your way to the top without putting in real, hard work. But in restaurants there are no set career paths or formal trajectories; Paul tells me some of the best chefs he's met through the years were originally KPs. They became chefs purely by helping out whenever unreliable chefs bailed on a shift or went missing altogether. After a while, they became the most valued, experienced chefs in the team.

Either way, the restaurant world is refreshing; a place where the ugly guy can win, and "fuck you" really means "I love you." There is no formality. When the kitchen flooded the other day, everyone—from the Head Chef to the new runner—stayed behind and pulled out the same shit from the drain. Because the hours are so long,

AN IN-DENIAL DALLIANCE

there is so much time to talk, to really understand the people you work with on a deeply intimate level. After enough late nights drinking in the restaurant, I got to know the waitresses, and my initial wariness has transformed into a stable fondness. And now I know that Marty, whom I was so scared of, only raises his voice because he has to, that's his way of running a kitchen and it's damn efficient.

But I still dislike Zack. He knows I'm shy and he doesn't like it; he wants to unwrap me like I'm his private game of pass the parcel, like he's the spoiled birthday boy and everyone must watch him play his stupid game. What if I don't want to unwrap myself and bare all in a room full of men that I've just started warming up to? Having said that, Zack is nowhere near as bad as Omar; at least Zack wants to make my presence more known in the kitchen, whereas Omar often dismisses my presence entirely.

When I forget Zack and Omar, when I forget about my nerves and my shy character, I love this job. I am doing well, and I'm being trusted with things more than the people who started at the same time as me, or even before. Initially, I did Larder with Paul by my side, monitoring me. He trained me up over a few shifts, but it was fairly easy to get the hang of it and now I'm flying, running the section just as well as he does, or so I like to think. For someone who is dangerously competitive, being given new tasks is like a drug, and I want to do more. I have always liked a challenge; I suspect it's linked to something unhealthy like needing validation, but who cares? Doesn't everyone want to win? Perhaps not.

"That pumpkin dish looks beautiful," Zack says, peering down over the indestructible rim of his thick glasses at my plate on the pass, with his back facing me. He is trying to make me like him. "Cheers," I respond flatly.

Paul arrives just in time to witness the awkward exchange. I'm glad to see his cheeky face.

"Hello, hello," he shouts toward the general vicinity of the kitchen, as he walks to the changing room. He gives me a wink and I grin back at him. We're both gearing up for our routine tomfoolery; he is also averse to Zack's boisterous kitchen ways, so I like it when he comes to join my side.

ZZZ zzz ZZZZ zzz ZZZZ.

"Fuck's sake, I thought we were done. Okay, this is the last check for lunch, people," Zack shouts, as he tilts his head forward to read the check. He's now on the Hot section with Omar, the new senior Sous Chef.

"Check on," he bellows. "One radicchio salad, one kimchi to follow, two pork secreto." He is getting louder and louder, proving to me just how easy it is to use your voice.

"Yes," I shout back at him.

"Yes, what?" he says, looking through his section toward mine, glaring into my eyes.

Does he want me to do the chef thing?

"Yes, Chef?" I say it like a question. I check my pants to make sure I haven't wet myself out of embarrassment. Using the phrase "Yes, Chef" makes me feel like I'm an amateur porn actor, a lady seduced by the man with a knife.

"That's it!" He shouts back at me with a big smile; he's clearly embarrassing me for his own entertainment. Bastard. But fine; maybe he's not that bad.

Paul wanders over to the Larder workbench, which

AN IN-DENIAL DALLIANCE

we both use; it's *our* section but he is my maestro, the one who teaches me the recipes. He always shares little tricks for each one. He watches me plate dishes, he tells me to "think less and feel more," and I tell him he's a pretentious loser while secretly taking note.

"You alright, matey?" he says to me, with a fatherly slap on the back.

"Yeah, good, you? You had a good morning?" I say, as I go fishing with a slotted spoon for kimchi and Gruyère croquettes that I'm frying in an ocean of oil; they look perfectly golden. I rest the piping-hot croquettes on a wire rack to drain off any excess oil while I prepare the rest of the dish. I lift a spoonful of saffron mayonnaise and dollop it on the starter plate and use the back of the spoon to spread it a little. I take the croquettes and balance them on the purée, then I sprinkle some kimchi salt and grated Gruyère over the top. It's done. It smells warm and funky. It's a dish that people want after Christmas to help with cheese withdrawals.

As I walk to the pass with the croquettes, Paul says to me, "Make sure you leave that under the hot lamps, yeah? Ideally, you should've done the salad first, because that is served cold so you don't need to worry about it cooling down, unlike the croquettes." He talks to me in a serious tone when he is teaching, and I appreciate it.

"Okay, yes, that makes sense. Will do. Thanks," I say.

"So funny how you thank me every time I tell you to do something. So posh."

"Fuck off." I grin at the floor, feeling shy, still, but unashamed; I don't need to hide my studious ways so much anymore.

I get to the salad fast: I take a handful of radicchio

leaves from the fridge beneath my workbench and, in a bowl, I dress it with guanciale oil, fried cubes of guanciale, a dash of some expensive quince vinegar, and a pinch of salt. I am delicate when mixing the salad, to avoid crushing the form of the leaves, or saturating them with dressing, making it look ugly and floppy when plating. That's another little hack Paul taught me. I pile the leaves effortlessly onto the center of a pristine white plate and off to the pass I go.

I look around the corner and see there are no waitresses waiting to take the dish. That means I must call for one myself: "Service," I say, a little bit louder than before. If only Zack could hear me now, but he's preoccupied with Ella. One of the Spice Girls comes to take my dishes; it really is the last check, it's time to close down and have a beer. Another shift done. I'm turning into a real chef, even though Marty likes to remind me that we're all just cooks—*he's* the only chef.

"What are you doing tonight?" Nathan, the dopey but cheeky chef, asks. Nathan doesn't really belong to a section, I suspect because he's not all that sharp or proactive. He leans in, watching me clean my knives.

"I don't know, I might go for drinks with Ella and that lot. You want to come?" I ask him.

"Oooh, friends," he says, taking the piss. I worry for a split second. Shit. Have I been that obvious with my relief at finally making friends? Nah. Who am I kidding? These men don't pay that much attention to me, especially Nathan. He doesn't pay much attention to anything, hence he's stuck at the back doing prep, or making pasta, or exploding bags of veal stock down his trousers and taking three hours to clean it up.

"Yeah, I'll come. Are we going to get a bag in?" he asks me.

"Hmm; I'm on double tomorrow," I say.

In my old nine-to-five office job I had evenings off, weekends off; that is a lot of time to doss about, to socialize, to do drugs, and then recover. Now I am working sixty-hour weeks and for the duration of my shift, whether it be ten hours or sixteen hours, I am standing up, moving about, lifting pans, beating mixtures; there are no moments of respite when I can hide behind a laptop screen and just be still and quiet, or go and sit on the toilet to scroll on my phone for twenty minutes without my boss noticing. And in the minimal time I have free, I'm either drinking or hungover, so it all kind of merges into one. It's like I never really leave the restaurant.

I often question if I can do this job long-term. But then there's this part of me that wants to conquer it, to get better at the thing I love most—cooking. It's the only thing I have real interest in, cooking and eating; and boys and sex, I suppose. I'm stubborn, I don't want to give up. I want to make a career out of my favorite thing in the world, cooking, and working in restaurants seems like the noblest way to do this.

Paul tucks his cloth into the waistband of his apron and removes the pen from behind his ear to review the mise-en-place list I've written for him.

As he leans forward, I spot the muscles in his upper arm contort beneath his skin. I don't really pay attention to men's bodies in the real world, but in the kitchen, you can't ignore it; the physicality of someone's body is right there in front of you. You begin to recognize the cooking scars on their arms, the way their shirt hangs by their chest, the bulk of their shoulders. I didn't think muscly men were especially attractive, but it turns out that when the muscles are right there in front of you, there is something enticing about them.

"How many on the books tonight?" Paul asks me, still reviewing the mise list.

"I think Marty said seventyish covers." Paul taught me to say covers. I used to say customers. I don't really know the difference.

He has taken me under his chiseled wing, he is kind and patient with me, like a babysitter, and I'm the child that fancies him a bit but I know it will never happen. Besides, I've got that new lover now, much to my dismay.

"Alright, I'm going to head off then, if that's okay," I tell him.

He widens his eyes.

"What?" I say, curious.

"So . . . I've heard about your new guy. How's that going?" He starts to laugh.

Paul has somehow found out the thing I wanted *no one* to know.

"I'm not sleeping with him!" I say as my face goes beet red.

"Yes, you are!"

"Okay, fine, I am, but please don't tell anyone. I don't want Marty finding out, he will never shut up about it," I say.

I don't want the guys in the kitchen knowing about my new dalliance because it shines a light on my womanliness; I worry that they'd see me differently if they knew I was sleeping with anyone, using my lady body to do lady things.

"So where are you going with lover boy tonight? You

going to go to the club and then snog on the streets of South London?" Paul asks, knowing the younger staff always go to this bar in Camberwell because Axel's friend owns it and often keeps it open late for us.

"Don't be revolting," I say. He's probably not far off the mark.

I firmly reiterate that he must not tell anyone at work; I am embarrassed. The other reason I don't want people knowing about my lover is far more important than gender politics: the man I'm sleeping with has a topknot.

In December, much like a new kid in a playground, I latched onto someone and it was the barman with a topknot. He brought me into the bar, the jungle gym of the restaurant, where the kids had fun and got silly, and I clung to him to feel safe. We kissed and then I accidentally fucked him.

Unfortunately, the sex was pretty good. Weeks passed and we had sex again. And then accidentally again. And then a couple more times. And he has done something important for me and I appreciate it; he has brought me out of my sex slump and reminded me of just how impactful a good shagathon can be on one's sensibilities. But I can't go on, I just can't. When I see him in the sober light of day, my attraction does not merely dissipate, it flees my body at such a great speed that I am hit with a wave of nausea.

Him having this topknot is a major issue. Why must all barmen feel the need to be so spectacularly unique? If it's not attention-seeking mustaches, it's tight floral shirts, or dangly earrings, or audaciously cropped, bollock-smothering trousers, or, worst of all: a topknot. Where did the hipsters go? They left their wavering music careers and now they're standing right in front of us, pouring us a drink in our favorite neighborhood restaurant. And they like to make really manly drinks—brown liquor with the butchest of citrus fruits: navel orange; dark, dehydrated grapefruit.

"Okay, but at least tell me this. In sex, does he ever untie his . . ." Paul signals toward his hair. He bends over in fits of laughter.

"SHUT UP," I say and run away.

The worst thing is, there are moments where I think I might quite like Topknot Barman. He is kind and generous, and he takes such earnest interest in my life. When we have sex, there is a moment afterward where I feel completely comfortable being naked next to him, and I unveil all my insecurities both physically and mentally. When I do, his ripped arm reaches out to touch my soft one, and he brushes his thumb against my hip. But as soon as I turn my head to face him and I see the topknot, my stomach turns inside out.

Personal lives and romantic happenings are not something that the chefs discuss with any kind of discretion in the kitchen, and I'd rather avoid my story being one that is analyzed.

And the last person I want to find out about Topknot Barman is Marty.

I like Marty, kind of, but his unpredictable mood still scares me. When he is angry, he can be a little rude, a tiny bit spiteful, but when he is happy, he is a lot of fun, maybe too much fun—he gets hyperactive like a fun dad and he starts spanking the guys' arses. Never my arse, though, which I suppose is a good thing, although it does make me feel slightly left out. Every time he passes my section, I find myself almost hoping he lands a large clap right on the center of my arse cheek. But yes, probably best he doesn't.

"What's going on with Marty, by the way? I saw him having an intense conversation with Omar out front when I arrived," Paul says to me when I return to the section.

Omar, the new Sous Chef, has been here for just a couple of weeks. He is a quintessential "chef" character: smelly, hairy, and the size of a boulder. He has a bald head and dark shadowed eyes, and his skin is gray-tinged, like his liver is failing or he hasn't slept, ever. He is covered in chef tattoos. Not the whimsical ones, like a branch of rosemary or a minimalist knife and fork; instead, he has the type of tattoos that should be reserved only for weathered sailors at sea. One of his forearms is completely covered in a fish, no particular fish, just a big girthy fucker with scales that have faded beneath his bushy arm hair. Then on the other arm there's a chunky lock and key with a banner painted across it reading CHEF. He's a slimy bastard, always telling the front-of-house girls how beautiful they are or making politically incorrect remarks about race and religion. Marty clearly wants him gone.

In restaurants, the staff turnover is high. In the three months I've been here, I've seen several chefs and front-of-house staff come and go, Emil being one of them. For chefs, it's always a telling sign when they take their knives home with them instead of leaving their knife-wrap in their locker; it means they're not coming back. Omar's knife-wrap has stayed, night after night, in his locker.

"Oh, fuck. Can you hear that?" Paul says to me.

"What?" I say, shuffling over to him.

"I swear that's Marty shouting," he says.

Nathan enters the kitchen, walking through the back door where all the noise is coming from. He's holding a big, deep Gastro—the stainless-steel containers that come in varying sizes and are used as a vessel for most things in the kitchen—full of ice, and his mouth is shaped in a perfect O, giddy from the drama that he just witnessed.

He fills us in: "Marty is going nuts with Omar. It sounds like he's about to fire him."

We all scurry over to the door and hear Marty going apeshit: "You fucking cunt. Who the fuck do you think you are? Coming into my fucking kitchen and acting like you fucking run the place."

"What did he do?" I ask Nathan eagerly, not as sensitively attuned to the word "fuck" after three months of working here.

"From what I heard, it sounds like Marty gave Omar some kind of warning before service last night, and apparently Omar told him to chill out. Think it was the last straw," Nathan tells us.

"I mean, I don't blame him," Paul says. He walks back to our section, unfazed by the kitchen gossip.

Nathan and I, the young bucks, follow him; we head back into the kitchen to keep busy so we can stick around and hear more of the drama. I've already packed up my knives so I help Paul pick some mint while Nathan blanches spinach and then dunks it in his ice-filled Gastro to keep the vibrant green color.

"What are you still doing here?" Paul says. "You can go, I'm all set."

"I know, but I want to listen," I say. He laughs, emptying roasted peanuts onto a chopping board.

Marty's rage is not petering out; if anything, it's growing. I'm not sure if Marty is aware that we can hear the argument word for word in the kitchen or if he just doesn't care.

There is a loud bang outside and Nathan stops blanching.

"What the fuck was that?" I say, delighting in the warfare.

Nathan and I crawl back to the doorway to see if we can hear. Paul gives in and joins us to listen at the door.

"I understand why Marty wants him gone," Paul says as he stands with his hands on his hips, leaning on the pass like he's kicking off a mothers' meeting.

"Yeah. He's a knob. He's so gross to the girls out front," Nathan says. "And he's a bit of a knob to you," he says while looking at me.

I'm surprised that Nathan noticed, but I don't say anything. I want the boys to know I can handle men like Omar.

Omar often stands at the pass and critiques my dishes with no real rhyme or reason. I suspect he wants others to hear him exert his authority, and he only feels comfortable demonstrating that with me, the only girl. "Re-plate that, please," he'll tell me, with no indication as to why. He'll swipe away splatter marks from the side of my salad bowls with his sausage fingers, and suck the sauce off them. "Too salty," he'll say, and then go back for another bite. I guess the boys noticed he's a wanker too.

As the team huddles by the door, sharing horror stories of Omar, Zack walks back into the kitchen from the dining room. He always likes to go and schmooze out front with the Spice Girls the moment service ends.

"What's going on?" he asks. We explain and he joins

us at the door. I am pleased; it feels like this is a thing we can all reminisce on as great friends in a few more months, when I finally make it all the way out of my shell. We all lean closer like we're outside the headmaster's office, rejoicing as we hear the loud-mouthed kid finally getting expelled.

Marty's voice is only growing louder. "You think you know everything. You don't. You know fuck all. Just because you've got those shit tattoos, it doesn't make you a good chef."

Toxic kitchen behavior sounded scary before I started at the restaurant, but this is a damn riot! It isn't pots and pans being thrown; this is more like a performative WWE fight, it's quite funny, really. I suppose if it was happening to me, and I was having abuse hurled at me, maybe it would be different. But this is exciting because we've all seen the tension build up for weeks, and finally it's imploding and we have front-row seats.

I begin feeling fearful that Marty is about to burst through the door and I'll get caught in his firing line, so I grab my Sharpie and knives and get going.

"Alright, you off, then?" Paul asks me.

"Yeah. I'm almost tempted to stay to see how this plays out," I say.

"This is only ending one way," Paul replies.

"What do you mean?" I say.

"Omar's gone," Paul says.

So, there is no formal HR procedure, no exit interview, no probation period. The WWE match has settled things; the loser will go home with his sweaty belongings and tear-stained cheeks, never returning to the fighting ring. I feel a bit sorry for Omar, but then I remember he's a slimy cunt.

AN IN-DENIAL DALLIANCE

I say farewell to Paul and even Zack, and I let Nathan know I'm going to get changed before we get our pints.

Nathan joins me in the changing room. It's not awkward anymore. We're used to the bareness of each other's backs as we hobble about, leaning forward as we undress—me hiding my tits, him his bollocks.

"The dining room is pretty quiet; we can probably just have a drink at the bar?" Nathan says. Again, he's asking me to make the call—I am rising in the ranks one way or another.

"Yeah, okay," I say. There is no reason I wouldn't want to do that, other than the fact that my dalliance is on shift and I can't bear to be around him in front of others. But Nathan doesn't know about that, so I must agree.

We leave the changing room and walk discreetly through the dining room toward the bar. There he is, Topknot Man doing "his thang," as he would say in this satirical American accent he likes to use for laughs.

Nathan and I take a barstool each and briefly check our phones after being off-grid since 8 a.m. Unlike everywhere else, phones in kitchens are superfluous tools; they cannot help us cook, therefore they're irrelevant for most of the day.

I'm hoping my lover will play it cool in front of Nathan, but in the past couple of days his affection for me has been spilling out all over the place. He comes to the kitchen to get fruit from our walk-in fridge and hangs around me like a needy child; and when we go to get drinks at the bar, he gives me more booze than anyone else. The latter part isn't so bad, but I'd still prefer him to do it more subtly.

He has spotted me. I see him quickly look at himself in the mirror behind the long row of bottled spirits, and then he does it: he adjusts his topknot. He is as reverent with it as he is with his penis, which in truth is quite a good one.

He swans over and looks into my eyes as if we're standing at the altar. I glare at him, signaling him to tone it down.

"How was the shift, guys?" He addresses both me and Nathan in a performatively nonchalant way, like he's hiding a birthday present for Nathan under the bar and I'm in on the secret.

"Yep, fine." I'm not drunk enough to talk to him yet.

"Yeah, good, you?" Nathan asks, unaware of the awkward red heat between us: anger radiating from me, infatuation from him.

He pours us our complimentary pints and hands them to us. The boys converse while I look at my phone like a moody cow.

"Can I have a top-up, please?" I say.

"Yes, of course." He takes my already basically full pint to the tap, gazing at me all the while.

"There we go, milady." Ew. For fuck's sake. He's already given up any attempt at discretion; am I that irresistible? Does the sun truly shine off the chip oil running through my golden hair?

Nathan clocks Topknot Barman's flirtiness toward me and smirks.

"Let's go for a cigarette," I say to Nathan quickly, pretending not to hear my lover's tender remarks and whisking away my free-of-charge beer. Nathan and I head toward the front of the restaurant where there are a couple of tables and chairs; I feel guilty so I turn to look back at my lover and smile. That should keep him happy for a while. He gleams back at me, the poor bugger.

AN IN-DENIAL DALLIANCE

Nathan and I sit outside to smoke and drink. The front-of-house girls join us at five-ish, just as they finish their shift. We sit out front, only going inside to do lines of coke or to plead with Topknot Barman for free drinks. It's cold, we're sitting under a dark, bleak January sky, but we've all spent too long inside so the fresh air feels good.

As I get tipsy, I start traipsing in and out of the restaurant by myself, dodging customers and heading to the bar where I know my lover will wait on me hand and foot. For a moment I stop and look at him. Nah, I definitely don't fancy him, I tell myself; oh, fuck, maybe I do? I squint my eyes; I tilt my head and lift up my hand to cover up the topknot. "So much better," I mumble to myself.

"And how are *you* doing this evening?" he says as I lean on the bar. It irks me when people start a sentence with "and," but I don't notice things like that when I'm drunk.

"Yes, all fine. Are you coming out tonight?"

I ask him because I'm drunk now and I just want a bit of fun; is that too much to ask?

"It depends. Are you going to go?" he asks with a sparkle in his hopeful and really quite beautiful eyes.

"Yep. You should come." When I'm sure no one is there, I kiss him behind the bar and ask for a cocktail. He says, "Okay, missy." I swallow a big wave of nausea. Missy? I am so clearly not a missy. "And I will see *you* later," he says as he hands me a margarita. He knows margaritas are my favorite cocktail; how can he know me so well, but know so little about my fickle feelings for him?

I walk away with my free drink. As I leave him behind,

I miss him a little. I am experiencing that God-awful feeling that happens to women after they sleep with a man where we feel warm and fuzzy around them, like we're connected. But I can't; it is imperative that I don't lead him on any further. Sex is sex. Booze is booze. God, I'm a bit drunk.

"Where are we going?" I say to Ella, as I scooch up next to her. We're the best of friends when we're drunk, she takes intoxication seriously like I do, no falling over or crying; just focused, professional debauchery.

"You know the one we always go to in Camberwell? Axel's friend's place. We'll leave in a couple hours," she says to me.

We drink for free for hours, watching tables come and go. At about midnight, Ella tells me and a couple of the Spice Girls to finish our drinks: "The Uber is six minutes away." The customers and senior management have left, it's just my lover boy closing down and the KPs locking up.

Six of us, the Spice Girls plus me and Nathan, pile in the back of a taxi with half-empty bottles of restaurant wine and cans of Red Stripe from Tesco. Zack is going to pick up more drugs and meet us there. I'm sure Topknot Barman will be fine making his own way. I'm too drunk to feel any guilt about abandoning him.

As we drive down Farringdon Road toward the Thames, I notice just how drunk I am. I'm slurring my words and I feel like I'm about to tell someone about him, and I can't have that. The secret is one of the things making it hot. We pull up to a bar that starts with the letter T. It's dark and busy with blue and black lights; there are still lots of people, but it feels like the scene might be beginning to peter out. I need coke; I don't want to start sobering up and thinking about my shift tomorrow. Maybe some ket as well, why the hell not, it's a Wednesday. We all rush in, excited to do an immersive tour of the toilet cubicles.

Ella knows Axel's friend well, of course. "Darling!" she calls out while she spreads her eyes wide open. The hugging in hospitality is rife, it's the hugging that will kill me. The endless onslaught of affection is just too much for me.

"Oh, for fuck's sake," he says as he sees all of us, clearly not wanting to serve six gurning drunks just as he was starting to think about closing down. But like a good sport, he chooses to have a good time instead of a good night's sleep. "Okay, you can all come in, but just for a couple," he says to us all. I've never met him, but he lets me shuffle past him toward a cramped room at the back, behind a little purple rope. I feel like royalty, restaurant royalty.

"Line?" Nathan says to me, the minute we sit down.

"Yep." We go to the girls' bathroom together and sniff some coke. I don't feel bad about the excessive drugs because I know I'll be soldiering through the comedown tomorrow alongside everyone else.

What a time to be alive. I have a shift tomorrow morning but even if I were to go home to sleep now, I'd still be tired, and what's the difference between tired and very tired? Plus, it's only a morning shift, not a double, I'll be fine. We head back to the room. I sit next to one of the Spice Girls, who all look and sound the same in the dark.

"What's it like working with the guys all day? Do you hate being the only girl?" she shouts in my ear, a lot louder than necessary. It's Georgia, I think, the drunkest waitress of them all.

"It's fine, I don't mind it," I say. I really don't mind who I work with as long as they are not mean. Marty and Zack don't *really* intimidate me, they just make me feel on edge. But Omar makes me feel sick and, at times, a bit scared.

"I think it's so cool that you're a chef," she goes on, gently swaying her head as if she's reaching full climax in a meditation class.

"Why?" I laugh, knowing her opinion already but wanting to make her articulate it so I can get my coked-up ego stroked.

"Because it's just cool."

I'm as incoherent as she is, so she sounds pretty profound to me. "Yeah, fuck it, babes, you're right," I say and we both laugh.

We continue to talk about nothing in an impassioned way. We can't spit out our sentences fast enough, and it's like we're saying the same thing over and over; like my words are traveling straight into her ears, then they travel up her throat and straight out her mouth. We are stuck in a never-ending loop of talking total utter detritus. But right now, at this moment, I am totally gripped by what model of Volkswagen her mum drives and why it reminds her of her ex-boyfriend. It feels like valuable information to me; I must learn more.

At about 3 a.m., the general public is kicked out of the bar but our group stays. It seems we have a good old-fashioned lock-up on our hands. Close the doors, turn off the lights, and light up the ciggies: this is our home for the night.

Finally, he arrives, my lover with the flamboyant blond

pineapple on his head. His eyes are wide and he's all jacked up.

I ask him, "Have you got coke?" before even saying hi.

"Yeah, sure, here we go." I take his bag and leave him by the bar. I go to the bathroom with Georgia, who is inspiring me with her Volkswagen-related philosophies.

When we close the door to the toilet cubicle, it feels like we're giggling girls having a sleepover and it's the most exhilarating night of our lives! Let's stay up even later! And let's have more sweets before bed!

And then I reach the level of inebriation where I stop caring what people think. I can no longer remember why I would. My heart begins to drown in sentiment, like I'm stuck in a Christmas movie. If you look for it, I've got a sneaky feeling you'll find that love actually is all around. Now where is the leading man in my drug-fueled rom-com? You know, the one with the weird hair? I let my desire take over and, now that my inhibitions are set free, it feels good. I choose not to think about any subsequent damage; when I leave the bathroom, I walk straight up to my lover, gazing at him like I'm in a Kelly Rowland music video, but instead of "When Love Takes Over," it's "When Coke Takes Over."

"Hey, do you want to be my girlfriend?" he shouts over the music. My stomach drops. What the fuck?

I turn to him; he is staring at me, with desperation in his eyes, begging me to love him. I don't know why the fuck he would think I would want to be his girlfriend. I feel sick but also a little flattered.

You know what, maybe we're meant to be. You're supposed to be with someone who challenges you, right? The thing on his head, well, that really, *really* challenges me. I lean over to him and shout, "What?" pretending not to have heard. He does not ask again. All I can hear is music and giggles, and the beating in my chest telling me: *Fuck it, one more drink.*

When we get kicked out at about 5 a.m., I grab my lover by the hand. I don't want to go home alone. We walk away together, not saying bye to anyone. There is no need. Because really we are all strangers at this point, the only thing that binds us is the toxins in our blood and our dread of tomorrow's shift.

"I'm getting an Uber. Want to come to mine?" I ask him. The night is over and the reality is hitting me that I have work in a few hours. I need someone to put me to bed and to comfort me when my alarm goes off.

"Sure!" he says.

As we drive parallel to the Thames, I look out the window of the Uber to the sparkling dark blue water and the leafy green trees; London looks so healthy and vivacious compared to how I feel. It's like London is shaming me for my bad choices. Fuck you, London! I feel this sense of liberation, this thrill: I am happy where I am in life after months of being anxious about whether or not I can do my new job. But I also feel like it is all temporary, like it's all going to come to an end somehow and maybe that would be a relief.

Maybe that's the end of the high. I can feel it slipping away. I know what's coming on the other side; my jaw aches and my head hurts at just the thought of tomorrow. Topknot Barman is tapping his thumb rhythmically on his thigh; I hold his hand to make it stop.

We get back home and we crawl into my childhood bed. Usually we go to his, but I needed my own bed tonight.

I'm tired, and I don't sleep well in boys' bedrooms, especially his, which is tarted up with a load of shitty wall art and cliché boyish memorabilia. He gazes around my room, wanting, I think, to look for clues about me, to appreciate my personality and to learn of my interests before we fuck.

I ignore all of this, and decide it's time for fun, for detached sex and the last line of coke that's stuck in the corner of the baggy. I always struggle with the end of a night out, with stopping the fun and going to bed. Sex means it's not over yet; the best is yet to come. And if we do it quickly, we can still get an hour of sleep before work.

I turn onto my side and look at him, feeling unsure of what's going on in my heart but quite sure of what's going on in my knickers. The lighting is perfect: my closed curtains cast a shadow over his head but there is a crack of early sunlight sneaking through, lighting up his ripped body and hard cock. He is a good man with an earnest soul. He shouldn't be with me . . . I am far too cruel.

I kiss him and taste coke and cigarettes. I feel his breath on my neck as I close my eyes and lie back like the pillow princess I am. With other boys whom I actually fancy, I try to do more of the work, but Topknot Barman takes care of me. He worships all of me, especially my pussy. He always asks me if I'm okay. He speaks tenderly but still fucks like a man, thank God. If he were to "make love," it would remind me of how much more he cares for me than I do for him.

It is slow sex, then sensitive sex, then hot sex, then amazing sex. He can't make me orgasm because my body is numb from the intoxicants, but he doesn't give up; he is gallant. With his face, and even his damn topknot, secured between my thighs, I am in heaven. I pretend we're in love, just for a moment, and then I cum. After I orgasm, I am done with him—but I stroke his arms as a meager sign of gratitude. It's only fair, I think, knowing full well that nothing about the way I treat this poor son of a bitch is fair.

When I roll over an hour later, at 7 a.m., I look at him. There it is, the deconstructed topknot; the beast is at rest. I actively grimace at the shiny, soft hair sprawled across my pillow. I've never seen the topknot deconstructed before. I take all of him in; he looks like the blond guy from *Lord of the Rings*, the one that so many women fancy. Fuck's sake. I feel for my phone as my head pounds. A text from Marty. I open it immediately. He sent it at midnight last night; I must've missed it. Fuck.

Hey, can you work a double shift tomorrow? Omar has left so I've had to switch up everyone's shifts a bit. Hope that's cool.

Jesus Christ.

The only reason I went out last night was because I thought I was just working a morning shift. Now I'm on for a double shift on one hour's sleep. I ignore the text.

"Come on. We need to go to work now," I say to my lover.

"Hey, you," he says, as he rolls over and needily reaches for me like we're teenagers in love, when really we're adults in denial.

Jesus Christ.

I put fresh clothes on and spray on some deodorant.

The potent floral smell makes me gag. As he puts on his too-tight trousers, I avert my eyes. I can't bear to look at his form now, though I am so drawn to it when I'm intoxicated. We tiptoe down the stairs so as to not wake my unsuspecting parents; I don't need them meeting the man I am hoping to be rid of shortly, though they'd probably approve of him, seeing as he's so enamored with me. We drag ourselves into an Uber and travel in silence, my hand in his and my head on his shoulder.

As we get close to the restaurant, I tell him to get out a couple of streets away, so no one sees us together. He does as he's told.

I brace myself to start my double shift. I can feel the toxic, sour air swirling around me with every movement I make. My head feels heavier than my whole body and my limbs are moving in slow motion. My chest feels tight. I am scared.

I walk through the doors of hell. I am met with a loud, energetic, pumped-up Marty shouting at me from the kitchen.

"Hey. Where the fuck have you been? You're twenty minutes late," he says. I know he's joking, but in a kitchen where every minute counts, twenty minutes is quite significant and requires an excuse. I don't have the brain power to think of one in time; I'm too exhausted.

"Sorry!" I call out, with death sleeping in the bags beneath my eyes.

"Lunch is looking really fucking busy today and I had to bin loads of your mise this morning, because one of the dickfaces out front turned your fridges off. So, you're going to need to bulk all your mise. Just prep double the amount of everything you usually would—especially loads of the tartare; that's been super popular—and get it done quick so we're all set at twelve."

Jesus Christ.

"Oh, and thanks for doing the double shift, you're a star."

He's right. I am a goddamn star. But I am part of the team and this is what it takes. This is my final initiation. If I can survive this, then maybe I'll feel like a real chef.

I never technically agreed to the double shift, but I know I don't really have a choice. I head down to the changing room, walking into the dungeon where my satanic punishment will begin. The space is damp and dark. I take a breath through my blocked nose and taste the remnants of coke in my airways. I feel scared. I sit for a moment on the bench of the changing room. My shoulders sink as I close my eyes. How the fuck am I going to stand up, let alone work from now to midnight? My body is exhausted from my job and my mind is exhausted from convincing myself I can hack this world of big personalities, big nights, big highs, and big lows. Maybe I'm just not cut out for all this. It doesn't feel like a hangover, it feels like terror.

Panic fills my lungs. I slap myself across the face.

"Okay, here we go," I tell myself. I just have to think about the times I love my job. I love my job I love my job I love my job.

3

Massive Attack

MAY

I'm at work, but in a toilet cubicle, not in the kitchen.

Nausea is swirling around my insides, but the waves are made of toxic air, not liquid.

My heart feels heavy but no tears are coming, they are stuck somewhere. Maybe in my throat, which feels blocked.

Turbulent thoughts are rushing through my head a mile a minute, moving too fast to interpret. My mind is being swallowed up in the eye of a hurricane.

My back crawls and my eyes widen.

Everything around me is a threat.

My breath is deep but not in a performative Hollywood way—in a hollow dark way. I am not rocking back and forth like they do in the movies. My limbs are fairly still; it's my insides that are erupting.

I sit on the toilet seat and attempt to steer my way out the door and along tis winding, dark road of panic. With every passing breath, my heart sinks a little further. I keep going and find no solace. There is no petrol station to fill my tank; it's just infinite nothingness until I reach the end of the earth.

This is a different type of fear; it is far from my day-to-day fears. It's not a fear of getting shouted at by Head Chef Marty. It's not even the ultimate human fear of dying; it's the fear that I am not really here, that I never really existed in the first place. My skin feels alien, like it doesn't belong to me. And my head feels as though it is malfunctioning, like a red-eyed rat has gnawed through the fundamental wires in my brain.

I have a split second of relief where my system momentarily reboots and I see some form of light in the distance, but then a moment later, I realize it's a demonic black SUV charging along the road, flaring its bright lights in my eyes as it speeds right through me, winding me in the gut.

I need to get the fuck out of here.

I lift my so-called body off the toilet seat. I exit the cubicle and look back at myself in the mirror. My face has gone all gray. Does it always look like that? It feels like I'm seeing my face for the first time, but from someone else's point of view. A customer washing her hands next to me asks if I'm alright.

I need to leave work. I walk directly over to Marty and tell him I just puked.

"What?" He can't hear me. Massive Attack's "Unfinished Sympathy" is blasting from speakers.

"I just puked," I repeat, a little louder, loud enough.

"What the fuck?" he says. I say nothing.

Then he really looks at me. He must see the terror in my face.

He tells me to go home. He tells me to feel better. I

can't interpret any nuance. I can't tell if he believes me or if he is pissed off; I can only hear words he is saying. I don't care what he thinks.

In the changing room, my brain is blank. I am just moving my body in the ways I need to so I can get out of here. I lift my arms. I take off my work clothes. I change into my normal clothes.

Now I am ready. Oh, wait. My knife-wrap. It's sitting on the bench. I need to put it in my locker. I should put it in my locker. But I don't want to.

A moment of clarity hits me, a small junction offering me an exit from that dark road of panic. If I take my knives with me, that means I never have to come back.

I swallow the rock-solid lump of tears, collect my knives with my shaking arm, and walk out of the restaurant while avoiding all eyes.

I don't remember how I got here but I know I'm safe. I'm swaddled in soft blue-and-white stripes from M&S. My face feels damp with tears, finally. My head is being held and my hair is being stroked. I am in my mum's arms.

While my dad is my best friend and therapist, my mum is my guardian angel, my original protector, the landlord to the little red room where my feeble fetus grew. I want to start life over again so I can spend a little bit more time here with her.

4

MICHELIN STAR PUSSY JUICE

AUGUST

There's a gentle gurgling sound as seawater slips in and out of my ear. I am lying in the Cornish sea, pushing my stomach out to keep me horizontal so I can float without my legs sinking. I am bobbing about on the waves and my body is at peace; my limbs are relaxed, unlike when I was in the kitchen, when they were tense and aching from real labor. My mind is nearly at peace, it is getting there, but I am interrupted every now and again by memories of London; giddy laughter during service, racing in the fresh air for the Tube home, Marty's proud smile when I got faster than him at pin-boning mullet. I left about three months ago, and any regret I felt then—little seeds I planted—is beginning to flower. I worry that I gave up too soon. I worry that once again, my bloody impulsivity might've led me up the garden path.

I tell myself that seven months is a good stint at my first restaurant, but my inner critic tells me that I should've stuck it out for a year. When I sit on the sand or float in the sea in silence, it tells me that I am a failure and I'm not cut out to be a proper chef.

Marty was reasonably nice when I called him to hand in my notice. He was almost unfazed, like he expected it, or he'd seen it a million times before.

I gave him my fake reason for suddenly having to leave and never come back, which was that I, an incredibly junior and inexperienced chef, was called upon by a friend as a matter of urgency to help out in his newly opened and chefless restaurant. He saw straight through my lies. "You're just burned-out because we're a little low on staff right now," he said. "I understand it's been difficult, but you're doing so well." I didn't know what burnout meant, but I didn't care. "Why don't you just take a week off and see how you feel?" he said.

To which I responded with the lie: "I've already told my mate I would do it, sorry."

He asked me if there was anything he could say to make me stay and when I said no, he gave up.

I lean my body forward in the seawater and let my legs fall. They anchor me upright. I lift my hand and look at my waterproof watch, which I bought from Argos. It's one of my new accessories for a life by the sea, along with some B&M sunglasses and a loyalty card to a local nautical-themed coffee shop. The clock face tells me it's 10 a.m. and nearly time to go to work. As I glide through the water to get back to the shore, I am swimming further away from my former life; paddling away from the muddy River Thames and the South London bin juice.

I turn for a moment toward the dark Atlantic Ocean. There are acres of shimmering space in front of me, everything so pretty and clean, so calm and tranquil. There are no tunneled train tracks, no one telling me to mind the gap; there is only the beaming sun, the lapping waves, and the breezy silence. Maybe I can hear the answers to my problems in the wind; am I supposed to be here? Was it the right choice to abandon ship, should I have stayed on deck like a stoic captain drowning with his job?

I reach the sand. From the trepidation in my walk, the Cornish locals on the beach can tell I'm from London—unlike the lonesome fisherman, the old guy with a metal detector, and the lifeguard who is Cornwall's take on Adonis. My feet press gently into the sand like I'm reluctant to leave my mark; I am a visitor, not a native. But a bit of me is starting to seem like I belong: the freckles on my skin, my sea-soaked hair, and my desire for peace and quiet. Every day my body and mind heal a little, and with every passing tide that creeps back and forth, new ideas of what I want from life wash up to shore. Like the tides, the ideas are ever-changing.

I sit for a moment and look out to sea. It's Tuesday but I'm not tired from a Monday double shift, because my new restaurant, here in Cornwall, is only open three days a week. When it's open, we only do about thirty covers, or forty on a busy day. It operates like a slow cruise ship, unlike my old restaurant, which was more of a speedboat. The food is seasonal and served as a set menu, the beer cans have funky graphics and statistics about sustainability, and the art on the walls is donated by local artists—the homemade kind, not the pretentious kind. It's all a little too feel-good for me, but perhaps that's why I feel good.

I head up the beach, toward the remarkably handsome lifeguard, whom I nod at from a distance. I wonder what he thinks when I walk up and down this beach every morning by myself, wearing my dad's old swimming trunks and a Speedo swimsuit from 2012, when I first got breasts and needed a grown-up-lady swimming costume instead of a totally-transparent-when-wet flowery thing. Despite my mismatched outfit, I feel good in my body. I am rid of Topknot Barman, and I don't miss him. I let the poor bastard down gently but I still feel guilty about how I used him. At first he sent me some follow-up texts, seeing if perhaps we could make it work long-distance, but I told him it was over and eventually he gave up on me. I've been alone, without family and friends, for three months now and it has felt empowering, my summer of solitude and solo sex. I haven't relied on restaurants or men for either thrill or pleasure; I have been self-sufficient in sourcing both.

Without distractions, I am left alone with my fickle thoughts, my ever-changing ideas. I thought I was coming to Cornwall to find a restaurant where I could thrive as a chef. Maybe I was supposed to be not a city chef, but a seaside chef, and my destiny was to live by the sea cooking fresh fish and having beach sex with beach boys. But now I wonder if I was wrong, if I might've jumped the gun. The restaurant is quiet and there is no service rush, no militant order, no long mise lists; it feels more like we're just putting on a spread for a beach barbeque. My job, which was initially fanny-fumbling frivolity and dandy fun, has become tedious, and when I have wanked all that I can in the endless hours of free time, the questions about my destiny begin to creep up on me. I am empowered, yes, but I am also fucking bored.

I avoid making eye contact with the hot lifeguard as I walk off the beach and up the hill that leads to my dead grandmother's house. My swimming costume is drying in the heat but the wet board shorts are clinging to my body. I notice my legs are getting more rural, my thighs are muscly in new, meatier ways, my skin is bronzed from the sea and sun, and there is some new color on them, a pale beige albeit. I look up at the lime-green bungalow that my granny gave to my family when she died—to my parents, my aunts, my uncles, and my cousins, plus four dogs and three babies.

The house is in a valley, isolated from any other houses, and I've been living in it by myself since I left London. I packed my clothes and my knives, shoved it all into a suitcase, and got on the train. En route I gazed out the window, ate crisps, and squashed any feelings of guilt about running away, about abandoning Marty and the boys, but also about being a young person with the privilege to have a place of solace outside my life in London, somewhere safe to land when my job sent me spinning out of control. I have another chance to start afresh.

I reach the bush outside the bungalow, turn the corner, and walk through the house to get to the front porch. As I pass through the kitchen, I switch on the radio that I have started using because, while there has been an abundance of wanking, there is complete absence of Wi-Fi. Craig David's "7 Days" is playing on Kiss FM. Bit of an obvious choice, I think. But I turn up the volume so I can hear it outside and head out to the garden. I strip myself of my wet and wrinkled board shorts and my damp swimming costume, lie back in the grass, and feel the August heat on my naked body. I sing "7 Days" to myself, a story of two people falling in love over the course of seven days. It sounds nice, I think, as I stretch my limbs out, reminiscing on my London life, on making love on Wednesday, and Thursday and Friday and Saturday, and chilling on Sunday.

When I moved to Cornwall I expected to take a lover. Before arriving, I'd dreamed up ideas of a striking, tall, rugged man with thighs of steel, rough salty hands, and a soft heart. But I haven't found him. I have had very little contact with eligible men, other than perhaps the hot lifeguard, although he is unlikely to take a DFL (Down From London) for a mistress. I don't care too much, though, after my spell of having sex with a man who, in part, I was repulsed by for months. I have come to the realization that it is better not to settle for someone else, but simply to have sex with oneself.

It's too hot outside. I walk naked to the bathroom and start running the shower. I catch a look at myself in the full-length mirror. My body is softer than before and my hair is wild; I look like a Renaissance woman after a bender at Berghain. My skin is tight from the sea salt and my nipples stand to attention. My face has a healthy glow, while my lips are cool and pink. I'm rediscovering my authentic self, a woman who has grace, not a woman who drunkenly gobbles up barmen.

There's something that feels erotic about my isolation, like I'm Rapunzel left alone in my lime-green tower. Alas, there is no prince to rescue me, to climb my long golden hair and reach the top of the tower where he'll make love to me. Instead, I have had to rescue myself; I have to climb the long pipe of the shower hose and make love to myself.

I step into the shower and stand beneath the waterfall; the sand slides off my arms and legs with ease, but I must be more thorough with the tender nooks and crannies. I take the portable shower hose and use it to rinse the sand from my pubic hair. The water drips down between my thighs and tickles me. I feel aroused but I've got no memories of men in my mind to use for inspiration. I need to make something work; I need to expel this tension pulsating in my pussy. I'm watching a good TV series, and the actor would get it for sure. Alright, I'll just think about him, and me, and about us in the throes of amazingly classy and unpornographic sex. There's a whole narrative I can create, a great story of love and romance. One where the man rescues me from my lime-green tower.

He knocks on the door of the bathroom and finds me dripping wet in the shower. He asks if he can come in and of course there is no need to question who he is or why he is here, because the chemistry between us says it all. He rips off his clothes and joins me; I don't pay much attention to his body; I'm more turned on by the way he is focused on mine. He looks at me as if I'm a mermaid, a mythical creature that he didn't believe existed until right now. I am a mythical creature, but I'm not a mermaid. Instead of a tail, I have two meaty thighs, a sun-kissed arse, and a perfect pussy. His weathered hands stroke my body and I feel the roughness of his palms on my nipples; he is a real man. His hands are used to build things, to lift things; to drill and bang, then fill and fix. He takes the shower hose from me, turns me around, and reaches from behind to place it just where it needs to be. He burrows his face in my neck, his beard scratching at my smooth skin. My senses are more alive than they've ever been; I'm so grounded to earth that I'm almost sinking through the floor. Okay, that's enough of that, I haven't got all day. Straight to the nitty-gritty, I say. In my fantasy, the man's hands are everywhere, in a way that wouldn't make sense in the real world. They are on my hips, my tits, and in my hair; he is like an octopus with eight tentacles. He clings to the flesh on my hips and clasps my plump tits. I used to hate my body when I was a teen, but now I feel the full force of it. I am a woman who has a lot to offer, who will feed your desire, like a Tesco meal deal. But I won't give it to anyone who doesn't deserve it. I've learned that lesson. And I won't work in a job I hate. Another lesson. Stop thinking about damn work, I tell myself. I focus on my fantasy octopus lover; he makes the waves come crashing down and I drown in ecstasy. It's amazing what I can do as a woman.

Then the post-nut clarity: I am a serial wanker, a woman with a part-time dedication to being a chef but a full-time dedication to my vagina. Another day in the lime-green tower where I am imprisoned with no friends, just myself and my long golden hair to play with.

I step out of the shower, tingling all over. I get dressed in my work clothes, grab my headphones, and head out the door. I begin my commute; I go down the stony hill, pass the beach, and then climb up the steps of the opposite cliff. My new restaurant resides in the nearby town. I put my headphones on and listen to music from my teens: Amy Winehouse and Lauryn Hill and other ladies reveling in their quest to find real love, even if it comes with mounds of pain. I feel like I have reverted to my childhood self. I am a teenager again, dossing about in the sun, working a part-time job, and romanticizing any and all aspects of life while avoiding any and all reality.

Soon I'm on the other side of the cliff and the restaurant is in sight: a small neighborhood seafood spot, with a minimalist matte-black exterior and lots of hanging plants. It's a fairly new opening in town—the owners renovated the previous space, which was a weird toy shop. It looks like a clichéd small-plates restaurant in East London. The restaurant interior is artfully effortless and the staff are all good-looking; it could be in Broadway Market. But to the right of it, there's a beach and a fairground, not London Fields. The restaurant has been around for a couple of years and they always seem to be hiring, according to their Instagram, which was why I messaged the Head Chef. He replied, asking me for a phone call on the same day, and we chatted. It was refreshing to speak with Sean, a Head Chef who sounded a bit, well, soft. It would make a nice change from macho Marty. I told him the name of my old restaurant and he said, "Oh, okay I understand," in a knowing way. He asked when I could start work, and I had my first shift the next week.

I turn up the street which leads to the restaurant's back entrance and brace myself for another day of pretending to be a chef. It doesn't feel like real chef work here, it feels more like the cooking you do when you're stoned, sleepy, or sun-soaked. Or the cooking I did with my dad in August of last year, while my friends were frolicking in London Fields but I wasn't in the frame of mind to see anyone. I had moved out of my flat, quit my office job, and crawled home to my parents. I was depressed and anxious; only my dad could get me out of the house. We would go to the fishmonger; he would speak and I would stand next to him observing the human interaction like a newborn baby. He taught me to be human again. We would buy all the cheap whitefish to make Rick Stein's fish soup. I would cook for hours while he watched; occasionally he would talk to me, or talk to himself if I didn't feel like it. With Sean, he does all the cooking and I do the talking to myself. But it's fine, I'm not broken anymore, I don't need Sean, or any man, to mend me.

"Heya," I say to Sean as I walk through the door. I hang my bag up, change into my Birkenstock Bostons, and tie up my hair. There is no grim changing room here—I arrive from over the cliff, in my work outfit, ready to go.

"Hello, mate. How's it going?" Sean says. He is tall, though he has a hunched back from prepping fish for too many years.

"Yeah, all good, absolutely beautiful day out there, the sea is so blue," I say, exercising my finest Cornish small talk, which differs from London small talk in that there is not just the sky to talk about, but also the sea.

"Did you go for a swim this morning?" he asks.

"Yep, for a couple of hours. It was lovely."

"What a life, aye," he says jokingly. He knows now that I left my job because I couldn't handle it. He refers to it as burnout, like Marty did, but I don't like to call it that. I avoid the topic altogether. I can't help thinking that chefs who have worked for years and years are justified to use the term, not me, a newbie who fled her first restaurant after having a panic attack in the toilet. Sean also ran away from London restaurants because of burnout, but unlike me, he put in the work and he earned his diagnosis. He tells me his horror stories, Head Chefs instructing Commis to heal open wounds by scorching them on hot planchas, or countless chefs who sexually assaulted staff and retained their employment. Together we laugh at the dismal world of cunty kitchen culture. He makes me feel better about abandoning ship.

Sometimes I wonder about fucking Sean. It's just me and him in the kitchen, and I think it could be quite fun to use the space in a creative way; for me to sit atop the workbench and spread my legs while he goes down on me with the same obsessive focus he has when filleting a trout. Jesus Christ. I must get my mind out of the gutter.

Sean gives me my first job of the day. "Right, if you want to get on with the flatbread first, that would be great."

In this kitchen, I don't get a mise list or a rota. I only know when I'm working because Sean will text me the day prior, saying, *Does tomorrow at 11 a.m. work?* and I only know what I am to do when I arrive in the kitchen: he will instruct me there and then, one job at a time. It's nothing like my last restaurant. I feel like a helping hand, not staff. It's not so much a brigade as a ballroom pair.

"Yeah, sure," I say, as I move around the kitchen, now familiar with where things go. It is a small space and everything is shiny and new, but in a plastic, IKEA way, like they've just built the space from cardboard boxes. There is no fancy equipment—no Pacojet, no vacuum-pack machine, and no Thermomix; there is no walk-in fridge, just two domestic fridges standing next to one another.

I get out the great big tub of bubbling sourdough starter labeled "Mother" from the fridge. I weigh out flour, milk, yeast, salt, and sugar and get my hands sticky. I know the measurements by heart because I have made this bread every day for the last three months. I know there are monotonous tasks in all kitchens, whether it be kneading flatbread, podding broad beans, peeling onions, or trimming asparagus, and I don't mind that; monotony is when I go to my happy place. But I want to cook new things, too. Instead, I spend most of my time here chopping peaches for the courgette stracciatella salad, deep-frying baby squid, curing sardines, or just unpacking produce. And making this flatbread, of course. These are all things that could be done in a matter of minutes but I have learned that there's never much else I get tasked with, so I take my time. I often look over at Sean, longingly watching him pin-boning trout or dispatching lobster or butchering chickens; I'm jealous of him working with the real ingredients, rushing toward lunch service with purpose.

"Do we have trout on the menu today then?" I say, hoping to get involved with cooking new things.

"Not today, I'm going to age it a little. Today we have pollock on, cooked over fire as per. And I'm making a classic beurre blanc sauce with that. Then I'm going to do roast Cornish hen with mushrooms. Oh, and a lobster special with chili butter," he says, ensuring I have all the fundamental information so there is no need for me to ask further questions. I feel like he's keeping me quiet, like I'm a child on a car journey asking, "Are we there yet?" every ten minutes.

After I shape the flatbreads, I put them in the oven, where they will rise. Even in the midst of my dull shift I am enthralled by the smell of baking bread.

"What do you want me to do now?" I ask Sean, feeling like I'm inconveniencing him by working quickly and being of service.

"Um, you can get going on prepping the peaches for lunch?" he says, as if it's a question.

"Okay!" I say, committed to maintaining my peppy, can-do spirits. Really, I am disgruntled. Surely there is something more useful I can do? Slicing peaches an hour before service starts is ridiculous.

"And you can go a bit smaller with them than you've been doing, they should be thumb-sized," he says.

Is he just trying to keep me engaged within the set boundaries of my one remaining task? Or perhaps I have been slicing the peaches wrong, but if I did, why did he not just tell me the first time? My frustration gathers at my eyebrows and makes me frown. I want to learn! And help! He seems to have no interest in this.

"No problem," I say.

I will take my time with the damn peaches. In my old kitchen, I worked as fast as humanly possible. Here, it's the opposite; my goal is to work slowly, to look busy when I'm bored. I know I had to take a break from that restaurant, but maybe I just needed an afternoon in the fresh air, eating crisps by the Thames, not to uproot my life and move to the edge of England.

At this moment, one of the front-of-house boys saunters into the kitchen. I can never remember their names because they all look the same. They are beautiful Cornish pedigrees, tall and slim with sandy skin and sun-bleached hair, highly proficient at surfing and skateboarding and all of the other sex-appeal sports. The front-of-house are young—eighteen to twenty—and they are all hot, but they are too young for me and our personalities conflict; I have been tainted by the cynicism of London's dark clouds and long bus diversions. While I love swimming in the sea and enjoy drinking on the sand with them on occasion, I am not a beach girl; I don't like being naked around men in casual settings and enduring endless hours of "hanging out."

"Are you all good for service?" the handsome boy asks me, clocking my slow pace as I slice the peaches methodically.

"Yep," I say with an accidentally loud sigh, which signals to him I'm bored out of my fucking mind.

He giggles and then swans out of the back door, barefoot, to smoke a pre-service fag in the sun.

"We've got two tables in, you all ready?" Sean asks me at 12:01.

"Yep," I say. Does he think I'm a sloth? A blind mole rat? A human with no hands? All I had to do was chop some peaches; of course I'm ready.

ZZ zzz blank.

The check machine is tame and muted here, like a monster retired from its life of disruption and torment. It doesn't set my heart alight like it did at my old place.

"Okay, right. Two covers," Sean says while sticking his check beneath the check machine; there is no magnetic rail for him to stick up his orders, to keep track of what he is cooking. There's no need for one.

"Yep," I say.

Because it's a set menu, each customer always has the same three small plates to share; that's my job. Then they will order a main course, which Sean will cook: chicken, pollock, or lobster. I'll do the sides: chips and a green salad.

Sean doesn't even read out the check or tell me the main courses that each table chooses, all I hear is two covers, three covers, four covers. Occasionally it's one cover: poor lonesome holidaymaker.

I put the flatbread in the oven to flash it. While it warms up I start plating the other dishes. All I do is plate. First the peaches that I so diligently diced over the course of sixty minutes. They are tossed with grilled courgette—which is prepped by Sean as he clearly doesn't trust me with the grill yet—mint, basil, roasted almonds, a little olive oil, salt, and pepper. I then pile the fresh and fragrant aromatic mix on top of stracciatella (the inside of burrata). The next dish is fried baby squid with aioli, which Sean makes before I arrive in the morning. My mise is merely to make a dry and wet batter, which takes all of three minutes.

Then finally, my third starter on the set menu is cured sardines. The sardines are filleted by Sean and cured by me; I haven't been told what the ingredients are for the cure because my Head Chef says he "sort of makes it up as he goes." But it tastes like thyme, lemon, garlic, and chili. I pile three fillets of fish on the plate, skin-side down so the flesh absorbs the sweet and sour chili juice that I generously scoop on top. I put my three starters on the pass and then pivot my body to get the bread out of the oven, onto a plate, and drizzled with olive oil. Everything is ready in about a minute. What now? I stand back and watch Sean as he cooks, basting a plump chicken supreme in mushroom butter while resting a fillet of pollock on open charcoal, patiently waiting until the white flesh turns opaque and iridescent. I glare at him with envy.

Time passes at a snail's pace. It's like we are sailing on an old people's cruise ship and it's moving so slowly I can barely feel it. I plate dish after dish of the same three things. I only wish there was an iceberg ahead to smash into, so there would be a little panic in the room;

I could jump off my sunbed and bring in the lifeboats, and cook something for the women and children. As my boredom boils, my thoughts clarify and there is no skirting around the truth: I miss the urgency of my old restaurant. I miss the loud noise of the check machine and the rush that flooded my body when I heard it. I miss reading the checks. I miss cooking different things. I miss working with others to feed a table of six with three allergies and two intolerances and one birthday. I miss being on a ship that would sometimes sink; we would go down, but together we would resurface and celebrate with barrels of beer and cartons of cigarettes.

While we are on the subject of things I miss, I miss sex too, sex with a man. Even if the sex was mediocre, the human intimacy would suffice.

Once we have sent the starters, my job is done and the rest is left to Sean. I head over to the sink section to keep myself busy; the teenage stoner KP left it in a tip when he bailed on work early because his girlfriend just finished her GCSEs and is saddened by her results.

As I do, Sean calls out, "Hey, by the way, I don't reckon I'll need you for dinner service tonight. We haven't got many covers." He wipes down *his* pass while avoiding my eyes.

"Oh, okay," I say.

"It feels like it would be wasting your time, and we can't really afford to pay staff when it's not necessary."

I've only been here for four hours. I used to work ten to sixteen hours a day. Not only am I bored, but I am making *no* money.

"Sure, that's fine," I respond, feeling defeated. I have enjoyed being here, in Cornwall, and working for a small neighborhood place. I like the ethos and I like

Sean, but that's not enough to keep me here. Nor is my sea swimming, nor are my daily wankathons. When I'm in this kitchen with Sean, I realize just how much my life has slowed down; the tides are so calm, I'm almost sailing backward.

I wipe down my already-clean surface and pack up my knives. "Right!" I say, hanging up my apron, slipping off my Birkenstocks, and sliding my feet into my sandy Asics. "I'll see you tomorrow! Oh, no, wait, I'm off tomorrow, I'll see you the day after," I say, laughing at my dire situation.

"Nice one! Thanks so much!" Sean calls out with his back to me, busying himself with his real-chef jobs: gutting fish, emulsifying sauces, pin-boning chickens.

I huff and puff across the seaside town to the pub to join the holidaymakers sparking up their Benson & Hedges; their eyes are glued to the footy and their round red bellies are hanging over their seaside shorts.

I order a pint of lager. I tried to drink Tribute, as it's a good Cornish ale, but in the sunshine I favor golden bubbles and fizz. I march my pint outside, sit at a picnic bench, and roll a cigarette. I light it and then take my hair down from its bun; my golden locks fall to my shoulders, clean and untainted by graft, sweat, or oil. When I untied my hair after a shift in London, it remained on top of my head, like an abstract statue molded in grease that I'd have to manually deconstruct with hot water and soap. This is not real kitchen-work hair.

I phone my dad.

"Hello?" he says, surprised, I'm sure, to hear from me in the middle of the working day.

"Guess what? Sean just told me to leave early *again*. He says he doesn't need me there tonight."

"Wow, really?"

"Can you believe that?" I say. "He just said the restaurant doesn't need two people tonight as it's too quiet. He has been sending me home more and more, the last couple weeks."

"Well," my dad says, "you should just see your time at this restaurant as a break." He usually avoids telling me what to do outright because he knows that my heart changes constantly. I can't help but have fickle thoughts when I have so much time to think.

"Yeah, I guess," I say. "But I don't know how much more of a break I need. It's been months since I did any real work." I realize just how fed up I am as I say it out loud.

"See how you feel later," he says.

I stub my cigarette out and roll another. Cigarettes are most enjoyable when emotions are heightened.

I'm sure he can hear the frustration in my voice.

I continue: "I'm alone in the middle of nowhere with fuck all to do."

"Why don't you do some cooking, seeing as you didn't get to do much at work. What about that Rick Stein fish soup we made last summer?" It's a good idea, actually. Even though he doesn't like to tell me what to do, when he does, he's generally right.

"I don't have the book with me. Do you remember the recipe?"

"I'll send you a text of ingredients."

"Alright," I say. My mind is already turning. I plan my route home; I'll go to Sainsbury's, followed by the fishmonger, then I'll pick mussels on the beach.

"Talk later, darling," he says. I am now occupied with the fish-soup idea and am no longer in need of his guidance.

My dad is so well acquainted with my ups and downs that I should really be paying him a therapist fee. He knows, as I said, my constantly changing heart; he knows that for me, the grass is not just greener on the other side, the grass is also shinier, softer, and brighter, and I will always race toward it, even if I slide through pools of hot steaming cow shit on the way. He doesn't say earnest things like my angelic mother might; instead he makes light suggestions and he listens to me rage, then we have a laugh at the end of it.

A few minutes later I get a text from my dad:

Fennel orange pepper tomato onion leek fish. And you should make the rouille too. And you could pick some mussels from the beach to add more flavor.

My phone is going to run out of battery. I pull out a napkin from my coat and write a shopping list on it, fag in hand.

At the local Sainsbury's, I race through the aisles with all the pent-up energy I have from doing sweet fuck all. The London in me returns as I charge past slow people to race for what I want: onions, fennel, and other things the old ladies don't need as much as me. Then I visit the fishmonger and buy the cheapest whitefish they have, dogfish and skate, and ask for a spare plastic bag. I'll use that for the mussels I collect at the beach.

I plow my way over the cliff. My body is working; my heart is pumping, my mind is turning, and I feel excited to take off this stupid fake chef costume and cook in my pants. When the beach is in sight, I jog down the steep stairwell to the rocks. Momentum helps my body move as I gather speed; my knees go all loose and feeble, just like my chef career.

I race across the sand to find the mussels, as the tide is coming in fast. I clamber on rocks with no hesitation. I rest for a moment at the peak. I see bigger and better mussels on the next rock over; I want those instead. It's a bit taller, and a bit steeper, but that's not a problem. I climb onto it and look upward; there is a monstrous patch of shining, wet mussels. I am climbing further on my hands and knees. My hands grip onto the sharp shells and bear my full weight—the force leaves an imprint on my hand, pink and sore. I take the scrunched-up fishmonger bag from my trouser pocket and hold it open in one hand; with the other, I pluck the mussels from the rock. I am picking only the biggest ones. If you're going to do something, you might as well do it properly. I see an especially big bastard right at the top of the rock, and I reach for it to no avail. It's not budging. The bastard. I yank it again. Finally. As I pull it out, the neighboring mussel scrapes my palm and leaves a deep gash. I am bleeding. I look down at my hands. There are no other cuts there. The rest of my skin is unscathed, my nails are long and clean. I am not a chef anymore, but I wish I was. I miss being a chef. But I can't indulge in this revelation, I can't cry. I can't allow myself any more feelings of discontent, I've had too many feelings for one day. The taps are turned off and now it's time to cook.

I walk up the hill to the house. I lob all the bags I've been carrying the ingredients in onto the kitchen table. I grab a beer from the fridge and sit down for a moment. My arms are a little achy, which feels good, like the ache in your abs after an onerous orgasm.

I play the radio. This time, Gold FM. They are broadcasting all this wacky country shit. That'll do me fine. I no longer have need of romantic music; I am full up on thrills at the thought of proper cooking. I scrub the mussels and dream of a life in London; of finding a new restaurant, a new lover, and a new existence. It's time to start over, again.

Soon the mussels are clean and I move on to chopping the veg for the fish stock: onions, fennel, and leek.

Rick Stein's recipe lists specific volumes for the ingredients but I feel confident eyeballing everything my dad texted me. I scale the amounts up, using all the vegetables I bought. With great gusto, I roughly chop three onions, two bulbs of fennel along with the fronds, and one leek. I chuck everything in a big pan over the stove. I add a big pinch of black peppercorns, a couple of bay leaves, and a small bunch of thyme. I pour in some cheap white wine, then take the whitefish out of its plastic bag and lay it on top of the bed of chopped vegetables. Then, as if I'm running it a bath, I pour on a blanket of water, just to the point where the fish is covered. I turn up the heat and wait for it to come to life, to simmer and steam. Some say you shouldn't cook a fish stock for too long—the water will become cloudy—but I'm not worried about that. The clarity of the stock won't matter when I'm blitzing it later on.

I call the shots here, after all. This kitchen is mine and it feels empowering. I haven't cooked properly since I've been here, but now there's a fire in my belly. Today something feels different. Today I am done waiting for someone to tell me what to do; I'll just figure it out myself. If I'm not cooking and learning at the restaurant, then I'm going to cook and learn in this house. If I'm not getting sex from the lifeguard, then I'll get sex from myself. Sometimes you have to go it alone.

I make the base of the soup by chopping more onions, fennel, and leek. They are even, thumb-sized chunks, but I am not pedantic with it; I'm in control, not Sean. Again, I know I am going to blitz everything after so nothing needs to look perfect. Perfect is boring. Calm is boring. Serenity is boring. Some people like to keep vegetables pale when they cook fish, but I want the soup to be rich and deep in flavor, so I brown the veg in sunflower oil in a pan and whack up the heat; I want it *hot*. I want the soup to mimic my life back in London, where there was passion, tension, and spice. I chuck a red pepper under the hot grill and let it blacken, along with a couple of big bulbous tomatoes. I am beginning to forget all the nothingness from today, and the last three months. I'm relieved that my instincts are still intact after all this time.

I use a serrated knife to remove two large pieces of peel from an orange and save the flesh for breakfast tomorrow; I carve slowly and delicately so that I don't cut into the pith. I follow the orange's round shape closely, caring for it like a good lover tends to my tit. Oh, those were the days! The smell of citrus mist fills my nostrils. It smells like Negronis. Fuck. I miss Negronis. Oranges, booze, sticky lips, pink cheeks, bright lights, and warm pavements. I miss London. I miss feeling stressed. I miss being around people my age. I miss being drunk and dancing. I miss flirting with strangers. I miss cooking at a proper restaurant. I miss having plural-people sex. I miss the night bus and I miss McDonald's.

I open the grill and smoke bellows out in my face; my eyelashes curl and my skin dampens. Oh, to cook with heat! I peel back the skin of the red pepper, and in my eagerness I burn my fingertips. The pepper's flesh is soft and slippery; it's wet and wild, dying to join the pleasure party in the pan. I chop the hot tomatoes deftly, sweet juice exploding across the chopping board, and I slide it all straight into the pan, collecting the hot wet seeds with my fingers. Then I add a pinch of saffron and the amber color disperses from it and, through the red pepper and tomatoes, spilling passion across the pale, fragrant onion, fennel, and leek. Soon everything is glowing orange.

I feel like a sexy witch making potions. I am ready to poison the village with pleasure.

I lift the skate wing from the stock and place it to the side on a big tray for a moment. I bring the pan full of stock over to a sieve hovering over another pan. Wow. My wrists are strong. I wonder why? Oh yeah.

As I pour with conviction, steam clings to my face. I think about the volume of stocks and potions in my old kitchen. I'm beginning to think of that restaurant like an ex; I'm nostalgic and pondering whether I ended things too soon—if I didn't put in enough work. The passion was there! I just got scared. I could've stuck it out; would something beautiful have flourished then? A happy ending, with lots of steamy nights.

I put the pot of shimmering stock back on the heat, to let it reduce a little, and then I take my sticky, hot hands to the opaque white frame on the tray. I peel back the flesh from the bones; it moves with ease. I want someone to undress me again, to peel back my clothes from my flesh. And then eat me. I chuck the fish flesh into the bubbling orange mix and I loosely stir it around, so the white flakes get a go on some of the red-hot romance. Now it's time for mussels. I get an empty pan on the gas hob; that's three pans on the go now, it's the most action I've had in months. I warm the empty pan on a high heat and let it fester like the burning rage of a jealous woman. Then I chuck in the mussels, and she lets out a loud hiss. In goes the wine: there you go, love. Drink it up and forget your worries. Glug, glug, glug. I put a lid on her, I let her do her thing.

Once the mussels, bubbling in the liquor, feel drunk and promiscuous with their shells wide open, I drain their juices into the orange mix. I put the mussel flesh aside as something to eat tomorrow, maybe in a seafood salad or pasta, something elegant after tonight's vulgar banquet. Finally, I pour the stock into the soup base, the white bubbling potion into the orange oily one. This soup is stubborn! Like me, it refuses to meet in the middle—it's a deranged mess, not sure of what it wants. What if we add a little more heat? Just like that, and a slow demonic stirring: *Bubble, bubble, toil and trouble*. And I, the sexy witch, I am amused.

All the empty pans, dirty knives and chopping boards are dumped in the sink, to be cleaned up tomorrow morning.

Time for a quick beer and a smoke, I reckon. I head out and look at the view. I can see the sea, which is now a sheet of shimmering blue; the horizon is made up of warm pink streaks of sky, as the sun is setting. It's pretty nice, but it's not really doing it for me. My knees are tapping away and my cigarette is burning down fast. I am having a nice time, but it's because of the cooking, not because of the pretty views or the low golden sun. It's the cooking that I've been missing, and it's the cooking that makes me feel good.

I head back to the kitchen. It smells like the sea.

While the soup heats up and the fish bathes in all its different flavors, I make the rouille. I use a recipe from my old restaurant. I know it by heart. I know how to treat the ingredients, how to handle the mix. I won't cut corners or skip the foreplay, I want to make it all worthwhile. If you're doing something, you might as well do it properly.

I pull out the food processor from a cluttered, dusty cupboard. It is old and stained yellow from years of use. I give it a quick rinse and add anchovy, garlic, egg yolk, harissa, and lemon to the bowl, where they pool at the bottom, acting shy and not really interested in getting to know each other. But I blitz it and soon they're all touching and dancing and snogging. I pour in vegetable oil, watching it disappear into the mix. I miss making emulsions at work. I long for it all, again. The rouille comes together now, like a wobbly, orange mayonnaise.

I scoop out the rouille and put it to the side. Next, I slice a few rounds of French baguette, which will act as a romantic rowboat for the rouille, floating its way through my silky soup. I chuck the bread under the grill to toast.

Now back to that soup. I blitz it with a home cook's hand mixer, then sieve it into a fourth pan. I am dirtying up all these pans with no regard for tomorrow. I am not worried about any feelings; they are one-night-stand saucepans. The soup is the perfect consistency, thick like double cream and now golden orange in color, a little paler than the rouille.

I take a shallow, chipped bowl from the cupboard and wipe away the dust. It's been a while since it's been filled with anything hot and creamy. Me too.

I pour, slowly. The soup cascades into the bowl, taking up the space it knows it deserves. It is rich and opulent. It's shining and golden. It's Michelin Star Pussy Juice.

I spread a thick dollop of salty, fishy rouille atop the crouton boats and send them sailing on the soup; off they go into the sunset. The final touch: a little sprinkling of Gruyère grated on top.

I take my bowl and a hefty glass of cold Albariño to the bench outside where I will eat.

It's now dusk, almost dark. It's cold without the sun, and with the sea air blowing beneath my T-shirt, but I'm warm from the kitchen.

I look at my Argos watch. "Fuck, it's ten p.m.," I say out loud to myself. I didn't realize just how much time had passed in the kitchen. I was in a parallel universe where you don't measure time by hours, but by the blackening of a red pepper, the simmering of a stock, or the smell of a soup.

I drink the soup. It is my favorite mouthful of food: rich and salty from the stock, sweet from the peppers and tomatoes, fragrant from the herbs, and savory from the fish. I want to swim in it. Not like this morning, where I was paddling around in the shallow end with silly waves lapping at my feet; I want to go out deep in this soup until I'm so far out that I can no longer see the shore. The rouille is punchy; garlic and harissa cling to the roof of my mouth.

MICHELIN STAR PUSSY JUICE

The soup is excellent. I know it, but still I wish Marty was here to taste it; I want someone to teach me, and to be strict with me and tell me where I fucked up. There is only so long you can go it alone.

On my visit back to the kitchen to get a refill of soup, I grab a hoodie and some tracksuit bottoms so I can stay outside a little longer. I am making a dent in the pot, but there's still too much to go around. I am used to cooking restaurant quantities, not seaside-spinster-witch quantities.

As I finish off my last bowl of the night, my stomach anchors my body to the bench with overindulgence. Half an hour passes and my happy delirium fades; the discontent buzzing is back, bitter and irritating, like acid reflux.

I want to speak to someone, but I don't want to exhaust my normal friends. Fuck it, I'll call my dad back. He picks up; of course he picks up.

"How was the soup?" he asks.

"Fucking great," I say.

"So are you working tomorrow?"

"Nope," I say, with a large sigh.

"When are you next working then?" he persists.

"The day after, unless Sean cancels that shift as well, which is probably quite likely." I'm not ramped up like I was at the pub, I'm depleted.

"Well, what's the plan?" he asks.

"What do you mean?" I say, defensively, irritated by his question because he is reminding me I am in a state of limbo, that my life isn't really a life but more a nice day out for a retired lady of leisure.

"You're clearly not very happy cooking in that restaurant, it doesn't seem enough of a challenge," he says. "I think you should leave." He offers me a rare direct opinion.

"Really?" I say, sitting up in my seat a little. If my dad thinks I should go, then maybe I should.

"I think you should come back to London and find a restaurant that works for you. Just give it a go, do a couple of trial shifts. I think you'll start going insane with boredom if you stay there much longer. Yes, you had a bad moment toward the end of the last place, but you were drinking a lot and I'm sure doing drugs too. That will have had an impact. But for a lot of the time, you loved it," he says. "Mum and I have never seen you happier, or seen you care so much about anything."

He is right, I think. Maybe it wasn't *that* bad. And maybe I can handle it. I had some pretty shit times after a big night out when I'd do a double on two hours' sleep, and of course there was my last day, when I had the panic attack and I felt like I never wanted to set foot in a kitchen again. But for the most part, I loved my job. Now that I'm hearing someone else say it—my dad, my unofficial therapist—it's decided. I will go back. I will try again.

"Okay, fuck it, yeah, you're right," I say. I feel both excited and relieved.

"Just talk to Sean tomorrow. Then use your last couple of weeks there to set up a restaurant trial in London."

"Okay. Fuck it. Yes. I'll do that."

I hang up the phone. I roll one more cigarette before bed.

I am so grateful for my dad. And I'm grateful for cooking. And I'm grateful to have forgiven myself for running away and for everything that happened at the restaurant, including stomping on the nice boy with the bad hair's heart. I am a good person with good intent, and carrying all my wrongdoings is of no benefit to anyone. I have clearly had one too many sunset strolls on the beach; I'm starting to sound a bit too spiritual for my liking. But I *do* feel better, and I look better, and it is time. Now, take me back to my damn city. I sit on the loo and pee, a bit tipsy. I scroll through a playlist on my phone and then play The Clash, "London Calling." I turn it off after three seconds because it's a bit clichéd and trite, all this awfully mushy sentiment.

5

Eating Kebabs in London

OCTOBER

I'm back in the Big Smoke, the beating heart that pumps pollution and lust through my veins. I love the pie-shop ladies cackling and telling me to "Sit down, we'll bring your tea over"; I love my local off-license guy, frowning until I make him grin; I love seeing the streetlights flicker on in the early evening; I love the pubs calling last orders, the people lending lighters, the doner meat shaving, the garlic sauce squirting, the cars road-raging, the bin lorries moaning, the buses switching lanes, and the tall bridges towering over the shitty Thames. I wake up every day with a feeling of warmth and contentment in my gut and I know that I'm in love. It is only when I get on my bike and cycle to my new job that I realize with whom. Or what, really. I'm in love not with a person, but a city. Cornwall is wonderfully pleasant, but it's the bright lights and the big city for me. Less is never more. I'm in love with London.

It's been a little over a month since I left Cornwall. The morning after I made fish soup, I got straight onto planning my return; I texted Paul, from the Larder section, and asked him for advice.

Hello, matey. Hope you're well. Sorry for the silence. I'm coming back to London and need a new restaurant to work at. Any ideas?

It was the first message I had sent to anyone from the restaurant since I left. Losing touch with people is one of my best skills. As soon as I don't have the bricks and mortar of a physical location to facilitate a friendship, I worry it won't survive, so in an act of self-preservation I pretend the friendship never existed in the first place.

Paul didn't call me out for it; he held no grudges. He texted right back.

Look who it is! Glad you're coming back to London. Let me send you a few ideas, just finished a shift with Zack. He's even more cocky now that you've left.

He guessed I wouldn't want to come back; he probably knew I wasn't the right fit, which I can happily accept now. I didn't enjoy being around the macho energy of that kitchen, with chefs like Zack making wanking jokes nonstop and chefs like Omar being a gross pest. I went out with the front-of-house girls and I had fun, but they just weren't my people. I enjoyed the cooking but not the culture, and I think Paul could tell. He sent me the names of a few restaurants that were hiring, and I emailed them all. I also replied to messages from friends, particularly my oldest normal friends, Ruby and Sophie, who don't work in restaurants and whom I'd ignored for far too long. I was ready to face it all.

Later that day, I told Sean I was going back to London. He didn't seem too bothered. He explained that he'd like to have been able to give me more shifts, but the financial situation was tricky. He confessed the restaurant wasn't doing all that well. Perhaps, I thought, because they were serving modern, stylish food to a town of tourists who would always opt for fish and chips and pasties. But I didn't say that. I left at the end of that week, the last in August.

I needed a new job, and I needed somewhere to live. The week I returned to London, I texted my friend Raquel, a chef whom I'd met once at Axel's friend's bar, which was basically a hospitality-industry brothel. We clicked immediately. Raquel sent the names of a few restaurants that were hiring, and she also wondered if I wanted to be her flatmate. Her flaky previous flatmate had moved out and she was desperate to make rent. Oh, how the stars aligned! I moved right into her flat.

Raquel is far cooler than I am or ever could be; she works for a new opening in Soho and somehow makes being a chef look easy. She always seems well-rested. She is Cuban and Italian but was born and bred in Balham; she's tall and slender and is blessed with God-given swag. She's a highly lucrative lesbian, bringing lovers back to our flat on a weekly basis.

Then I got another call, this time about a job. It was one of Paul's recommendations, in the end: a fine-dining restaurant with a big team and a well-known Head Chef running things. Paul told me the culture was great and people went there to learn. That was what I wanted really, to learn. So I went for it.

Now it's early October, and I've been at my new restaurant for over a month. I love London and I love my job and I love my roommate and I love my grown-up life.

I live in North East London, where I observe my new neighborhood's busy streets, its chicken shops, and its residents—mostly millennial gentrifiers. I clap from the sidelines, taking notes on how to look so self-assured, as if I had landed in my grown-up life effortlessly.

I approach this neighborhood as a greedy tourist: there's so much good food to be eaten. Raquel and I went on a proper expedition the other day. We walked from our flat to Stamford Hill. We stopped at a Jewish bakery called Grodzinski and bought a jam doughnut to share, then we crossed the road and visited a little Brazilian supermarket to buy some *pão de queijo* for a savory hit, then we made our way down to Seven Sisters and in a Colombian supermarket we drank guanábana juice and ate empanadas. Then it was lunchtime. We headed east to Green Lanes; I wanted to go to the spot that my new Head Chef, Lenny, had mentioned called Antepliler. Raquel and I ordered İskender, a ridiculously hefty, fatty offering for two women who have been eating all day. After lunch, we walked up to Finsbury Park and drank three Guinnesses at the pub while awaiting the resurgence of our appetite. When the sun went down, we got a table at Dilara, a Uyghur restaurant, where we split the "large plate chicken" and a couple of lamb skewers. Our stomachs were full, so we walked home, happy. Alas, at quarter to nine, we grew peckish again. I cycled down Kingsland Road to Peppers & Spice and picked up a polystyrene box of oxtail, butter beans, and rice and peas for me and Raquel to share. Alas, a sweet treat was missing, but we remembered our fruity-jelly-stick-things from Longdan which we keep in the freezer for a daily digestif.

Now that I'm cooking in London again, I want to eat all the food my city has to offer. With every new cuisine

I try, I realize how little I know. There's far more to learn about food in the real world than in the pompous cooking school where I paid to feign interest.

When I'm not eating around my flat, I'm cooking at work. My flat is a hefty cycle from my new restaurant, but I don't mind the journey; I'd take a long bike ride of solitude over a smelly commuter Tube any day of the week.

This morning, on my way to work, my phone rings. I scramble for it. I pause my music, temporarily silencing Gil Scott-Heron singing to me about Lady Day.

"What's up?"

"Where are you?" my dad asks me.

"Just cycling through Angel." I weave through the queues of cars. "Why are you awake this early? It's seven thirty. You usually don't awake from your slumber until, what, midday?" I am back to being myself again, with my obnoxious wit. I know that my dad will have noticed, too. He's pleased about this turn of events but remains on call for any bumps along the road.

"Very funny," he replies. "I am awake because your mum has a fucking knitting meeting in the kitchen at eight a.m., so now I'm having to have my breakfast in the middle of the night." He sounds as if he's genuinely distressed at the thought of having to have breakfast before his routine 9 a.m. sitting. He is a funny man with many anal rituals.

"Okay, right, and is that why you have called me, then? To let me know you're eating breakfast?" I ask.

"No! I was just calling to ask for a restaurant recommendation for me and some old Soho work friends. What do you suggest?" My dad always asks me for restaurant recommendations because his own references are limited to Pizza Express and the one Turkish restaurant my family have frequented my whole life.

"Just text me the details and I'll send you some options. Talk to you later," I say. "You interrupted the best bit of my song."

He laughs and then performs his classic English goodbye: "Okay, thanks very much. Bye, then. Okay, bye. Yep. Bye. Okay. Bye. Bye. Bye."

I click Play on my music; Gil fingers the keys of his piano while I race through the busy streets. The commuters in suits waiting for the bus look so miserable, the poor bastards. They queue in their black and gray work attire, looking identical and unanimously docile while staring down at their phones; a long trail of marching ants. I swan past them: Come on guys, give us a smile! My new zest for life is unbearable.

I cycle through Shoreditch and then arrive at a crossroads to take me into the city. I find myself deep among a herd of another breed of commuters; their flesh is meaty and their pelts are shiny. Fluorescent spandex cups every bulge on their body, bollocks especially. These are a strange species: the serious cyclists. Are their flamboyant outfits totally necessary? Or are they like peacocks, where the males boast their vibrant colors in a desperate attempt to seduce some females? They wait at the red lights with bated breath. They hate it when I break away first, without waiting for the green light. They tut at me; they roll their eyes. They puff out their chests like birds, too, but they don't make a sound. Silly boys. Perhaps they fear me, the eagle that belongs to no flock. In reality, I am more like a cocky city pigeon that flies right into the path of danger: the double-decker bus. A great big honk blasts in front of me and my heart beats fast. It's 7:33 a.m. and my blood is pumping, I feel alive! I turn right toward St. Paul's. There is beauty around every corner—pubs and Prets, coffees and cigs, harsh faces but hopeful hearts. I'm in London; we're back together and I'll never leave my love again.

I cycle with no hands on the handlebar like a truly obnoxious youth. The buildings get taller and the tourists spread like an irritating rash. As I cycle alongside another bus, I notice a blonde girl with a blazer looking out the window on the bottom deck. She must be heading to work. She looks so flat. Imagine feeling that way from nine to five, for five days a week, for the vast majority of your life. I am either up or down, never in between. I like it that way.

Though perhaps that's only because I'm currently up.

I realize that I am, in fact, quite looking forward to my day at work. I work hard for sixty-odd hours every week, but there is no dread. I don't really care about the long shifts. I don't mind missing social things that happen after 5 p.m. and on weekends; what is there that I am missing out on, anyway? In all my former jobs there has been some sort of reluctance to go to work, some sort of dread. I had to muster up the courage to act enthused before, but now I'm enthused in an authentic way, and it is a welcome feeling. I can still go out late in the evening, anyway. I am happy to skip the stagnant start of a night out; it's more fun to join at the peak of the night, when everyone is already drunk enough to dance and snog people they shouldn't. And I am also happy to miss all the things that happen in the normal waking hours: walking in the park, sitting in a flat, hanging out with infants, eating cereal, visiting the zoo, et cetera. Fuck it! I never liked that stuff anyway.

In Cornwall I was unsure about cooking as a profession, but something about London has refined my focus. It's all the never-ending activity, I think; it somehow calms me down. Restaurants are everywhere and I want to be in them, cooking. And I want the thrill of the unknown that comes with cooking à la carte, where you don't know what people will order, versus the familiar routine of churning out a set menu, like in Cornwall. Yes, there were a couple bumps in the road, but I'm back on track; I'm back in the race. My new restaurant is great. I am learning fast and with constant guidance from kind people. There is no patronizing or shouting. I worried I couldn't be a chef at my old restaurant, or even Sean's place, but I can be one here. And I feel excited by that; I feel excited by the prospect of having to care less.

I'm not far off now. Google Maps says it'll take me one minute, but I'll make it in thirty seconds. I skip the red lights at the crossroads and cut through the National Gallery. I lock my bike to a railing opposite St. James's Square. Two minutes forty-seven seconds.

My new restaurant is around the corner. It is big, with a dining room that seats about a hundred people. The aesthetic is timeless yet modern: white starched tablecloths, but clean, Scandinavian black chairs. It's on the third floor and the window seats look over the West End. And there's a small smoking terrace where the chefs and front-of-house team rendezvous after a busy service.

My restaurant is considered a new classic; if people are interested in food, they have heard of it, and my parents love name-dropping it to their most sophisticated friends. Our clientele is varied, with a mixture of old and young, nerdy and trendy, native and new; yet the one thing all our guests have in common is prosperity. It's not cheap.

I don't feel dread as I approach, like I have in the past. I don't fret about the hours that lie ahead; about how stressful and scary, or boring and long, they might be. I do feel a little nervous, but it's more like adrenaline than panic; like before you steal a can of Coke from Tesco.

I head toward the restaurant; it still shocks me just how big it is compared to the last two places I worked. Here I cook "British and European cuisine," whatever that means. The menu changes with the seasons and is slightly more traditional. It feels like a privilege to work here, like I'm a part of something exclusive. We, the chefs, wear starchy white chefs' jackets, like a team, and we operate like a team; we pool all our skills together and share tips and tricks. We have one common goal: to serve excellent food to the greedy gourmands of London.

The chefs' entrance is around the back. Lenny, the Head Chef, is standing outside. He waves, and removes his headphones with one hand; in his other hand, he clasps a lit Superking cigarette.

"Morning!" I say, with genuine enthusiasm. I'm in an excellent mood today; I'm only working a morning shift, which means the sun will still be in the sky when I leave work at around five.

"Alright?" Lenny says. He is an inherently grumpy man but tries to be sweet when talking with someone one-on-one, to let them know it's not personal. He's a nice guy, really. He welcomed me, a Commis Chef, into the kitchen with his open, awkward arms and made sure everyone else did too. "What did you do with your days off, then?" he says. I hang around out the front while Lenny finishes his cigarette.

"I went to that place on Green Lanes you recommended. Antepliler," I say with a grin.

"Did you have the İskender?" he asks. He told me to get that dish when recommending the place, so of course I did. We talk about food a lot, as all chefs do. Lenny and I are specifically passionate about highly calorific, processed food that's dense with saturated fat; we often pay more attention to it than refined, swanky restaurant fare. He is from one side of London and working-class; I am from the other side of London and posh, but our souls meet over the topic of doner meat and hash browns.

"Yep, fuck me, it was so rich," I say. The dish consists of thin slices of lamb doner on top of a slightly sweet tomato sauce, which is on top of thick, creamy yogurt, which is on top of bread. It's served with a portion of chips alongside. A sandwich was my favorite food growing up and my dedication to it remains, but now my definition of it has broadened. Any combination of handheld carbohydrate, meat, and sauce—whether it be a jerk-chicken *roti*, a lamb-and-cheese *pide*, a double cheeseburger, or a tuna-cucumber baguette from Pret—that is the framework for my most sacred meals. He laughs and stubs out his cigarette. "I told you, you should only order İskender if you're hungover. Either that or you've run a marathon." Together we climb the stairwell up to the kitchen. He leads the way, and I follow. He is Head Chef after all.

"I know, I know. It was still good, though," I say, my voice bellowing into his backside a couple of stairs above me.

"I admire your appetite," he says, genuinely. "That thing took me and my girlfriend down."

Lenny walks straight through the kitchen to his office, to do some admin, and I take a right to go to the changing room. Inside I find the boys. It is amazing to think how quiet and shy I was when I first joined; now, just a month later, these boys are my friends. I can be myself around them. We're all in the same team, but we appreciate each other's different skills.

I think running away to Cornwall dented my pride a little, but that's good because it put my arse in gear; now I am squashing my fears and going after what I want. I want to work in a kitchen, I want to be chef, I want to be on the team. All those shifts just watching Sean cook reminded me of that. I don't think I was ready to be a chef in Marty's kitchen, but I am now.

And it helps that my team is *really* lovely.

I should say that there are no women in the kitchen at my new restaurant, either; I'm the only one, but this time I don't really mind.

"Morning!" George says. He is the Sous Chef. He is in his late twenties, and has orange hair and broad shoulders, but not in an obnoxiously athletic way. His pink skin goes red when he's stressed. He has the kindest disposition of anyone I've met. Warmth literally radiates from his smile. I would never fancy him but I'm deeply jealous of his girlfriend having found herself such a noble man; I met her recently and she is also impossibly nice.

"Hello, babes," I say. I slip off my Asics and walk in my socks to the uniform cupboard. I sift through the stacks of folded laundry to find a size medium trousers and a size medium white chef's jacket. The trousers are uncomfortable because they are clearly made for men; there is too much space in the bollock area and not enough space in the thighs. But I like wearing a uniform every day; again, part of the team and all that.

   George and I proceed happily in silence, changing our clothes, collecting our knife-wraps, shoving our rucksacks into our lockers, and sliding our ciggy paraphernalia into our pockets: Rizlas, tobacco and filters, lighter. I hear a flamboyant whistle in the distance and in bursts the Chef de Partie, Finn, arriving just after everyone else as usual. You can't really get mad at him, though; he's always too joyous.

   "Morning, Finn," I say, while bent over cuffing my made-for-man trousers, which droop past my shoes otherwise.

   "Hello, mate," George says.

   "'Ello, 'ello, darlings. Sorry I'm late," Finn calls out like a songbird.

   I fancied Finn for about two minutes, when I first saw his face, but as soon as he opened his mouth I was put off by his offensively potent peppiness. I also found out he's gay. Now we are best friends; he's my favorite person to get drunk with post-service because we always end up talking about smutty things like sex with bad men. He's older than me, about twenty-seven, and has a bleached-blond buzz cut and piercing blue eyes. He's been working in hospitality since he was sixteen, and you can tell—as much as he is a beautiful boy, his skin is scarred, his face is gaunt, his eyes are tired, and he looks older than he is. Nonetheless, at heart, he is a child. Like a true hospitality veteran, he is immediately familiar with people, whereas I take anywhere from three to six months to warm up to anyone. I am shy when I first meet people, and my social battery runs out quickly, which is not ideal when your work involves spending anywhere between twelve and sixteen hours in precariously close proximity to other people on a shift. But I've got past that now. In the kitchen I am at the point where I no longer must pretend to be talkative; they all know the real me: stoic and cynical, like a middle-aged man.

George and I head into the kitchen with Finn trotting behind us. I spot Victor, another chef, who is always somehow at work before anyone else. He is a small man in his forties. I am told he is an agency chef and so he doesn't really have a title, but he is exceptionally experienced and he just does stints in a handful of restaurants for half the year, then cooks on yachts for the other half. I don't know why, but he gives me the creeps. He doesn't speak to me much, but it feels like he says things with his eyes, gross things.

"You alright, mate?" George says to Victor.

"'Ello, geez," Finn says, while rubbing him on the shoulders affectionately.

"Morning," I say.

Victor responds to us all with a solemn "Hello."

We ignore the awkward man and crack on with unpacking the supplies.

On the right-hand side, on the widest workbench, there are mountains of produce. There are dry-store ingredients, jumbo tubs of salt, big pots of spices, and gallons of olive oil, pomace oil, and vinegar. Then there are the fresh ingredients: onions, celery, and carrots for stocks, an enormous sack of potatoes for chips, bags of colorful leaves for seasonal salads, boxes of apples and pears for puddings, and kilos of butter. Everything is in bulk.

The meat arrives in a pile of blue plastic bags and it's put away by George. The fish comes in white boxes—it is sometimes stained black from a squid-ink explosion, or it might be dripping wet from the ice that it sits on top of, and Finn and I put it away. Today it's skate; I slide the wings straight into a Gastro and cover them with cling film. Into the giant walk-in fridge it goes. We scurry around organizing things. We start at the crack of dawn to bring together one of London's finest banquets in time for 12 p.m.

The kitchen itself—unlike at my restaurant in Cornwall or in Islington—is new, modern, and high-tech, with expensive equipment, flat shiny surfaces, monstrous extractor fans, and a long window overlooking the street below. It almost feels too glamorous to cook in, but after a few hours of getting our hands dirty, the glamour subsides. There are hundreds of steel containers; it seems like we could never run out but on a busy day, we do. There are three industrial gas hobs, each with six rings. There is a large island, where the Pastry section operates, at the front of the kitchen. We have two ceiling-high freezers, which are separate from the walk-in fridge where on one side the meat is piled up in excess, like at Smithfield Market, the dairy is in the middle, and the fish is on the right-hand side. The fruit and veg sits on a tall rack by the door, overflowing and looking pretty, like a Beatrix Potter illustration. We have two very cheeky yet highly proficient KPs, who have their own room a few steps above the kitchen but are somehow always hanging about with us while keeping on top of the mountain of dirty dishes that pass through the dining room every service, in addition to our onslaught of sticky tools, bloody chopping boards, dirty pots, and hot pans.

Once the supplies are put away, and we've piled up the

cardboard boxes and cleaned down the workbenches, we go to our sections. It's fairly quiet on a Friday lunch, so there are just four of us working on service while Lenny does a stock-check and makes the rota for next week. Today I'm on Pastry section, but I'm also working on the Larder section, learning from Finn.

George is on Hot Mains and Victor is on Hot Starters. I realized, when arriving here after my time at other restaurants, that sections vary from kitchen to kitchen. Each one is like a home, where the rooms are arranged based on the amount of space, the number of people living there, and the wealth and prosperity of the owners. My new restaurant is bigger and we cater to more people, thus we have more rooms, or sections. It is modern yet warm, and all the equipment is expensive. We are like a very civilized family living in a ginormous town house.

My mise list for Pastry reads: custard tart, blackberry compote, crème caramels, praline, chocolate mousse, apple and cinnamon ice cream base and churn, cheese biscuit base. Not too bad. I'll rush through that so I can work with Finn on Larder during service. The sooner I am proficient on both the Larder and Pastry sections, the sooner I should get a go on Hot Starters, where I imagine Victor will show me the ropes. Finn often cooks on Hot Starters, too, but Victor is better, quicker.

Finn has been showing me the prep on a few of the dishes each day; so far, we've made pork-chestnut terrine, tonnato dressing, cured sea bass, steak tartare, and celeriac remoulade, and he has taught me how to shuck an oyster. I prefer Larder to Pastry, partly because I prefer eating savory over sweet food, but also because you're cooking in sync with the other chefs during service, so when you send dishes out together, you're a part of it all. It's like a relay race, passing the baton to one another as you send out dishes. Pastry can feel like a different race altogether. It's the end of the meal: a solo sprint to get plates to the pass.

But there is something about the Pastry prep in the morning that I love. It feels like starting your day by sipping an herbal tea as opposed to downing a coffee. It is slow, methodical, considered. While other chefs race around chopping veg and stealing hob space for their big pans, I warm up by rolling pastry for a tart case. Pastry is precise; you pay more attention to weight and volume and temperature. There are many more ways certain dishes can go wrong. Take a custard tart, for example. You want a nice wobble in the custard, but you don't want it to spill out the sides; you want a nice golden pastry, but you don't want it to crumble; you want a confident amount of nutmeg, but you don't want it to dominate. If one of these variables is off, the whole thing is ruined. Pastry is teaching me patience.

"You guys know the *Guardian* was in last night?" George says.

"Oh yeah, how was that?" I ask.

"She turned up an hour late for her table, so we were waiting for her to order at half ten. It was fucking annoying," he says. He's normally so kind that this comment is a bit out of character.

"What a dick," I say.

"Fucking critics and their audacity," Finn shouts from the back, as he butchers chickens.

"And she ordered a grouse. We'd just sold the last one so she kicked up a right fuss." George sighs.

"Her fault for being late," I say.

Working in kitchens has made me realize how many annoying things customers do—which I used to do. One of the worst is being excessively late to your table. Every now and again, people will be ten or fifteen minutes late due to traffic or a train issue, and that is fine. But strolling in half an hour after your booking, especially if it's the last seating of the night, is wanky.

I realize now that the last table in a restaurant, the group just chatting, are single-handedly postponing a whole group of tired, overworked people from going home. While the last table is dilly-dallying about, undecided on whether or not they want dessert, a team of chefs are in the kitchen waiting, the KPs have accepted that they will be missing their last bus home, and the front-of-house staff are texting their friends, saying they won't make the pub for last orders.

It's almost always critics or people of media-influence who act entitled in restaurants, because they know their power. When they finally arrive for their booking, chefs are told their check is "VIP," and thus we should make *every* dish *extra* special for them. They make requests, too; to serve them a different cut of the same animal, to use oil instead of butter, to make a pudding vegan when it is made up of solely dairy—and then they want a long break between each course to take a call. Of course, it is in our interest to make sure people with influence have a nice time, but I don't like the idea of prioritizing them above other customers who might've saved up for this dinner out. I don't like the idea of leaving the smaller steak for the common man and giving the big juicy bastard to an Instagram influencer who won't even eat it, who'll just take a picture and then caption it as yummy but a little overdone (because they asked for it to be).

Nevertheless, I am conflicted. Because while it is often VIPs who make my job harder, their presence also seduces me; I want to cook in a restaurant that serves important people. It makes me feel like I must be a good chef if they're turning up. Maybe in the end I'm just an outrageous snob.

"How's your list looking?" George asks me. He always checks up on me, but in recent weeks he has done so less and less.

"Yeah, not too bad," I say. I worked hard to learn the Pastry section quickly, so that I could expand my prospects after the stunted seaside chapter, and in the past week or so I've begun to feel confident, like I'm at school again, like I'm top of my own made-up class.

I start my tart. I take a rolling pin and I bang it down on the fridge-cool pastry, forcing it to flatten. I push and mend any cracks. I roll it, and rotate it, and roll it, and rotate it. Some chefs in books tell you to be very careful with pastry, but if you're too hesitant, the pastry will tear. The more you touch it, the warmer the pastry gets, then the butter melts and then it will stick to the surface and then you will try to save it, and you will not.

I am impatient, and so when I first started on Pastry, I found myself feeling frustrated by how pedantic you have to be at times. But I learned all the different variables of what can make a crème caramel fail. Now, my crème caramel stands tall and proud, but will wobble if I ask nicely. It slices smooth and it tastes like sex.

I roll my pastry circle backward, so it wraps around the rolling pin, then I slide my tin forward and in one fell swoop, I lay the pastry over the top. The pastry hangs over the case like a super-king-size duvet smothering a single bed. I shuffle it into the ridges and then take a knife to trim the edges. Now that it's looking prim and proper, I can store it in the fridge while I make the custard.

George swings by my section on his way to light the charcoal grill. In hushed tones, he says: "I want to get you on Hot Starters before the end of this year, okay? Maybe even before Christmas."

"I would fucking love that," I say. "But surely that's not going to happen before we hire more people to do Pastry and Larder?"

"Lenny is upstairs in the office now, sorting out job postings; we're looking for two new Commis to do Larder and Pastry. We know Larder will be easy for you, so it would be good to get you on Hots to support that section over Christmas. The boss is really impressed with you," George says. I'm ecstatic. Big Lenny gushing over little old me! Marty very rarely gave me positive encouragement and Sean basically wanted me to stay clear of all cooking, so having a manager who is actively gunning for me to be promoted feels really good. The hours of hard graft this past month, trying to impress the boys, trying to impress myself, have been worthwhile.

I want to learn Larder quickly and then move on to the Hot section. I want to cook with fire; I want to have my own check spike. Pastry is great. But in service, I watch the boys working in sync, cooking fish and meat, and it looks like magic. I want to learn all the tricks.

"You'll be grand," George says, his faith in me evident. It makes me feel like I belong. Maybe this is my place and these are my people. What fun and games this chef thing can be!

Time flies by when you're having fun; chewing the fat and making pastry. Soon I am pulling my custard tart out of the oven to cool down and firm up a little, so the custard doesn't slope downward on the plate like a creamy avalanche. I take pride in plating. My dish is the last thing that people will eat at the restaurant; it is the cherry on top. I look forward to serving a pale, creamy slice of tart, and spooning the deep-purple blackberry compote alongside it: the color contrast will be magnificent.

The chefs are hustling around their sections, cleaning their knives, and tucking cloths neatly into their waistbands, awaiting the check machine. The front-of-house staff waft in and out to discuss counts with George, and he confirms we have no counts, we are on top of our game today. The restaurant is so big and spacious that the bond between the front of house and the chefs is a little less close here. Sure, we still have drinks after work, but we are more like normal work friends, as opposed to a tribute act for the cast of *Skins*.

Service is quiet, even quieter than expected. It feels like George, Finn, and I spent the majority of it congregating around the pass, picking herbs, and talking nonsense.

Before we know it the last check arrives for the Pastry section. The check reads: one crème caramel for Table Nine. I run a knife round the outside of a circular mold and, with conviction, I firmly press it onto a plate. I lift it up and there lies a perfect crème caramel, wobbling like a lovely bronzed bottom.

"Right, guys. That's it, that was our last check," George says.

"Fucking hell, that was slow," Finn says.

"Well enjoy it while you can. Next month, we'll start

getting busy," he says. The holiday season is approaching, and I remember just how hectic things get.

While cleaning down my section, diligently transferring my custards and compotes into new containers, wiping the sticky surfaces, and piling up my used utensils for the KP, I think back to last Christmas. I often felt scared, but not the good kind. I felt worried about letting my team down in Islington, drowning in checks and fucking up tables. But here it's different. I don't fear it because I know if I *do* go down, these boys will chuck me a life vest and then we'll all laugh about it after.

Finn and I head out for a cigarette. We can't use the fancy terrace because the customers are still in the dining room, so we walk down the spiral staircase and arrive at our established smoking corner by the bins, signposted by the fag butts on the floor.

"What a wildly thrilling Friday lunch service," he says sarcastically. I giggle in response.

"We should be able to get out of here nice and early." I roll my cigarette, filter in mouth.

I light my cigarette and then lend him my lighter. "What are you doing tonight?" I ask.

"Some birthday thing. I need to fit in a few benders before our hours get fucked at Christmas. You?" he says.

"Not sure, I'm off tomorrow so I might go have a few drinks with someone."

"Oooh, like a date?" he says, huffing on his chunky roll-up and winking at me. He loves gossip.

"Absolutely not. I don't really date much," I say. I dangle my skinny roll-up in midair like an elegant lady, pondering my continued state of singledom.

"Why? You're beautiful and you know it, you bastard."

He speaks with sincerity and sweetness, but he's also bitchy. I love him.

"It's just all a bit embarrassing. All the formalities make me nervous," I say.

"You're straight, right? How boring. I'm trying to think about who I can set you up with but the only two good straight guys I know live in Deptford, which is a bit far for you."

I laugh. "Yes, I am straight. And yes, that's too far away. It would be a logistical nightmare," I say.

To be honest, I'm not in the mood for men tonight. Being in the kitchen with men all day makes me crave female company; I decide to text my long-lost best friends Ruby and Sophie to see if they're around.

Later, back on my bike, in the opposite direction of Deptford, I glide through town. On my way to work, I sped; I am now able to take my time, to bask in the sunset and shuffle my Spotify. The sun is sparkling and I'm feeling happy; I'm in the mood for a little drink, perhaps a little dance.

"Raquel?" I shout up the stairs as I let myself into our flat; I like giving my flatmate a warning that I'm home in case she is in a precarious situation, like on the toilet or naked or secretly stealing a tampon from my bedroom. She isn't likely to be doing this, it's more that I'm trying to instill this habit in her in case she comes home and *I'm* doing this.

"Hey! How are you doing?" she shouts from the kitchen. I can assume she isn't on the toilet naked.

"Yeah, good." I climb the stairs, huffing, drop my rucksack, and join her at the minuscule table by our kitchen window.

"How was work?" I ask.

Because we're both chefs, Raquel and I always have good stuff in our fridge from our restaurants, like leftover côte de boeuf, expensive butter, and nice anchovies. We're also always stocked up with a wide array of instant noodles, a reliable and delectable midnight snack. We cook with so much fat that our kitchen has a thin but permanent layer of grease on the walls. We drink together a lot as well; day-drinking cans of beer on a Tuesday is not so shameful when you're doing it with someone else.

"Yeah, long day but good," she says. Raquel works harder than I do. She often does seventy-hour weeks because her restaurant only opened a month ago, and it's in Soho, and it's not fully staffed yet. It's a sort-of-Italian small-plates restaurant with a glamorous wine bar. It seats about two hundred covers. Raquel says she's tired but doesn't show it; her skin is clear and her hair is smooth, she looks as beautiful as ever.

"What are you working on tomorrow?" I ask.

"I'm off all day, thank fuck," she says.

"No way! Me too." I give her a grin, a knowing grin. "Well . . . maybe we should get a few drinks, then?"

"Yeah, fuck it," she concedes. I am delighted. We take beer to our respective bedrooms and put our phones on charge. I text Ruby and Sophie.

We're going to Mascara Bar at 6ish. Meet us there?

Ruby replies immediately: *On Tube now. Can't wait to see you!*

We take showers, one by one, washing the kitchen grease off our bodies, transforming back into young ladies with clean fingernails.

"What are you gonna wear?" Raquel shouts through the wall our bedrooms share.

"Don't know. Probably what I always wear," I say, which is black trousers, black top, black jumper, black Asics. I don't have any nice clothes anymore; being in kitchens means I spend the majority of my week in a uniform, or pajamas. My home clothes are merely functional. But what I lack in style, I make up for in sex appeal.

I drink a Tyskie from the can and then look at myself in the mirror. I look tired but pretty, the kink in my hair from having it tied up all day looks intentional, like I've had a blowout. My cheeks are pink, not from anger but from living a life out in the open; in the sunshine of my flat and the flames of my kitchen. I realize how far I've come in six months, the crippling anxiety that hit me in my old restaurant and the boredom that gripped me in Cornwall are things of the past. I'm so full up with self-love that I'm not even thinking about dinner, but I should probably eat before drinking. My diet is not healthy, perhaps the least healthy it's ever been, but I'm working fifty to sixty hours a week, walking twenty thousand steps a day, and using my body constantly—to beat mixtures, lift heavy things, and so on. My body has changed. I'm the slimmest I've ever been; my trousers are hanging off me and my cheekbones are poking out. I look like a damn supermodel. I know my insides tell a sad story, but I don't care about my lungs or my liver right now, it feels more important that I relish this moment of feeling hot as hell.

I finish my look for the night: I am wearing casual, if a bit shabby, clothes, but everything is black so it can pass as chic and glamorous. It's all in the makeup, you see; a little flick of liquid eyeliner, shiny pink lips, good eyebrows, and bronzer everywhere. I leave my bedroom looking hot and smelling nice, like expensive perfume and dry shampoo.

"You ready to go?" I say to Raquel.

"Yep." She is obviously ready; she wears no makeup and jeans and a T-shirt everywhere she goes. She is effortlessly hot.

We skip dinner. Raquel and I head to the pub just before it gets dark; my eyeshadow glimmers in the sunset. It is important for me to get in touch with my femininity on occasion; I don't need it often, but I do need it now and then. Working with a team of men and doing jobs which turn my skin blotchy doesn't necessarily lend itself to the sort of grace I sometimes desire, despite my new, kitchen-obtained BBL. But I feel good. I've been back in my city for a month now and I have yet to land even a snog. Maybe tonight's the night.

"My old friends Sophie and Ruby are coming to meet us," I tell Raquel as we enter the pub. "I've only seen them once, and for about twenty minutes, since I've been back in London."

They are my oldest normal friends, the type of friends I can go months without seeing and it feels like no time has passed when we're back together. I know Raquel will like them. She gets on with everyone.

I hear Sophie before I see her.

"Hello, ladies!" Sophie calls over to us, pretty face beaming. Glamorous Ruby is beside her. We've been friends since secondary school, and despite us all going in different directions since, there is something that bonds us now and forever: our love of talking shit at the pub.

Ruby and Sophie are both civilized and do jobs I don't really understand. Ruby is in fashion marketing, some sort of tech brand that helps people style clothes digitally, and Sophie works for an unknown start-up sports company that does events, or is it customer experience? They earn good money and seem to have the type of flexibility where they can go to TK Maxx for three hours on a Wednesday afternoon and no one bats an eye.

"Alright!" I say, giddy at the sight of two much-loved friends racing toward me after a long period of absence. I feel like their faces have changed; I'm only just realizing how old we are, how grown-up! I feel quite emotional seeing them, like when I used to get lost in the supermarket but then I'd turn down another aisle and see my mum waving at me. We hug, they meet Raquel, and we go to the bar; a bottle of white for us all to share, which lasts about seven and a half minutes.

"How are you?" they say in unison and then giggle at their harmonized enthusiasm.

Before I can answer, Sophie says, "We haven't seen you in fucking *ages*."

Since I started at my new restaurant, I really haven't seen my normal friends. I have thrown myself into my job and not just the work itself, but the culture. I spend what time I have off with chefs, either at the pub or at new exciting places to eat. My normal friends and I, we live such different lives.

"Yeah, good, just been really busy with work," I say.

"How's it going, the new restaurant?" Ruby says. Her nails are pristine and her makeup is flawless; she looks just like the type of woman I used to think I would be, but in recent years, I have learned I will never be. It feels good to accept that.

"It's great, I really love it. The hours are long but I've adjusted in a way I didn't at my old restaurant. And I'm learning loads and the chefs are fucking lovely. So it's great, yeah," I say, quite amazed that I have nothing to moan about for once.

"I knew you'd find your place. Think you just needed to shop around a little. Well done," Sophie says in her characteristically sentimental way. I grimace. I'm a little too sober to engage in ooey-gooey conversation.

"Thanks," I say. I may be proud of myself, but I show nothing to that effect—at least this early in the night.

When I ask Sophie and Ruby about their lives, they tell me about their nine-to-five jobs and how discontent they feel in them. They want a promotion, they want more money, they want to work from home more, they want to be able to go to Pilates on Friday afternoon and make up the extra hour on Monday. They think about changing career paths but they're unclear on what to do next.

I listen and nod. I am completely and utterly without judgment; these girls are precious to me, but I am happy not to have these problems. It all sounds boring.

"So I am thinking of maybe staying in tech but moving away from fashion. It's so cunty," Ruby says.

"Yeah, you have never been a big enough cunt for fashion, Ruby," I say. She smiles. It's true. Ruby is the nicest woman in the world; she has always been there for me in my darkest hour. And to top it all off, she is completely beautiful with a marvelous arse and long glossy auburn hair.

"I have no idea what I want to do, to be honest," Sophie says. "I'm going to stick at this place for another year because I'm about to get a pay rise, then I'll figure it out."

"That sounds good," I say, but it doesn't. Take a pay cut, move into a smaller flat, just follow your dreams! My newfound ambition is obnoxious and abundant, but I don't share it. I feel like I've just returned from a gap year in Southeast Asia and I keep having to remind myself that no one gives a shit about my flaky philosophies.

I am flooded with gratitude for my own life. Nothing could make me return to the world they are in, where you have to use acronyms like USP (unique selling point), and you have to say "best wishes" and "kind regards" over email, and where you have to book a Microsoft meeting to have a chat. I am so glad to have escaped it. Where's the thrill? And the fun? I would rather stick to an ever-changing workweek where my hours are never the same but my tongue is delighted with new tastes, my head is clear, and my arse is firm from stockpot deadlifts.

We talk about work, and love too. They're both in serious relationships, bound to men that they met years ago at university. Their men are different from the type of guys we fancied when we were teenagers; we used to like naughty, smelly boys with unkempt hair who smoked and drank before we did. But now Ruby and Sophie are dating grown-ups, men with well-fitting suits and good intentions. They are, in fact, nice. I am happy for Ruby and Sophie, happy that they evolved. I haven't quite got there yet; I'm still drawn to cocky, hot bastards. I realize Ruby and Sophie have left other things behind, too, whereas I have not, just yet. Things I was supposed to grow out of as a teen—giving in to dumb impulses, chasing silly thrills, prioritizing passion, and romanticizing life—they are all things that I have leaned into further. I don't know who is better off.

I know that in your twenties everyone goes at a different pace, but it's crazy just how quickly someone can feel far away. I used to feel a little worried that I was so far behind, but I realize now that I may never catch up in the way I thought I would—that's not a life I'm excited by.

"So what's this place we are going to tonight?" Ruby asks.

"It's very gay," Raquel says. She goes on to describe her favorite spot for cheap thrills and cheap booze.

"I'm excited," Sophie says, though I know she must be secretly disappointed to hear there won't be a crowd of straight guys fawning over her like there usually is. She still adores the attention, despite her matching-pajamas relationship.

"We'll find you and Ruby a nice girl for the evening," I say, grinning at them, wanting them to forget about their grown-up lives.

"You're the only one who's single, babe. We should be finding you someone," Ruby says.

"Raquel is too!" I say defensively. I do not want to reveal the fact I haven't had any cheap thrills in months; no sex, no attention, not even from middle-aged men on the bus.

"I am single, but I'm also wrecked from doing two back-to-back doubles, so I'm not wasting my sacred evening off trying to pull when instead I could dance to gay anthems for six hours and then get a kebab on the way home," she says.

I sip my drink.

"So go on, what about you, then?" Raquel says, looking at me. "You're off *all day* tomorrow. And you haven't got laid once since you moved into the flat!" she says. To my dismay, she has exposed my factually correct sex status.

Ruby and Sophie are grinning.

"I've been incredibly busy," I say, knowing I'm about to get ganged-up on. Actually, I am quite looking forward to the peer pressure. It's fun when your doing something stupid brings others happiness.

"Excuses, excuses," Raquel says. "We all know you're just too painfully straight to get with a girl."

"Yes, I've already told you I'm embarrassed about the severity of my heterosexuality. No need to shame me! I already feel great levels of shame," I say. I am embarrassed of how boring it is to only fancy men, especially emotionally inept ones.

"Have you seriously never snogged a girl?" Raquel asks.

"She hasn't!" Ruby says. She once waited with me while I hid in the toilet at a party where the girls kissed the girls to make the boys give them free beer. We were fifteen.

"It's true," I say solemnly, genuinely saddened by the great gaping hole in my sexual experience.

"Okay, well tonight you can change that," Raquel says. She has a stern look on her face, as if this is a matter of great urgency.

I laugh and roll a cigarette as I think about her proposition. "Is that not a bit offensive?" I ask. "Like a straight girl just using a queer girl for an experience?"

"Relax, mate, fucking hell. It's just a snog," Raquel says.

I feel giddy. That happens when I drink, not because of the alcohol, but because of the possibility. None of us know what could happen tonight, where we could end up, who we could meet, what we might eat when we're too drunk. It's a whole five to ten hours dedicated to venturing into the unknown. It's not an easy thing for me, to feel out of control, but alcohol helps. It lets me sit back and enjoy the ride, as opposed to asking exactly how the ride was manufactured—and in what year? And when? Is the ride likely to collapse? Or malfunction? No. Instead, I sit still and let my hair blow in the wind. I don't know where we're going, I'm so excited! I have to drink more!

I'm drunk when we arrive at the club in Hackney. It wasn't just the beer and wine from earlier: I feel drunk on feelings of sentimentality; I want to remember every moment of this night because I don't know when I'll next have a rota which allows me to see these friends. I really would quite like a snog. A snog feels vital on a night like tonight, in a city like London.

The club is vast but I can't really gauge the size because there's so much fucking glitter. In the center, there is a circular bar, and in the center of that, there is some sort of abstract artwork made of mirrors which distort our reflections. While I wait in line to order a round for the girls, I stare at my own—my cheekbones really do look sharp—and then I look beyond my shoulders at the dance floor; there are tits everywhere. I feel happy and safe; free of men!

I grab the four vodka tonics from the tall woman behind the bar and thank her. I head to the dance floor and there they are, my dear friends, going nuts. They all look beautiful and I'm convinced they are the best people in my world; I feel so lucky to be with them.

That's when I see her.

A girl is staring at me while I dance, staring at my face, not my body, almost like I've got food in my teeth. She is short and tanned with straight hair swept back in a neat, low ponytail. She is wearing baggy trousers like a skater and a black, brandless baseball cap; I like how she's dressed. She is androgynous, but also very pretty. She is not my type, generally, in that she is a woman, but everything else about her is just fine.

She edges her way over to me, trying to be casual, but she is overt in her desire. The staring! She is looking at me as if I'm something spectacular; but she is far more beautiful than I am; she looks like a perfect pixie. Alas, I am more than happy to pretend I am the prize.

"How's it going?" she shouts in my ear.

What the hell is that noise? I think. Fuck, it's a New Zealand accent. I don't think I'm into that. Get over it, I tell myself.

"I'm good, how are you?" I say, fluttering my eyelashes, signaling to her that I am a woman ready to engage in romantic relations with another woman.

"What do you do?" she shouts in my ear.

"I'm a chef. You?" I say.

"Ah, chef! Oooh. Nice!" She congratulates me like I'm a chicken that just laid an egg.

I cringe at her enthusiasm; I wish she would play a bit harder to get, but she's not going to. She has set her eyes on me; I am the golden goose.

We make googly eyes at each other, dancing around casually. She seems to be set on me, and it's making me nervous. I'm flattered. I am unclear on why she has picked me so quickly.

"I'm just going to go to the loo, be right back," I say to her. I don't want her to think I'm running away. I turn around before she can respond, and I group my friends together by their elbows and shepherd them to the toilets.

We all squeeze and bend our limbs to fit into one cubicle.

"I found my girl," I say, assuming they are all just as invested in my escapade as I am. It turns out they are.

"It's the short one in the black cap, right? Fuck me, yeah, she is really *staring* at you," Raquel says.

"And she came over to me to ask about you when you got a drink," Sophie says.

"She asked if you were seeing anyone."

"Fuck, how polite!" I say and ask her, "What did you say?" I suddenly feel like I'm on a dating reality TV show.

"I said no, and she was thrilled," she says.

"Oh, fuck! I just remembered," Raquel squeals in delight. "The bargirl I know gave me her ket." She pees and we shuffle our bodies around one another, each of us waiting for our turn for the loo.

"You guys want some?" Raquel asks.

We all say yes and then take turns with our individual keys. It makes me excited to see Sophie and Ruby committing to the night, not leaving early to see their boyfriends and return to their quaint nine-to-five lives.

"Are you ready for your woman-to-woman snog?" Ruby says to me as she takes Raquel's throne.

"Yeah, fuck it. Give me another bump for courage."

Raquel passes me the key. I scoop a little mound of white powder and I sniff it up my right nostril.

We file out of the cubicle and face the mirrors, sloppily topping up our makeup.

We head back toward the bass-heavy dance floor. It's

so loud I can feel the vibrations traveling up from the soles of my feet to the softest part of my thighs.

"Hey!" my admirer says, as she spots at me. "I didn't think you'd come back." Her hand brushes against my waist. I consider the feeling of her hand on me: if someone I fancied touched my waist, it would definitely make me feel hot, but I feel nothing.

She looks at me with a smile so genuine that guilt hits me. "I have to tell you something," I shout to her over the loud music.

"Oh yeah?" she asks. She pulls me closer.

Just at the exact moment the music stops, I shout back, "I'm straight," and my voice bellows around the club for what feels like five minutes. But then the drop comes and everyone starts dancing again.

But my admirer does not. She is taken aback. "What? Are you for real? You're straight?" she says.

"Sorry if I misled you," I say.

"What are you doing at this club then?" I like that she's turned on me a bit, putting a little tension between us. I'm more accustomed to this type of interaction, it's closer to the one I have with men; there's less of the staring and more of the teasing. Maybe I do fancy her.

"My flatmate, Raquel, is a regular here, she's always trying to get me to come," I say.

I look around for my friends. Raquel is over by the bar, drinking a shot with the bargirl, our ketamine supplier. It seems like Sophie and Ruby have found the only straight men in the room. I look back at my admirer. She is hot. If I were to get with a girl, I'd be honored for her to be the one. Fuck it. I lunge at her like I'm a fourteen-year-old boy.

My lips touch hers and they are soft like silk. It

doesn't feel like we're kissing, or at least, it doesn't feel like the kissing I have done with men. It just feels like our lips are meeting in an unconscious way: our faces lean in the right direction, our lips are in sync, and her hand is brushing my hair the way I like it to be brushed, I don't have to ask. I am so aware of her womanhood; it is not bad, it is just new. Gradually, the kiss deepens. It's like eating panna cotta for the first time; an interesting texture, a bit sweet and wet and nice. I wonder if there is a universal taste of women. Do I taste like it too? Am I just kissing her because I want to kiss myself? Am I attracted to myself? Is that a normal thing, or am I a dangerous narcissist? My manic inner dialogue is interrupted when Ruby and Sophie come and tap me on the shoulder.

"Hey, we're leaving!" They're grinning at me.

"What? You losers!" I shout back at them, with my admirer's arm still holding my neck.

"We have work tomorrow!" Sophie says.

"Alright, fair enough. Love you! Bye," I say, and turn back to my admirer. I realize I am alone with her now.

I turn and shout to Ruby and Sophie as they are walking away: "Wait, is Raquel still here?"

"Yeah, she's over there," Ruby says, pointing toward the bar. Raquel is still talking to the bargirl, who is seemingly besotted, using lots of hand gestures.

I decide to stay right where I am. I dance with my lover to Shania Twain and I wonder if we are going to fuck. I look at her and try to imagine her face between my thighs, or mine in between hers.

"Where do you live?" I shout to her; perhaps her answer will decide my destiny.

"Just around the corner," she says with a suggestive

smirk, giving me a glimpse of the way she'll look at me if we have sex. "Why? Are you coming back to mine?" She holds both my hands while we dance as if we're a married couple, which makes me feel a bit nauseous, but there's also the thrill, that thing I chase. The thrill cures the nausea.

"I don't know! I don't think so!" I say. "I haven't slept with a woman before!"

"That's fine, we don't have to do anything, but it would be nice to hang out with you," she says.

I've heard this line so many times, but from men. It's hard to determine if she is using it in the same way they do, that universal male tactic. But I suspect she has a genuine intention to get to know me. It makes my chest a bit tight; I'm not inclined to have deep meaningful conversations with people I've just met—I'd prefer a bit of oral sex, I reckon.

Suddenly the club lights switch on and the space is lit up like a dentist's surgery. I feel nervous. I worry that maybe I just fancied her because of the ambiance, and now that that's gone, I am going to pussy out, so to speak. But she takes me by the hand and leads me out to the front of the club, which is hot.

I roll a cigarette and ask her if she smokes.

"No, I don't, but you go ahead," she says, which is not hot; I wasn't asking for her permission.

We sit just around the entrance of the club so we can kiss more. She takes me by the hand again and leads me up a few steps near a fire exit, which is, again, hot. This time I feel it: fanny flutters. Now we're getting somewhere.

Her hand runs up the inside of my thighs, and I look down and note how small her hand looks compared to my leg. She really is petite; I have never been with anyone smaller than I am—perhaps skinnier, though. But she is small and skinny and elegant. She is good at what she is doing. She stares at me, still stroking me, looking for answers in my avoidant eyes.

Then suddenly I spot Raquel. She is standing on the road opposite us, waiting in the queue of a kebab shop. Fuck. I'd love a kebab, I think. I'm bloody starving.

I question it for a moment. Kebab or sex with a woman? I take a final toke of my cigarette and stub it out decidedly. It's got to be kebab.

"Hey, it was really nice to meet you, but my flatmate is really drunk so I'm going to take her home," I say, like the greedy, lying son of a bitch I am.

"Are you sure?" she says. "I was going to run you a bubble bath." What the hell? Hold up a minute, love. She sounds like she's reading the script of a Hollywood rom-com; the idea of someone I've just met pampering me makes my stomach turn.

"Sorry," I say. I kiss her lady lips one last time, then run across the road, toward Raquel and my kebab.

Raquel laughs as she watches my ket-induced gallop toward her.

"What? You're not going to go back with her?" she asks.

"No!" I say.

"Why the fuck not? You've been kissing her all night."

"If I'm honest, I saw you in the queue and I couldn't stop thinking about kebabs," I say.

"Just not her kebab?" she jokes, and I laugh.

It might be the ket but I'm feeling all sentimental. I feel like everything is coming together in my life; I am back in the city I love a little too much, seemingly rid of any residual self-doubt from the last time I was here. I feel braver after joining my new restaurant and now I feel braver after my new snog. I might even be ready for real love, you know? I don't want to go backward, though. I don't want another office affair, or another intolerable love with a barman, or another snog with a random person on a night out; I want something more substantial, something that will fill me up, something like a large doner and chips.

This kebab will sober me up, but I will remain drunk on female friendship and the feeling of not knowing what's next, not knowing who or what I will fall in love with. Could it be a new section at work, or a new lover in my life?

Raquel's first up in the queue. "Lamb doner, large with chips, please."

I'm next. "Lamb doner, large. And a Coke."

"Actually, can I get a Coke too?" Raquel says.

We sit on the pavement, side by side. I wrap my hands around my doner. I stare at it: the strips of meat really do look like a minge—not like a porn-star minge but like on a real woman. I take a drunken bite.

"Pass me a chip," I say to Raquel. She drops a handful in my lap. I continue to savor the mushy thoughts. I am happy and free, but I still want more. I'm addicted to love. Right now it's a city, but I think I want to love a person next.

6

Going Down

DECEMBER

Two months later it's December, and the kitchen is wrapped in spiky tension—like a Christmas tree draped in tinsel.

We, the chefs, are like actors waiting in the wings for the stage curtains to open, or stallions banging their hooves against the stable door, or pizza-delivery guys revving at the red lights. Suddenly we hear the sound that signals *go*; the audience is silenced, the gun goes off, and the traffic light turns green.

ZZ *zzz* ZZ *zzz*.

A few months ago, lunch service was so quiet and I was so bored that I longed to hear that sound. But now services are so busy that I'm holding my breath for every second that I don't hear it.

ZZ *zzz* ZZ *zzz*.

The check machine calls out demands; he is a loud-mouthed, smug bastard who tells me what and when to cook. He is like a pompous Father Christmas and we, the chefs, we are the reindeer. We no longer have any autonomy; Santa pulls on our reins, dictating our every move—we are to work tirelessly through the busy services of the year.

We're only fifteen minutes into lunch service and I'm already drowning.

Newly appointed Sous Chef Finn rips the checks from the check monster's mouth and calls out the orders: "Check on. Two oysters and bread. To follow, grouse, onglet, chips, and greens."

I have also recently been appointed Chef de Partie. Who would've bloody thought it? Me, surviving in a kitchen long enough to take one step up the ladder and leave behind my tempestuous Commis career.

"Yep," I say, under my breath, shitting myself on my new section. I rip the check from the check machine; now that I'm on Hot Starters, I have my very own monster.

I think back to my old job in a shiny silver office. My new job is still colored in metallic, but it isn't skyscrapers; it's stainless-steel workbenches, polished fridges, pots and pans, Japanese knives, the flashing gray of a mouse running past my feet, and the dull sheen of the moon when I leave at 1 a.m. I used to fancy men with soft hands and clean clothes; now I'm falling in love with a chef with sweaty balls and burn marks on his arms. I used to be managed by a French woman with nice pert tits and power suits; now I am managed by a monster, the check monster.

Zzzz ZZ zz.

I should've had my mise ready for the start of service so I could cook quickly and efficiently, but I didn't move fast enough this morning. I'm tired and groggy today, perhaps due to all the athletic sex I had last night. Fuck it, yesterday's euphoria was worth today's downfall, my new lover makes it all worth it.

Zzzz Zzzz.

My mise isn't ready but the monster doesn't care.

While I'm scrambling, the other chefs are admiring their amply stocked-up sections, the bastards.

Today, Finn is on Sauce and I am on Hot Starters, where I serve fish mains and the more expensive starters, like potato röstis and caviar. Our recently joined adolescent Commis Chefs, Jayden and Maggie, whom I've been training up, are on Pastry and Larder.

Today I am on Hot Starters by myself for the first time. I am without the support of Victor, the awkward old guy who has been training me on my new shiny section. Victor has taught me infinite kitchen lessons in a short period of time, but he has become a bit pervy and it is making me uncomfortable. So I welcome his absence, even if it means I am out of my depth during the busiest week of the year.

ZZ zz Zz.

"Check on," Finn shouts. He forgets to read the orders on the check because he's spotted Jayden under-whipping meringue, which should be out of the oven by now. Service has only just started and it's already a shambles.

I'm not set for service, but the monster waits for no one.

Zzzz ZZZZ zzzz.

I have to get my arse in gear. I push my half-finished mise to the side of my workbench: a chopping board of dill for the fried whitebait with mayonnaise; a bowl of puntarelle heads, sliced and swimming in water; a tray of potato-rösti mix which is oxidizing with every passing minute; and a bowl of mandolined fennel that is also rapidly turning brown. I quickly douse the fennel in olive oil and lemon to delay further discoloration.

In the winter months, especially December, the food we cook is heartier, more Henry VIII–esque. The sauces are deeper; the greens are darker and there's more demand for meat, carbohydrates, and fat. People let go of the idea of balance and instead embrace gluttony. There is something romantic about being in a kitchen at Christmastime, even if we are working our arses off to cook double the amount of food for double the amount of customers. Despite being stuck in a windowless, stuffy kitchen, we don't miss out on *all* the joy, because we have our own joy—our own traditions in the form of drinking cooking wine and keeping spirits high with sweets, drugs, or delirium. And this Christmas, life is even *more* romantic because I am in the midst of falling head over Crocs in love. The man I am dating is another chef, a handsome, burly one, with a firm arse and big hands. All I want for Christmas is him, and to survive this lunch service. I am dying to indulge in daydreams of him, but I have no time.

Finn shouts across the kitchen: "You got loads of cheese-en-place ready, Jayden? It seems all anyone wants to eat in December is fucking cheese." Finn is new to his role of Sous Chef so he has a lot to prove, and he thinks he should do this by micromanaging the young bucks Jayden and Maggie. Today he is the eldest son of the house, the firstborn of kitchens, the one to be trusted with the sharp, dangerous things. I am the younger sister trying to take the piss out of him.

I fancy a bit of micromanaging too, so I get involved. "Jayden, during December, just pre-slice all your cheese so it's ready to go when a cheese check comes on. It saves you from having to slice it in service, and you're guaranteed to sell loads," I tell him. Jayden is a green chef, with no experience; he's cheeky as hell but he knows when to be serious. I like him but I like telling him what to do even more. Maggie is quieter, but secretly better than him; she's cleaner and more organized, which is vital to thriving on both the Pastry and Larder sections. After my time being shy and feeling inferior in kitchens, I enjoy putting people, especially cocky boys, in their place. Jayden finishes his meringue and then races to his fridge to do as I say. Good lad.

He's a pretty boy, Jayden. He will grow up to be a handsome man one day. Alas, not as handsome as My Chef.

I can't stop thinking about him. My mind runs wild: right now I am wondering if we'll marry and bear two healthy children. He's so hot. He works harder than I do; he has more experience, he takes on more shifts, and he has climbed higher up the ranks. We meet up after our respective double shifts late at night, or early in the morning, and we indulge in our version of festivity: rushed *char siu* pork in Chinatown, cold beer, and warm kisses. We dine in anywhere that is open and then we dine on each other. The sex always stays with me for the next day; even as I move around the kitchen, I can feel the imprint of his hands on my arse like I'm a Wagyu cow and he's my keeper, massaging my body to relax my muscles. Only I am of course a lot sexier than a cow; I'm more like a thoroughbred pony.

As I stretch my arm across my section to wipe away the mise debris, I glance over at Maggie, whose body is tensely hovering over a blue chopping board as she tries to shuck an oyster. Her shoulders are tense and her hands are gripping her oyster knife so tightly they're turning pink. She is using the full weight of her body to pry the bastard open. I can see she needs help but she's not going to ask; she has too much pride. I'm the same.

ZZZ zzz ZZZ zzz ZZZ zzz.

"Okay, another check on, guys," Finn calls out unnecessarily loudly; he's acting tough but he's quaking in his Birkenstocks just as much as I am. "One puntarelle, one pumpkin soup. To follow, onglet, grouse, and chips," he says. I have to do the starters on that check, the puntarelle and the soup. The onglet and grouse come from Finn's section. Oh, I also do the chips, but that's piss easy.

"Who are all these people ordering lunch at half twelve? They need to relax," I mutter while organizing my checks on the rail above me; reading the ones Finn didn't call out. He's as scrambled as I am, but he's pretending he's got everything under control. Our older brother, our protector.

"Virgins," Finn hastily responds. I laugh.

ZZ zz ZZz.

"Okay, that's mains away on the trout and onglet on Table One," he says.

"Yep," I say. That's trout for me.

"Give me eight mins, yeah?" I say, predicting how long it will take me to have my trout and chips ready so we can have the food up on the pass at the same time.

"Eight minutes?" he asks, insinuating that eight minutes is too long.

His questioning irritates me; he knows I'm very new to the Hot Starters section and he knows I'm behind on my prep, but he's clearly going to run a tight ship to prove he is worthy of the Sous Chef title. Finn is usually sassy and flamboyant, and I find it funny, but today he's being serious and strict. His identity crisis is irking me.

Finn and I don't usually work on these sections together. The more senior chefs—Head Chef Lenny, Pervy Chef Victor, and now Senior Sous Chef George—aren't in the kitchen this morning so it's just us kids; it's like we've been left without a babysitter for the first time. I'm the younger sibling whose priority it is to have fun and Finn's my older brother whose priority it is to mediate our fun, so our parents don't retract our newfound freedom and punish us for messing about. Jayden and Maggie are the pet hamsters we must keep alive, one day at a time. "Right, I'm a minute up on those starters," I say to Pete, our very shy, petite Malaysian runner, who is studying business management at UCL; he is standing opposite my workbench, waiting patiently to take my soup and salad. He is a good runner; he listens and doesn't talk the hind legs off a donkey like the rest of the front of house.

I ladle out a bowl's worth of pumpkin, sage, and Gorgonzola soup from a large Gastro container in my fridge and pour it straight into a small saucepan. I get it on a low heat to warm and start on the puntarelle salad. Despite it being arctic outside, the kitchen is heating up; the hobs at the back of the kitchen are broken so I've had Finn's stockpots commandeering the hobs on my section since 8 a.m. This is only increasing my resentment toward him. A ginormous stockpot sits at my eye level; it is filled to the brim with veal bones, chicken carcasses, flaccid veg, and greasy water, all simmering away. My section is clouded with musky, fatty smells; like I'm at the spa, but instead of essential oils, it is gallons of meaty condensation clinging to my skin. To top it off, I am downwind of Finn's section where, in between serving food, he is butchering late-season grouse, releasing its arsey aromas for us all to enjoy.

I lift a handful of springy puntarelle from the bowl and shake off the excess water. I should have had it drained and packed away in my fridges but I ran out of time. I drop the leaves into a stainless-steel bowl, drizzling in some expensive extra-virgin olive oil and a squeeze of lemon. I add chopped anchovies, fine shavings of Parmesan, some pepper, and a tiny sprinkling of salt. I don't need much salt, the anchovies and Parmesan contain their own. I use a spoon in my right hand and the fingers of my left hand to toss the salad gently, so I don't squash and wilt the pretty leaves. The mixture of oil (fat), lemon (acid), and icy water from the leaves creates a little emulsification, making a thicker, more stately dressing than you'd expect. I topple the salad onto a plate with a limp wrist in an effort to achieve a look of effortlessness.

"Keep that out of the light," I say to Pete as I push the plate over to him.

"Yep," he says, already knowing not to put cold things beneath the hot lights. As I said, Pete is a good runner.

Next, I turn to my pumpkin soup, whack up the heat, and give it a mix. It's bubbling away now; it's ready. I take a bowl and ladle the soup in. I chuck on a handful of pancetta, a little Gorgonzola, a few fried sage leaves, and a drizzle of olive oil. Done.

"Okay, service, please, Pete," I say to the boy, who is still a little on edge around me despite my utmost efforts to prove I am quite pleasant. I push the bowl toward him and give him a smile; please like me! I want him to know that I'm kind at heart and that when I go all stern in service, I mean no harm. I don't like making people scared at work because I know how shit it feels.

"Can you get going on the trout quickly?" Finn says. "We got the mains away check five mins ago." A Mains

Away check from the monster tells us the table is ready for their next course. I'm not sure why Finn is spelling things out for me like I'm an idiot. It's not my first time in service.

"How long on the onglet?" I ask him, knowing it's not in the pan yet and thus, he's chasing me on my trout for no reason other than to practice his Sous Chef swagger.

"It's already resting!" he says, a little too aggressively. For fuck's sake. I feel bitter toward him: he's jumping the gun, cooking mains early and making me catch up.

I wait for my frying pan to start spitting fat, then I tiptoe my trout from the back of the fillet toward the front. The trout's pink body retracts; it is like a bad-tempered girlfriend stretching out in bed, subtly trying to arouse her beau. I'd never be bad-tempered with My Chef; I'm far too sweet. I drop chips into the fryer cage, ready to go when the trout is a minute off.

Right, quickly back to my mise. I crack on and ignore the chatter in the kitchen between Finn, Maggie, and Jayden; he's stopped with the swagger and is doing another Sous Chef thing—checking in with people, making sure they're mentally well. He leaves me alone, thank God; he knows I don't want to hear any trite kitchen sentiment from him, "teamwork makes the dream work" and all that.

I grab an empty tray and a sheet of baking parchment to bring back with me to my section. It's all about economizing every move, grabbing what you need as you go. I take the rösti mix out of the fridge and spoon little balls onto the tray, which is now covered with brown paper. I'll start by molding twenty, that should be enough for lunch service. I turn to look at my trout, it's cooking quickly. I have to hurry. I shape the rösti mix into little discs which, during service, will be turned golden brown in the fryer and then topped with a dollop of crème fraîche and a hefty mound of caviar. I'm meant to use a cutter to shape the rösti mix but I don't have enough time. The cowboy hat comes on as I mount my stallion to gallop past precision and patience. We say a chef is a cowboy in a kitchen if she or he cuts corners or compromises techniques.

I form ten röstis in the palm of my hand and then promise myself I'll do the rest later, using the proper equipment. I slide the tray back into my service fridge. God, it's all looking a bit messy under there; I'll leave that for later as well. Fuck. My trout. Fuck. I want to feel it, to see if it's cooked, but my hands are sticky from the rösti mix.

Z-Z-Z-Z-zzzzzZ-Z-Z-Z-zzzz. Z-Z-Z-Z-Z-zzzzz-Z-Z-ZZ-Z

"Check on. Six oysters, straight up." Maggie looks at me.

ZZZ zzzz.

"Straight up means that the table isn't ordering anything else, so we can send the food straight away," I say. "Go on."

"Four oysters, one whitebait, and bread. To follow, grouse, trout, and chips," Finn says.

"Yep," I say. I rip the checks from the mouth of the monster and shove them up into my rail so they hover parallel to my head, taunting me. I'll ignore the new checks for now.

Right, the trout, send the fucking trout. I quickly sauté some blanched samphire which I completely forgot about. I fry it in oil and butter, on high heat. I take a spoon and lop off some of my garlic-dill butter, chucking it into my trout pan; I turn up the heat and coat the pink in gold. When the fillet feels firm, I take it off the heat. I dollop wobbly aioli onto a plate, center stage. Then I lift the trout with a spatula and slide it on top. I place the samphire alongside it. I should've plated it before the fish but I'm fucked in the head, you see. I spoon the residual golden butter and pour it over. Done. "Service," I say to Pete.

"What about the chips?" Pete says. Fuck's sake. I pivot my body, reach out my hand, and drop a few handfuls of chips straight into the oil; hot fat spits back on my forearms.

ZzZZZZZZzzzz.

"Two secs, Pete," I say to him, signaling to hold off on sending the trout until my chips are done.

ZZZZ zzzz ZZZZ.

ZZZ.

It's December and people are greedy and needy. They are drunk in festive dresses; they are Veruca Salt, and they want it NOW. I group my existing checks on the rail to the right, and slide the newer ones to the left. I scan them all and plan my order of events; two chips, trout, puntarelle, and whitebait. There are three more checks in the mouth of the monster which Finn hasn't read out yet. Why is he on my arse when he's not doing his own job properly?

My trout is waiting patiently under the hot lights while my chips are cooking. My heart is beating fast but I tell myself to just slow down and concentrate. I am trying to learn the choreography of the Hot Starters section, the shortcuts, the ways I need to bend my body so that I am efficient with time and movement. On my new section I'm now cooking in conjunction with both Maggie on Larder and Finn on Hot Mains. Cooking with fire in service makes me feel powerful, like a proper chef. If only I was cooking like one.

ZZZZ zz zzzzzz.

"Check on," Finn says. But before he can read out what it says, more of them come pouring out of the monster.

ZZZ zzz ZZZ zzzz.

ZZZZZZ zzzz. "Check on—" he tries again, but he is interrupted by another check. *Zzzz ZZZ zz.* The monster is projectile puking checks all over the place; the paper is long and winding, like there's a snake on my section. I'm too busy to clear up the mess.

Finn waits a moment for the monster to silence. He rips out the checks. "Right, okay. Check on, Table Four: one soup, one rösti, one puntarelle, one whitebait, two oysters. To follow, grouse, turbot, onglet, chips, and greens. Check on, Table Seven: two soups, six oysters, one puntarelle, three chips, straight up."

"Yep," Maggie, Jayden, and I say.

He continues, "Next check on: rösti, pissaladière, smoked mackerel, oysters, Comté roast pear, celeriac gratin, onglet, chops. All straight up."

"Yep," Jayden and Maggie say. I give up speaking.

Zzzzz ZZZZ.

"Soup, whitebait, puntarelle, and rösti." Fuck's sake.

All these checks are for me; the bastards downstairs are just ordering food from my section.

I'm too far behind. I don't know my way around my fridges and my hobs; I'm unfamiliar with the escape routes.

I ignore all the new checks and keep working on the existing ones.

"Maggie, you up on those oysters?" I say. I realize I haven't spoken in full sentences in a while, and nor has anyone else. You can tell when it's a busy service because the sound of cooking drowns out the sound of voices. The chatter fades and you speak only to communicate your timings. The cooking soundtrack dominates: pans clank against others, plates spin, oil spits, water simmers, and knives chop.

"I'm up in thirty seconds," she says. Good girl, I think.

I quickly plate a puntarelle.

"Alright, puntarelle is up, Maggie. Send it to the table when you're ready." Now I can concentrate on my next table.

"Shout if you need help, yeah," Finn says to me. I am too proud to accept help; to me, accepting help is accepting defeat. I have always been like this, since I was a child. Maybe it's because I have a real older brother and I grew up competing with him, or wanting to compete. This is definitely not a healthy mindset to have in the kitchen, but fuck it: I don't want my kitchen brother to help me get through this Mario Kart racecourse, I want to do it on my own. Being slightly out of my depth lights a fire up my arse, it sends waves of thrill through my body. This is my favorite part of the job. I like being busy, too busy, because I don't have time to overthink, I just have to keep moving. Finally, I've found a job that stops my overthinking, even if it does stress me out; I'd rather drown in a tidal wave of thrill than sink in a corporate ship of dull doom, ruminating as it falls.

I respond to Finn with fake assurance so that he backs

off. "Just got a couple bits to send then I'm good, it's all good," I lie. I am not all good. Silly, stubborn woman.

"You got that mackerel working on Table Four?" Finn asks me. "It's been on for fifteen minutes."

"Yep. One minute," I say. Fuck. I haven't even seen a check with mackerel on. I scramble to get one from the fridge. While I hold the wet, cold thing in my right hand, I drizzle the plancha with oil and flaky salt to help crisp up the skin. I have butterflied all the mackerel so it is pretty and neat; that's one piece of the mise I did finish on time. If only I could enjoy this moment of cooking it. I place the mackerel skin-side down on the hot black surface and it seizes up; I feel about as tense as the poor bastard. I peek under the edges of the fish; when I can see the skin is golden and crispy, I flip the mackerel and "kiss" it on the plancha, heating the flesh through ever so slightly. I'll let it finish cooking slowly under the hot lights. I plate it, then spoon out a bowl of pickled apple and push it toward Pete.

"Right, I'm up," I shout, while wiping the edges of the plates clean. "Maggie, you got the toast ready to go with the mackerel?" I shout over to her.

"No, sorry, I'll do it now," she says quietly. I can hear shame seeping from her voice.

"Okay, as quick as you can. Mackerel is on the pass," I say.

Poor thing. It was my fault. I should've been communicating with her, but I can't tell her what to do when I haven't got a clue what I'm doing myself.

I find the mackerel check; it's still attached to the monster, that's why I didn't see it on my rail. I rip it from him and spike it with a little too much aggression.

I note Pete is watching me, clocking my irritation, and I wonder if he is feeling a little nervous about what might happen next.

"Thanks, babes!" I give him a wink to signal that my quiet rage is not aimed at him but at Finn, my bastard brother down the line who's not reading out the checks, and who's racing ahead and leaving me behind. I'm moving my body but doing nothing, just touching pots and pans, panicking.

"Right," I say to myself under my breath, in an attempt to calm down.

I remind myself that this will be my new reality. We're in the middle of the Christmas season, remember, and it's not going to ease up for at least two weeks. Everyone is eating out and everyone is feeling celebratory; we turn more tables, and people order more food. This means we are unloading greater volumes of deliveries every morning, we are preparing double the amount of mise, and cooking for a higher number of people. In short, it is harder simply because we are doing more work with less time. It makes me nervous, but I like the challenge. Each service is a game I want to win. Even now.

"How far off on Table Seven?" I ask Finn.

"Probably like three mins, cool?"

"Can we make it five?" I ask, resenting him for moving so fast when he knows I need more time.

"Yeah, alright, fine." Usually, Finn and I are a promising duo, moving with grace and gusto. We dance under the hot lights, him leading and me following closely behind. Usually we can read each other's body language. But today is different, today our chemistry is fucked.

Perhaps it's because I've been spending too much

time with my lover outside of work. I am cheating on my kitchen with *another chef*. I have been thinking too much of cunnilingus and too little of cooking. No wonder I am doomed. In this moment, I vow to change that.

I spin around on my axis, plating puntarelle, dropping chips, spooning caviar, warming soup, scooping dill mayo. I am working as fast as I can but I'm falling further behind.

Z-Z-Z-Z *zzzz*.

The checks are rolling in thick and fast. The check monster keeps puking big, long checks all over my shiny steel workbench. The pots of stock are bubbling away behind me, making the skin on my back itchy. The deep-fat fryer is spitting on my pink forearms. We have so much food going out that there is little space left on the pass. Our lineup of checks is growing, but our energy is depleting. The pans are smelling smoky; they're at the height of heat before it's hazardous. We need a reset but there's no time.

Finn and I are out of sync. We're getting in each other's way. Finn is over-communicating and I'm under-communicating. The dishes are looking weird on the plates, overly considered; a trout sitting slightly wonky with a mean amount of aioli puddled beneath it; Jayden's crème caramels are cascading off the plate; Maggie's oysters are looking like they've already been chewed up. Finn keeps talking to me but I'm no longer listening. I started this service on the back foot, hoping to catch up, but I've fallen and I can't get back up.

"Keep talking to me, yeah," Finn urges. He is using my lagging to prove his role as Formula One champion. Fuck off. I know how to drive.

"When are you on the pass? I'm up in two," he tells me. I pause as I squint at my checks, urgently trying to figure out what order we're sending these tables in and what I have to cook next. He walks over to my section to peer at them. I want to bat him away with my spatula. I am Mario and I want to drive my damn Kart by myself; I want to prove to myself that I can do this racecourse, that I'm as good as the boys. Even though Finn is a good boy, he's still a boy, a boy I need to beat. I've done it before and I need to do it again.

"It's all good. I'll be up in two," I say, with zero confidence. Miraculously he backs off.

"Service, please." We're sending out food but I have no idea where it's going.

The line of checks up on my rail is so long that I'm no longer able to fit any more. I am late on all my starters and I haven't even looked at what's coming up on my mains. Fuck. There are no more corners to turn, there is only one direction I'm going and it's *down*.

"Going down" in a kitchen means to sink beneath the surface of service, to lose control and to drown.

I have too many checks and too little time. I am going down.

The checks become fictional, like I really am playing a game. Finn is up ahead, leading the rally, and I'm swerving around like a drunk driver. I have röstis falling apart in the fryer, cabbage lying lifeless in water, trout turning grayish pink, and burned chips floating in oil. Nothing is making sense. I am wiping down surfaces to preoccupy my body, to buy me a moment to squash this rigid lump in my throat. Sweat cools on my body. I feel defeated: I am check-blind. Why the fuck do I do this job?

"You need help?" Finn asks, but really, he is telling me I *need* help.

"No, I'm fine," I insist. I'm not fine, I'm deeply fucked, but despite being on the verge of a breakdown, I am not giving him the satisfaction of rescuing me. I don't want to be the girl who couldn't hack the Hot Starters section on a busy lunch without her pervy professor. Perhaps my greatest downfall: pride over practicality.

"You need to start moving," Finn says. I ignore him while staring at my checks.

Pete stands opposite me on the pass—he's on the safe side. My dead eyes meet his nervous ones; I wipe my forehead with the back of my wrist.

Zzzzzz ZZZZZ.

"For fuck's sake," I say under my breath.

Pete whispers to me across the pass: "Trout on Table Three and Table Four? Ready soon?" That sweet, angelic son of a bitch. He's telling me which checks to prioritize. "And three röstis for Tables Eight and Three?" Fuck your Mario Kart, Finn! Me and Pete are playing a game of Tetris and we're going to knock the checks out layer by layer.

I get the trout on fast. Rösti, that's easy. I drop three rounds of rösti mix in the fryer and prepare all the plates for the dishes. A scoop of crème fraîche atop each rösti, bosh, bosh, bosh; a hearty quenelle—if you will—of caviar, and we're good to go. The trout is done in a few minutes. Done and dusted, kippers and custard.

"Service," I say. Pete takes the plates with a smile—he knows he's saving my arse. I spike the rösti and trout checks, and take a fresh look at my remaining lineup. Suddenly I can see what's in front of me. This isn't Mario Kart; this is Tetris. It's like those last checks were the block I was waiting for in our game, the long bendy fucker that wiped out layers and layers of chaos.

Things are looking up but I'm still down. I move my body fast. Why didn't I move it this fast at 10 a.m. when I was setting up my section? I was thinking of My Chef, that's why. I was daydreaming about our sex in slow motion, and clearly my cooking followed suit.

I keep going. I get a pan on the heat, I drop the basket in the fryer, I wipe down, I slice, I bend over, I nab a spoon of butter, bang it in the pan, rotate my body, pivot my heels, wipe down, plate, and call service. And again. And again.

I shout a bit too enthusiastically to Finn, "Okay, I'm clear on all starters now. Can we say three minutes on the mains on Four and Six?"

He turns to me with a smirk. "Okay, well done, let's go." I thought he was pissed but it turns out he's proud. Adrenaline is pumping through my veins. I feel giddy.

I avoid making eye contact with Finn; I don't want him seeing my relief. I couldn't do this a year ago. I couldn't cook this type of food for a lunch service this busy and get through it. The pace can be stressful, but it is this pressure which makes me feel worthy.

I am grinning down at my chopping board as I'm working the last remaining checks. Finn notices. He's having fun now, too. The check monster sings out Z-Z-Z-Z-Z and Finn is harmonizing as he reads out the orders; doing the type of silly voices that you only find funny when standing in a windowless kitchen for hours on end with a weird group of people.

"Check on. Two röstis, if you will, milady. To follow, your finest, fattest, plumpest trout."

Finn bites his cheeks, trying not to grin; he is thrilled

to have witnessed my catastrophic downfall, as well as my heroic comeback. He has realized he can run a service as Sous Chef, he can orchestrate a busy lunch and help his Chef de Partie down the line.

"Fuck off." I blush with embarrassment but you can't really tell; I'm already a deep fuchsia from the hot lights.

Finn mouths, "Love you, man." He knows the L-word will break me, the son of a bitch.

I lose it. I start to laugh. "Please fuck off," I say.

We keep working through the checks, but now we're setting the pace. Finn and I are back together, doing the dance, hand in hand. Oh, my Sous Chef!

And this is where I actually fall in love. I expected it to be with my new chef lover, but it's not. It's with the damn kitchen. I fall in love with this job, with the service, with the up and the down. It is something different from my love of food itself. In the kitchen, I am in love with working hard. I am in love with the way my body feels after a busy service; the shaky feeling is unique, it is not like the one after Pilates, but more like the one after me and My Chef fuck; when our bodies become giddy and floppy.

I can't wait to see My Chef this evening and tell him about this service. I don't have many people in my personal life who understand my job, and why I want to do this, but he does. That's what makes our thing special.

I spike my last check and I glance over at Maggie. She is the only girl I've worked with in kitchens. She is a few years younger than me, and I like to look out for her. She doesn't really need it, though; she's quiet, but she's braver than I was when I first started. She doesn't creep around the space like a lady dormouse hiding from the fat tomcats.

"How was your service?" she asks. I smile. I want to ease any concern she might have felt about how things went for me during service. I might've been affected by it in the old days, but not now.

"Yeah, I went down pretty hard, but I'm still learning the section so it should get better soon," I say. I continue with a louder voice, "It would've been better if Finn wasn't being such a massive bellend." I turn to look at Finn and he's grinning wide.

It's Christmas and we're all exhausted and irritable, but nothing can ever get too serious in the kitchen because you are with a group of people who have all opted to spend way too much time with their arses in the air while they scrub fat and other things from the back of a fridge.

It is all about camaraderie. Finn was an irritating dick in service, but I was stubborn and self-righteous. The thing we have in common is neither of us care as soon as service ends. How can we? The job consists of short-term thrills and long-term treachery with so many hours of laborious work, but once you fall in love with it, you're fucked. You think only of the magic.

I guess I've fallen in love in more ways than one, and now my insides are wobbling like jelly.

There is only one thing to accompany a shaky body and sentimental thoughts: a cigarette.

"Never needed to smoke more," I say longingly. We've only just finished lunch service but it's already 5 p.m. The tables of rich old men will be finishing their cigars right about now; after having their dessert course, cheese course, coffee course, cocaine course, and digestif course, then the dinner tables will be arriving straight away.

"C'mon, soldier," Finn says.

"Ew." I cringe at this nickname, but it secretly it makes me feel like I'm a part of something.

We diligently fold our service-stained cloths in sync and leave them on our respective workbenches. We lift our aprons above our heads and fold them, resting them next to our cloths.

We grab our jackets, wrap them around our chef whites, and head out the door to face the December air.

Stepping outside is like cracking open the window by the bed after sex, fresh air hitting our skin while we are still totally absorbed with the warmth from moments prior.

I sit on the edge of the pavement and Finn comes to join me. "Jesus, look at me," I say, after seeing my reflection in my phone. Finn chuckles at my flushed face and wild, untamed hair.

"Haha. First time going down on your new section, hey? Well done," he says, lovingly and giggly.

We light our cigarettes. And now it is the silent, comfortable bit—again like after sex—where we gaze down at our phones, not acknowledging how much thrill we just felt.

Cooking in a restaurant is not always like this service. I endure weeks of thinking I might be bored of it, or I can't hack it; there are services that are dull. There are times when I want out.

But then, when I least expect it—the chemistry is back and I fall in love all over again.

I didn't realize when I went to cooking school that restaurants were going to consume my life like this. It is hard work and the money isn't good. It might not end well but, like my romantic entanglement with My Chef, I tend to avoid thinking about the longevity and sustainability of things, as well as the potential damage to my ever so achy-breaky heart.

"So, you seeing that chef hunk tonight? George's mate? What's his name again?" Finn asks.

"It's Kit. Yeah, I am!" I say, smiling, unable to disguise my enthusiasm for all conversation related to him.

"You are so in love, aren't you?" he says.

"Fuck off," I say.

I might be in love with Kit, or I might just be in love with everything else in my life; maybe he's merely a bonus.

7

IN LOVE WITH ANDREW EDMUNDS

DECEMBER

It was shortly after my night out with Ruby, Sophie, and Raquel that I met him: My Chef. It's been manically busy at work in the lead-up to Christmas but in the little time out the kitchen I do have, he is the only person I see. My lovely, very hot Chef.

The sex is mighty, but what is even more impressive is the way this man is making my heart swell up and shine red like a tacky balloon on Valentine's Day. He is lovely and wonderful and extremely rugged. I find it peculiar to think that I ever settled for anything less. What the hell was I thinking? Oh well. I've won now. A proper, full-throttle, deeply romantic relationship is destined for me and him. It's practically a done deal. There is absolutely nothing that can go wrong, I'm sure of it!

"Fucking hell, be careful!" I say to a waitress rushing past me while I'm holding a whole tray of hot duck fat, enough to splash third-degree burns across her tiny body.

"Sorry!" she squeals.

"All good," I say. "Say 'backs' if you are behind someone, yeah?" I remember I felt shy about saying "backs" in my first kitchen, like it was over the top, but it isn't. It's just basic decency at this point.

"Yes, of course, sorry," she says.

It's the week before Christmas, so leaving work in the daylight is a thing of the past, as is working any less than sixty hours a week. Today is a Thursday lunch service, which can often be busier than a Saturday dinner service. It's when all the City folk come in with their clients for a corporate holiday meal—the talent agents, the creative brand consultants, the bankers. They order everything with special requests and then explain with a fake grin and sympathetic eyes that they are waiting for others to join them.

Lunch service moves faster when we have the same number of tables to serve in less time. For most of the year, lunch usually ends at about 4 p.m., but in December, when the streets are colder and people are feeling more festive, the tables stick around for longer; they walk out the doors full of too much wine and cheese at five, just as the evening reservations arrive. That means we have no time to prepare for dinner service; we just roll straight into bulking up our morning mise, which miraculously vanished during lunch service.

I got in late this morning because of My Chef. We were up last night shit-talking our restaurants. And then I rushed all the way to my restaurant; riding through the West End, I nearly skidded on some roadside puke from the night before. At this time of the year, I cycle into either puke or shattered glass being swept away by our unsung heroes, the KPs, at the front of the restaurant.

I hustle hard because I want to leave on time today. I've had enough of these chefs, I want to see My Chef. I am in a state of fury because Jayden, the new sleepy teenage boy whom I'm training up on the Pastry and Larder sections, didn't pull his weight last night, so now I'm having to speed-cook two duck and pork terrines for dinner that were meant to be pressed overnight. I am now permanently on Hot Starters, which I am delighted about. No more shucking oysters for me.

More experience means you take on more responsibility, ensuring the newer junior chefs have their shit together and their sections bulked up on mise, clean and ordered. We have the health inspectors coming in any day now, and Jayden keeps leaving his service fridge in a state. Thankfully Maggie, the other Commis, is slightly better than Jayden.

I'm working hard to get the new kiddies set up as much as possible for dinner service. The terrines are cooling, now I just need to finish off the smoked mackerel pâté and get some salmon curing. And make a double batch of brandy-butter ice cream for the Pastry section. I'm looking over at Head Chef Lenny, who is realizing halfway through lobbing a load of butter into his seared onglet that the check says "dairy-free" in red capital letters. "Fuck's sake." I'm glad he realized in time. I can't have a customer going into anaphylactic shock—I really need to leave on time today. I observe Lenny as he fetches a new onglet from his fridge at the pace of a snail. Come on! It's like no one appreciates that I'm in the throes of a new love affair. I've got places to be: specifically, a table for two at Andrew Edmunds.

I'm tense. There isn't enough time to do the things I need to do and still leave at 5 p.m. to see My Chef. I wish

Maggie and Jayden would hurry up so I can get them working on some mise for their sections. I shouldn't be doing this for them; I should be doing work on Hot Starters full-time now.

But I have to fill in the gaps on the kids' section because they're still a bit slow; I'm making mackerel pâté at the speed of light. Fuck, I also told George, who has been promoted to Senior Sous, that I'd organize the dry store for the imminent inspection, but he's off today so I might leave that for tomorrow. The fridges need clearing out too. And Lenny has also asked me to trial a new crème caramel recipe because, apparently, I'm not doing them quite right despite glowing reviews from many influencers.

We've all been constantly on our back foot leading up to Christmas. There is tension in the kitchen, but we all love each other dearly. It's the customers who are pissing us off; the corporate work parties asking for cheaper Christmas-themed canapés and the late-night drinkers drowning themselves before Dry January. I'm not going to see the sunlight for months; I'm ghostly pale but at least My Chef still fancies me.

"Where are Jayden and Maggie?" Finn shouts over to me.

"They don't realize they're supposed to be in the kitchen cooking at four, not showing up to work and finishing off their fags at four," I say. A joke, but not really. Paul, from my previous kitchen, taught me that the hard way, by shouting "About fucking time!" if I walked into the kitchen at 4:05.

Right, focus. The mackerel pâté. I need to grate some horseradish and blitz it with crème fraîche, cream cheese, and lemon zest. It's a quick job, but we need great big vats of the stuff because it's our most popular starter, which means the task takes longer. It's grating the horseradish that's the annoying bit. I've done six sticks but my arm grows tired eventually; this is the job for a serial hand-job-giver, or a teenage boy. Fuck it. I'll leave the rest for Jayden.

Instead, I rush-slice some red onion for the pickles to go with the pâté. Fuck, I slice my thumb right next to the scar that just healed over. There isn't time to deal with it, I want to see My Chef. I whack on a plaster and a blue plastic glove; in seconds my blue rubbery finger floods with blood. This little nick in my finger means another few weeks of me modifying every single movement to avoid the pain of lemon juice dripping in the cut.

I still love working at my restaurant, though. Even after a busy shift, there is light at the end of the tunnel. There is satisfaction in learning something new with every single task you carry out, attaining lifelong skills that will bring pleasure to both you and complete strangers. We are using our hurt hands to make nice things. That's why it's so special dating another chef; we both have this desire to learn, to get better, to seek and give more pleasure in life. It is unifying, and it is sexy.

Together, My Chef and I are a stinky, sleep-deprived match made in heaven. I can't believe he wants to see me again this evening. We only just saw each other last night. Maybe I am more than a tasty snack, maybe I'm a whole meal.

I remember thinking about love while eating my kebab at the end of my night out with Raquel, Ruby, and Sophie, and I think it might've put out some sort of doner meat manifestation because the following week, I met Kit.

In chef dating, it seems you do things backward. There is no phase at the beginning where you can fool the other person into thinking you are perfect or your bedsheets are pristine; there is no time for that charade. Kit and I had sex the first time we met. I was at the pub with George after work one day, and it turned out that the handsome man at the table next to us—who was of course Kit—used to play football with George in school. I bet he was damn good as well, My Chef.

Kit joined us; his restaurant was just down the road, and he was enjoying his ritual post-work beer all alone. The minute he sat down across from me, our chemistry was excruciatingly evident in that horrendous way where the third person suddenly feels like they are unwanted soggy cucumbers in a sandwich. After a knowing wink in my direction, George left us, and three became two; it was just me and Kit. We decided to cycle together through Central, but we ended up carrying on until we made it to East. We skated around the streets, trying to find a place to drink that was the right type of sexiness for the occasion. In the end we glided right past Dalston Superstore, and I suggested we pull up at the Irish sports bar near where I live (yes, the proximity to my bed was a contributing factor).

We chatted about our industry until we couldn't *not* kiss any longer. Then two chefs became one, under the yellow spotlight of a twenty-four-hour Morrisons sign.

I couldn't remember his name at this point and we'd both been up since 6 a.m., but we went back to mine and fucked. We were sticky from the deep-fat fryer and bloated from the pints. We didn't do the thing people do at the beginning of relationships—where they tentatively have sex, figuring out what the other person's preferences are, so that after weeks of trial and error they create a personalized and perfected body of work; all we did was fuck. And it worked.

He asked to spit in my mouth. I thought this was unbecoming, but I, like most people in their twenties, try to broaden my horizons, not wanting to miss out on what others are getting up to. So I said yes and what a thrill it was. He spoke to me in a way that was not romantic, but heavily erotic. I remember concluding: this carnal sex style must be because he is a chef. It was becoming apparent that fucking a chef is similar to working in the world of kitchens: the more you do both, the more the idea of going back to your former life of boring desk jobs and mundane sex seems completely impossible. I knew I fancied him because of the chef thing, I knew I was fetishizing him, but who gives a fuck? There are worse things to be fetishized for.

Afterward, we lay in my clammy bedsheets, exhausted from our lives of never-ending physical labor, but rejuvenated by the orgasms. Then we took a shower.

"You smell nice somehow," I told Kit before it was his turn to wash.

"It's my shower gel, I've been using it since I was eighteen. It's mint and tea tree," he replied with a shrug.

"That one with the green bottle? I know that one. Every eighteen-year-old boy used to use that. Did you never fancy switching it up?"

"Nah, it makes my balls tingle, it feels good." I'd only known Kit for about six and a half hours before he divulged this information. It was refreshing. The idea of dating backward, to be privy to the grossness first and for the romance to come later, makes sense. If you bear witness to my week-old McDonald's delivery bag scrunched up on the floor of my room, my Bridget Jones pants hanging off my chair, and my overflowing bin at the beginning of our love affair, and you still want me, then you know it's worth taking it to the next step. It is exciting to have the romance to come.

I would've been happy to have stayed with Kit from that first night on, to never leave his side again, but I suppose adult relationships are more civilized than that; there is less lying around in sex-juice bedsheets and more existing independently, only to be more infatuated when reunited.

But Kit and I text each other throughout the workday. We send each other pictures of what we're doing. We're both trying to prove to the other that we're good at cooking. Right now, I'm plaiting bacon to line that duck-and-pork-terrine mold. I made an extra effort so I could show off to him. I drape the slices over one another with painstaking precision; when every inch of the mold is covered in beautifully symmetrical slices of plaited bacon lining, it looks like a woven blanket.

I text him saying, *Come and lay in here with me, lover boy.*

And he replies, *No probs. Let me finish butchering fifty rabbits and I'll be right there.*

He sends a picture of fifty dead, skinless rabbits. There are only two things that disturb me in kitchens so far—birds when they come in with their heads still intact, and rabbits. Their bodies are so human-like. If you get them on their front and spread their legs, they look almost identical to me on a hot summer evening, naked atop bedsheets.

And still, I'm turned on. The way Kit and I work with our hands all day is hot. It's all very carnal. We are both on a mission to make beautiful things. We want to learn and we want our hands to perform.

This translates so much to sex: after a day of handling dead meat in the kitchen, we can't wait to handle each other. Our hands are better than laymen's. They are strong and firm, but also light and considered. The way he plates a dish reflects the way he goes down on me, teasing shapes around the dish before finding the perfect angle. The way I grate six sticks of horseradish a day gives me the arm muscles to bring him to climax with patience and gusto.

Sometimes I wonder if he'd like another girl whose arms are less solid, but I realize for the first time that I am in a relationship with someone who likes me not because of the way my body looks, but because of what my body says about me; my hands are scarred because I cook with fire, my arms are strong because I lift pots and pans, my face is pale because I'm tired, and my eyes are smug because I'm falling in love.

"Where the fuck are Maggie and Jayden? They're taking the piss now," I say.

"What's the rush? You got somewhere to be?" Finn asks, winking at me. He knows about Kit and he's excited for me. Alas, this excitement often translates to taking the piss.

"Shut up," I say. I focus on the pickled red onions for the pâté, the glove protecting my cut from the vinegar.

"Are you going out with him tonight as well? You clearly can't get enough," Finn says, a little quieter so Victor and Lenny don't stick their nose in.

"Yeah. Andrew Edmunds," I say, smirking a little from excitement for my big date.

"Oooh, very nice. Perfect for Christmas." I love Finn and his relentless enthusiasm, especially when it comes to love. He's the only other chef who obsesses over boys like I do.

Maggie and Jayden walk through the door in their pristine chef whites. "Finally," I shout. "What time do you call this?"

It feels good to be teaching someone else the ropes now. It's validating to be able to actually help other people using things I've learned. And it's gratifying to finally unveil my secret bossy side. But I'm not being a dick for the sake of it; I need Jayden and Maggie trained up on Pastry and Larder pronto so I can finally start having some fun on Hot Starters. That's the motivation.

"The Larder fridges were in a fucking state, Jayden," I say. "You need to leave them cleaner. Maggie, yours was good, well done."

"Unlucky," Maggie says to Jayden.

"Biased! Sexism!" Jayden jokes.

I walk them over to the Larder section, open up the fridges, and show them what's what.

"Right, so the terrines are cooked and in the blast chiller. You should've done that last night, Jayden—"

He interrupts me. "It was super busy—"

"Yeah, yeah, whatever, babes," I say, giving him the same treatment Paul once gave me.

I show him three sides of salmon I cured and so perfectly sliced that it almost looks machine-made, and the pickled red onions, and a tonnato I made, too, and leaves I washed for the Stilton salad. "You just need to finish the mackerel pâté for service, yes? You got that?" I say to him.

"Yes, all good, boss," he says.

"Excellent," I say. I give them a little pat on the back. "I'm getting the fuck out of here now. See you lot tomorrow." I'm at the door before I remember. I poke my head back around the corner and say to the kids: "And Jayden and Maggie, leave the sections clean, yeah? Good. Bye!" I leave for the Foyles on Charing Cross Road; the bathrooms have become my Central London Salon, where I doll myself up before meeting with My Chef.

Tonight's mine and Kit's first proper date. Despite us seeing each other for over two months, we don't go on proper dates, we see each other for rushed yet thrilling post-shift sex. We always talk about going for dinner, for a proper date, but we haven't yet had the chance. We're both working longer hours than usual, and his rota always conflicts with mine, hence us meeting strictly in the early morning. Either he is at work or I am at work, or we've both finished work and are meeting up for sex.

We always find time to talk a lot about restaurants, though; my restaurant and his restaurant.

He cooks at an old, iconic restaurant with fine dining, white tablecloths, red booths, tinted windows, and some real old-school cheffy cuntery. His Head Chef throws both tantrums and pans. My restaurant is like its younger, sexier sister. We cook similar food—it's fine dining too, and classic British and European dishes—but we're a bit more modern in terms of plating and political correctness. His restaurant is one that all the legends in hospitality fawn over and treasure, even Nigella posted about it on her Instagram. I am truly besotted; it feels very thrilling to be in romantic relations with a proper chef who works in a proper restaurant. Yes, I suppose I am a proper chef too, but fucking one is becoming more thrilling than being one.

We're going to Andrew Edmunds in Soho, where a classic European menu is served at candlelit tables in a snug eighteenth-century town house. It is one of the last of its kind. We have both wanted to go for a long time, but with *some* restaurants you need to wait for the right person or the right occasion. I still haven't gone to St. JOHN because I am waiting for Anthony Bourdain to come back from the dead, take me by the wrist, and march me in there for four hours of carnal feasting, seven bottles of wine, a couple of lines of crushed aspirin, and then a great big fuck for the final course.

Finally I am at a place in my life where a restaurant like Andrew Edmunds is an appropriate dining choice: a place where the lights are so low and the atmosphere so intimate that only real lovers are allowed in, or retired aristocratic men filling their bulging bellies while slurping bourgeois Burgundy. Kit and I are real lovers; but we are also two chefs on our days off, two piggies deeply passionate about eating, two lustful shaggers apprehensively entering the romance stage, two twentysomethings who will dress up all swanky. It is a Special Occasion dinner, and we are taking it very seriously.

He phones. "Where are you?" he asks me.

"I'm just leaving work now. I'll be there in half an hour," I say. I'm lying, really; I'm in the loos at that Charing Cross Road Foyles, putting makeup on and changing into my date outfit. I didn't want to get ready in the changing rooms at work in case one of the boys came in and saw me. They've never seen me all glammed up and I worry they would take the piss again, or even worse, fancy me.

I look at myself in the mirror. I've done light makeup

to complement my stress-induced, blushed cheeks. As I apply some browny-red lipstick, a mother and her toddler enter the bathroom. He's in tears. Babies freak me out. I am so pleased to be far away from having to care for a child; I am still a child myself and I still want people to care for me. I'm wearing a high-neck, black lace top and straight black trousers; my Asics can stay. I look at my hair; it looks a bit dodgy, with all these weird kinks that must've formed as I ran, sweated, and almost spilled duck fat in the kitchen this morning. I coat it in dry shampoo, rustle it about, and then tie it up in a disheveled bun. And for once it works; whenever I want a bun in my hair to look good, it never does, yet when I'm lazing about at home, hungover, without a care in the world, I wrangle my hair atop my head and suddenly I'm bloody Brigitte Bardot. But the gods must be looking down on me right now because my hair looks sensational. Right, I'd better go.

As I walk toward the restaurant, I see him waiting outside. I can barely hide my smile; what a div. "Hey!" I say.

"Hello, you," he says, but in a sexy way, not a goofy, rom-com way. He embraces me. Shitting hell, I love him.

A waitress welcomes us and steers us to our tiny table. "Go on, take the side with the booth," he says as we approach. I do. I only date real gentlemen, you see.

Kit struggles to get his legs underneath it. My beau is a hunk of a thing, with curly hair and jet-black eyebrows; he has nice lips and the kindest eyes I've ever seen and very long big legs.

"You okay there?" Seeing him squash into this space is endearing, it makes my heart swell, but Kit remains oblivious to my adoring gaze.

"Why are these tables so fucking small?" I feel his legs taking up 90 percent of the space beneath our table, but I don't mind. He shuffles around and wraps his legs around mine so we are locked in like a jigsaw puzzle.

"I don't think they're that small, I think it's just that you're a big man," I say, gazing at My Chef.

"Yeah, I suppose," he says, smiling back at me.

We're excited to be on a real date. It's been a long time coming. But we're still exhausted, with neither of us getting more than four to five hours' sleep a night in months, less if we're fucking.

"You haven't been here before, have you?" I say.

"Nope, I have wanted to for ages, though," he says.

"Yeah, me too." I think we've had this conversation before but we're usually drunk when we see each other so I can't remember all the finer details in our exchanges.

This time, it's not alcohol, but the formality of it all that is making me delirious. "I'm not used to seeing you out in the real world," I say.

"I know, it's weird, isn't it?" He whispers the next bit: "It's so nice." He isn't talking about the restaurant; he is talking about being here with me. I guess he is delirious too.

Our conversation is slightly stunted; it's like we're both realizing this is our first date and we're a little nervous. But our bodies tell a different story; we lean forward with our elbows on the table, we want to be as close to one another as possible—without touching of course, this is our first date after all.

Here we are, sitting across from one another in our Sunday best. I can tell he's made an effort for me and it makes my heart pang. I've made an effort for him, too. "You look nice," I manage.

IN LOVE WITH ANDREW EDMUNDS

"So do you." He takes my hand across the table. Fuck, well, we're really doing this romance thing, aren't we? I look down, suddenly shy. I am new to this world, and I always thought it would make me nauseous, the whole dinner-date thing of dressing up fancy and holding hands in a candlelit restaurant, but it's quite nice, actually. It feels like when you tell your mum not to come to school sports day because you think it might be embarrassing, but when you spot her face in the crowd of mums, your heart fills with so much love that you might cry. Kit showed up for me tonight and I think I might cry.

After an elongated yet comfortable silence, I ask what he wants to eat. We peruse the menu in silence. Laymen can never appreciate a restaurant like us chefs. Kit and I sit there, peering around and acknowledging every minute detail; how the tables are set, how the menus are arranged, how the waitress smiles; this is a version of the front of house that we never get to see from the other side. We know the stormy cloud of chaos that is brewing behind the kitchen doors, we can interpret the weather signals between general manager and floor staff; we know all about the rudder that needs to turn in order to make this old rickety ship sail smoothly into a tempestuous tide: a busy Thursday night in central London.

Chefs take their time at dinner. We are tortoises and you lot are hares. Where you would race through the menu, disregarding anything that sounds too dodgy, we over-order, especially the things that we're unsure of, or that are new. Last week, Raquel and I went to dinner and had braised duck feet, fermented eggs, and cold boiled pork belly.

"Rabbit?" he suggests.

"I was thinking that too." We know what we want. We know how to eat good and fuck well. "And maybe the Dover sole?" I add. He smiles at me. Kit likes that I am greedy and have extra fat around my hips; it means I love food more than I love most things, just like he does. It's almost like we're in an arranged marriage—two chefs brought together by their community—and we're one of the lucky couples where there was no need to let the love evolve, because it was there from the start.

Before ordering, we ask the waitress how she is, and we actually listen to the answer. We sympathize with the nineteen-year-old girl working in a restaurant full-time; she, like a lot of young people in hospitality, is trying to pursue a career in something creative but is having to fund that dream by waiting on old white guys.

"You guys work in restaurants, don't you?" the pretty young thing guesses after the initial pleasantries. We both grin. Immediately the waitress's professional facade drops and she starts complaining about the other customers. Even though we are the scruffiest people in there, with the least amount of money, suddenly we are VIPs and all these King Charles lookalikes wonder if we might be rock-and-roll nepo babies or young artists.

Kit and I pour gloopy red wine down our throats, our arses meld to our chairs, and our hearts escape our tight chests to hover over the white tablecloth. We enthusiastically await a meal which, as a one-off treat, we are to eat sitting down with knives and forks, not standing over a bin with a spoon.

"How was your lunch service?" When I feel nervous around him, like now, I often fall back on our work as a topic of conversation. Kit is more comfortable in silence than I am. He is helping me learn to relax.

"Yeah, fine. Although Tom is being a prick again. He thinks he's better than he is; he hates it that I've been asked to train him." I wish Kit would train me instead of Tom, a young chef he's just hired who has no interest in cooking.

We relax into our chairs and talk about everything and nothing: restaurant socialites, our favorite pubs, the color green, and his cock. He speaks briefly about his ex and looks down at the table as he does so.

"A big point of contention in our relationship was that I was a chef. You know what it's like. The hours are long, and you never really know what the next week is going to look like until you get your rota. It's hard to make plans with your partner, to make them feel prioritized." This is a bittersweet moment for me. I feel slightly smug at the prospect of me understanding him and his lifestyle in a way she couldn't, but I also feel depressed at the reality of how hard it might be for our relationship to flourish, for our minimal time out of the kitchen to overlap.

"Have you been to the Quality Chop House before?" he asks me.

"No, it looks great," I say.

"We should go there next," he says.

Knowing that this date isn't some sort of test, and that I will see him again even if I am acting a little quiet, reassures me. He definitely likes me a lot, I know it. Sometimes I forget but looking at him now, I can see it all over his face.

Before we can do any more buttery bumbling, our new friend arrives at the table. "Here's the rabbit," she announces. She puts the food down in front of us and I am sad because it means we have to stop holding hands to eat it.

"Thank you so much," we say in unison.

We chefs get to know the food before we eat it, we admire the plating, we delight in the colors and the shapes; laymen squash their food down their gullets, never taking a moment before hurrying along to the finish line.

We both take a bite. "Fuck, that's really great," Kit says. My mouth full and eyes wide, I nod at him. Being on this date is like waking up from a dream that I don't want to leave just yet, but instead of desperately shutting my eyes in an attempt to return to fantasy world, I am able to leap up from my bed, pinch my arm, wash away my sleep, and still be here, existing in this exact moment, in this dream, on this date, with him.

"You have a bit of rabbit sauce on your chin," Kit says.

"For fuck's sake." I laugh, immediately trying to wipe the spot. "I thought you were looking at me like that because you were enthralled by my beauty."

He laughs, too. "I mean that as well." He says it casually, but my heart goes haywire. "But you also really do have sauce on your chin."

"Well, I can't locate it and I look like a dick, so can you just get it, please?" Kit reaches his big chef hand across the table and brushes my chin with his thumb, holding on to my jaw a little longer than necessary.

"I like you a lot," he says, looking down at the stem of his wineglass and then looking up to meet my eyes. I bloody knew that was coming.

"Yeah, well, I like you too," I say.

We both grin like kids on Christmas morning.

"Even if we don't get to see each other at normal

times, or go on many proper dates, I still really enjoy our time together," he says.

He's saying all the right things. It fills me with glee; it's as if he's rehearsed it in the mirror, yet it sounds so considered and genuine. If he is a bastard, I wouldn't be able to tell.

I guzzle up the romance between sips of wine. I want to drink it up. I am lapping up all the nervous flirting and sweet words that we missed out on at the beginning by skipping straight to the sex. I didn't necessarily long for this traditional dating, but now that it's arrived, I am addicted, I want more.

The mains are excellent. The rabbit is tender and the Dover sole is beautiful. But there is only so much attention I can pay to the food when I'm falling in love with the man watching me eat. When our plates are clean, I am sad. I don't want to say goodbye to him, I don't know when I'll next see him because our rotas always clash.

"Are you working tomorrow?" he says.

"Yes," I say. I wonder if he will want to go out with some friends instead of going home with me. "Are you?" I ask.

"Nope, but I want an early night." I wonder if he'll ask me to sleep over. We haven't really planned anything in advance; this is different from when we meet up after work at 1 a.m. and inevitably fuck. My heart is full but there's still space for pudding, for him lying next to me in my bed.

Fuck it. "Well, do you want to come back to mine?" I ask.

"Definitely," he says. Perhaps he had been nervous, too. Perhaps my suggestion reassured him. I forget women are allowed to make the first move. He continues excitedly, "We could watch a movie or something. Let's go to your corner shop and get you a mint Aero." He's planned it all out, I realize. And he knows my favorite chocolate bar. Fuck. I'm done for.

Our first real date, our first dinner at Andrew Edmunds, and we are giddy. Instead of dessert wine, he leans over and kisses me across the table in the middle of this snug restaurant with all the customers watching us, rather displeased. His lips are sweeter than any Riesling. It is the perfect end to our blissful meal. Plus, there's mint Aero and sex to come.

"Shall we go?" he says, after we split the bill. He tried to pay but I forced him to split it with me. This was not in feminist protest; I'm not against men paying for women, I am just too awkward to deal with the whole debacle of thanking them afterward. Also, I know Kit earns the same shitty wages I do; we both can't afford this meal, so we might as well split it.

We thank the waitress, we give her a wink, and we go on our merry way like a Christmas rom-com. It's pitch-black and freezing outside; he tries to give me his coat as we wait for the bus but I decline. This isn't a damn movie, I think. But fuck it, maybe I should lean into it and just play along.

Something in me shifts when we sit down on the top deck of the N38; I melt into the chair, I stop thinking, and I actually live in the moment. My whole body is warm with food and love. I am sleepy from the wine and from my heart working overtime. Before now, when

I was with Kit, or any other guy, I was always half distracted by an inner dialogue where I would question his actions or try to immortalize certain nice moments by memorizing them. But in this moment, sitting with him on a full stomach on the N38, I'm not.

I have work tomorrow, but I'm not thinking about that either. Even if I did think about it, I wouldn't fret. My job is merely to use my hands to give people pleasure and joy for Christmas. I'm basically Father Christmas, if Father Christmas was about to have sex with a handsome chef.

8

Ready Steady Cock

MARCH

It's a sunny afternoon in March when I think I'm getting the call that I have often ruminated on since My Chef and I started dating in October. He calls me after work. I pick up. He begins with "Hey," followed by a drawn-out "So . . ."

My heart—forever feeble—drops as I hear the hesitation in the word "so." I immediately assume he is calling to tell me it's over. My brain instinctively formulates a plan to deal with the breakup; I will get a couple of cans of beer from Tesco and sit among the pigeons in a patch of grass by Westminster Bridge; I will listen to Etta James and cry into the River Thames until the water is no longer brown but crystal clear.

Despite the fact we have been seeing each other for many months, my brain sometimes overthinks things, and makes me question Kit's pursuit of me. Sometimes I worry he was swept up in a spell of winter romance, employing me as a doting companion through cuffing season, and now that the weather is shitty and gray, he's over it. I worry I am a rich gooey Camembert he bought as a one-off treat. I am initially delicious, with oozing melty sex appeal, a change from his usual mature Cheddar. But after a while my free spirit seizes up and I can become a little too intense: he opens the fridge door and *bam!* the Camembert is invading his nostrils—he unlocks his phone and *bam!* ten texts from me, asking if he wants to hang out.

Kit continues, "I just went via the butchers at Quality Chop House on the way home from work and bought a fucking massive côte de boeuf." I squat on the pavement outside my restaurant. I laugh tentatively, waiting for the blow, for him to tell me it's over. "Do you want to come over and I'll cook it for us?" he asks. Bloody hell. It appears I got the wrong end of the stick; it seems My Chef is not dumping me, he is in fact in love with me. I knew it.

In the past, I have only ever experienced pathetic romantic gestures like "I bought you an extra pack of Rizlas because you always pocket mine." Never proper ones like this. I never expected this, especially from a chef. I thought chefs would be cold bastards with superiority complexes and no desire to court a lady before laying with them. Before I started working in restaurants, I thought that they were incapable of love, that they'd all have toxic pasts which didn't allow them to have normal functioning relationships, like Scar from *The Lion King*. I thought they'd all have substance abuse issues, anger problems, or a roster of mysterious women whom I could never compete with. Kit is not like that. He has a big heart, one I would like to slit open with a Swiss Army knife and squeeze my body inside to take a nap. My Chef is sweet and kind, but not overly affectionate; he is introverted but quietly opinionated, sociable but happy in his own company. He is cooler than me; he knows about music, film, and fashion. Kit offering to cook this steak for me is a moment that feels too good to breeze past. I want to bask in it. Despite us both being chefs, we have never cooked for one another. We prefer going out to eat, to explore restaurants in London that aren't our own. But I am thrilled by the prospect of him asking to cook dinner for me; I want to remember this feeling forever, before something goes wrong and I fuck it up by being too keen. Perhaps I should decline, I feel like I've been too available recently. In fact, yes, I'll do that.

I respond casually, "I don't know. I'm so tired after my double yesterday. It sounds nice, but I think I'm just going to eat cereal and get an early night." I'm playing the game. We're six months in and I probably don't need to, but something unnerves me about Kit; I feel like he's not all that serious sometimes, or like he's holding something back. I've never inquired about whether or not we're exclusive; I suppose I'm a little too afraid of the answer being one I don't want to hear. Instead, I will continue as things are, but I will control myself. I must recalibrate my feelings for him.

He sounds defeated but accepts my answer with a simple "All good," and hangs up. They never bloody fight for me. Moments later he sends me a picture of the great big hunk of beef; his muscular thumb grips the corner of the meat, making a dent in the red flesh. He's so hot. I fancy him more than I've fancied anyone.

I text him, saying, *Okay, fuck it, I'll come. I'll be there in an hour.*

Kit replies to my text, *Great. Can't wait.*

I stand up from the pavement and cross the road to unlock my bike. The steak date is officially on. I feel thrilled. My Chef is cooking for me. I've only been in the restaurant world for a short while compared to him; I didn't expect to be gallivanting around the elitist circles of London hospitality so quickly. The more people I meet, the more exclusive it feels. Kit seems to know someone in every restaurant, he seems to belong, whereas I still feel like I'm playing a part in some sort of social experiment.

I cycle fast back to my flat so I can fix myself up before our dinner. Yes, he's already seen me looking disheveled, but I still want to catch him looking at me in that obsessive way; the way a guy looks at you and registers how beautiful you really are incrementally more each time he meets you.

    I take a look at myself in the mirror. My hair is doing the Vivienne Westwood thing it always does after work—the humidity and sweat makes it go wild. Sometimes it looks good, other times it's a disaster and I need to wash it and start over. I reread mine and Kit's text conversation to try to decipher the theme of the evening and thus figure out my outfit. I have bags under my eyes from yesterday's double shift and my skin feels tacky from sweating over a stove, like a plaster that's lost its stick.

    Fuck it. I jump in the shower; hot water washes away the oil and soap scrubs away the residual animal protein from my fingers. A shower after work is like being born again. I decide against washing my hair and instead just zhuzh it up using dry shampoo. I am no longer Hagrid, I am a sheared sheep, curly and cute. I put on black trousers, a T-shirt, and a hoodie, and slide on my worn-to-death Asics. Must get some new shoes. No time. Too busy being in love. Plus, I have realized recently that comfort is sexier than putting on an outfit that isn't authentic to you. Dress for yourself, I tell myself, not for him. I make the final closing statement to my inner demons: this guy likes me. He's asking to cook for me. No chef wants to cook in their free time if it's not for someone special.

As I walk up my road, my phone vibrates in my pocket. It's a text from Kit.

Do you wanna make a sauce or something to go with the beef?

Fuck no. I absolutely do not. Fuckity fuck. The moment I've been dreading since we first started dating: the great cook off, Chef Lover 1 vs. Chef Lover 2. We've been too busy to cook for one another, and when we do have the same day off, we like exploring other restaurants and pretending to be a normal couple. I can't imagine anything worse than cooking for another chef who is better than me, especially when I am using every ounce of my energy for that chef to retain interest in me. At all times I must be funny, at all times I must be smart, at all times I must be HOT. The cooking is just one step too far. I know how much we judge other people's food; I don't want him having those mean thoughts about me. Plus, I've talked about food in such an arrogant and entitled way whenever we've gone out, I've probably given him the illusion that I'm an excellent cook, whereas in reality I'm still learning fundamental things every day.

I reply: *Yeah, sounds good*

A lie a day keeps the sanity at bay.

I leave my flat on foot, march to Sainsbury's, and think of England. What can I cook that is easy? But that is also impressive enough to ensure this chef will want to be with me forever and ever? I remember the Café de Paris–style sauce that my former Head Chef, Marty, taught me how to make. I quickly settled on that: a classic crowd-pleaser. I will need to pick up anchovies, an egg, a lemon, chervil, parsley, tarragon, butter, Worcestershire sauce, and mustard. I buy the ingredients and head to the bus stop.

What was going to be a highly romantic evening with me sitting at his kitchen table, looking effortlessly beautiful, drinking wine, and watching him cook, has now turned into an episode of fucking couples' *MasterChef*. My stomach is doing somersaults. I ponder whether it would be easier to just leg it home, put my phone in the bin for five working days, get on with my life, and forget Kit ever existed. But I get on the bus to Hackney. For every minute of that bus ride, I think about how I can avoid fucking up the sauce, and equally, how I can avoid fucking things up with him. At least it's just me and him. The bus pulls up to the stop on his road far too quickly, and soon I'm standing outside his front door.

I text him: *Outside*

Moments later, there he is. He opens his big arms and the smell of his skin, which is becoming my favorite perfume, wafts all over me. "Hello," he says in that flirty way boys like to say hello.

We go into the kitchen and I immediately hear noises from upstairs. For fuck's sake. Kit lives in this house but doesn't own it—his friends do—but I could've sworn Kit said they were away.

"Are Maria and Ben here?" I ask, with very little attempt to hide my discomfort. I am tired from work and I feel vulnerable in his home now that I know I'll be meeting new people. I feel as if my hoodie is sitting weirdly on my shoulders, my hair feels like it's hanging in an ugly fashion, I worry the light is falling on my face in a way that highlights my kitchen-blemished skin. The inner demons are back and particularly loathsome. I've met a few of Kit's friends out and about but we're always drunk and he's always draping his body over mine to make me feel included, which I do because I'm drunk too. But this is different. It's almost as if this is a proper girlfriend-boyfriend thing. Is this guy my boyfriend? I just don't know. I should ask my friends later.

Kit interrupts my demon thoughts, "No, no they're still away. But Haseem is here. You know that chef I was telling you about who started at Grit. I said he could join us, hope that's cool."

Get me out of this chef hellhole. They're everywhere. And they're all better than me. With more years in the kitchen, more strength, more resilience, and more penis.

Kit is ignorant of this; he thinks I'm brave and that I don't care what people think. "Come and have a look at the steak," he says. He takes my hand and I am conflicted. I want to run a mile, but I so badly want us to flourish into this hot, hospitality power couple. If I'm too nervous to cook for him and his friend, then perhaps us dating won't work, and perhaps me being a chef won't work either.

The côte de boeuf Kit proudly places in front of me is indeed massive, but right now there is nothing I care about less. I quickly glance around the space, and wonder where I will make my sauce. The bag of ingredients is still in my hands; I feel like I'm wearing fancy dress to a normal party.

Kit opens a bottle of red, pours a glass, and looks over at me. "You okay?" he asks.

I muster some grit from the bottom of my stomach, the same grit I use when I'm in the kitchen on a sixteen-hour shift, serving several tables at once, spinning out, and getting lost in the checks. It's the grit in the stomach that makes me a good chef, a good lover, and a good pretender. It's not to be confused with Grit, the swanky new restaurant in Peckham that Kit's friend Haseem works at.

"Yeah, yeah, I'm fine." I grin and poke him in his stomach. Fuck.

Kit's house is some sort of chef commune. It belongs to Maria and Ben, the co-owners of a very sceney pub in Haggerston that I went to with one of my poshest friends a few years ago. After entering the industry, I quickly learned that the restaurant world is just as elitist and exclusive as the fashion, art, and film worlds; it is not what you cook, but who you know. And, as I mentioned, Kit knows a lot of people.

I put the Sainsbury's bag containing my sad, limp little ingredients on the kitchen counter and sit down to have a sip of my wine. My legs fumble, as if deciding how to hang on this damn barstool. I hate barstools. They are innately uncomfortable.

"How was your day?" Kit asks me. I look up at him; he looks hot, like a trendy young dad relaxing in his massive swanky house.

I ignore his question because all I did with my day was dream about him. "This place is ridiculous."

"Yeah, it's pretty nice," he says sheepishly.

While Maria and Ben are away doing some sort of ayahuasca retreat in Ecuador under the guise of a food-research and recipe-development trip, they let chef friends stay here. Kit explains to me, "They are just renting it to me, and now Haseem, for cheap because they're never here, so it's helpful for someone to look after the cat, Lily—she's very cute." I'm jealous of the cat.

"How did you meet them?" I ask.

"I can't really remember, ah . . . actually, think it was on a night out." This is a true sign of a social butterfly, someone who can't remember how they met their closest friends.

The place is beautiful, with contemporary artwork and retro furniture, all positioned in a way that screams, "We like to host!" Everything is so informal yet considered; it says: *We are extremely sociable, but we and our friends, we go against the grain, we exist outside societal norms, we probably won't like you, we are creative, we will be young forever, we are secure in open relationships, we can work a double shift after a coke bender, we are real chefs.* There are endless pictures of friends and family on the wall, the sheer volume of pictures is so excessive it's almost entering gloating territory; if I had this same wall, it would host about seven pictures featuring my parents, my brother, Ruby and Sophie, Raquel, and my family cat. For the most part I am fine with my small circle, but when I'm around Kit, I feel jealous of his ability to make friends so easily. The more I hang out with people in hospitality, the more I feel like I should probably have more interesting friends. I should probably be living in some weird, cheffy halfway house like Kit.

The kitchen is like a chef-themed *Where's Waldo?* First, I see the industrial-sized blue kitchen roll atop the kitchen counter; perhaps the most fundamental bit of kit in any restaurant kitchen. Next, I see the jumbo-sized tub of Maldon salt. Then, the great big six-burner gas hob (thank God it's gas; if it was electric, where would we get our heroin-chic burn marks from?). And right above it, a knife bar holding a collection of ten to fifteen of the most spectacularly macho knives I've ever seen.

"It's mad how there is just no one here to use all this stuff," he says, glancing at a very expensive-looking blender.

Kit stands by the counter unwrapping his knife-wrap; he is always buying new knives. Chefs love adding to their knife collection, but in reality, they mainly use one chef knife, a Victorinox bread knife, and an OXO peeler. Perhaps Kit only bought the steak so he could test out this new knife, perhaps inviting me was merely an afterthought, and perhaps I should stop being so self-deprecating and insecure.

I hear footsteps. "Hey," a voice comes from the staircase. It's Haseem. Here we go. As if the pressure of cooking for two chefs wasn't bad enough, it's also the first of Kit's friends I am meeting sober, and I'm desperate to make a good impression in the light of day. I want Haseem to tell Kit how amazing I am when I go to the loo later on, how I am the perfect balance of pretty and hot. I am seriously regretting not amping up my hotness when I got ready earlier. I was at the time dressing for comfort, but if I knew Haseem was here I would've changed strategies: it's always good to have sex appeal when meeting your lover's friends—they become blinded by jealousy and your personality becomes almost totally redundant.

Kit introduces me. Hearing him introduce me to his friend makes my heart flood with warmth. He doesn't say "girlfriend," but he doesn't say "friend" either. More to dissect with Ruby later.

"Hey, nice to meet you, how's it going?" I say, with totally fake nonchalance.

"Yeah, alright, thanks, I just got back from a trial shift at Grit. You're a chef too, right?" Haseem is sweet and engaged; I am relieved. What's also sweet is the fact that he is aware I am a chef, meaning Kit has told him about me. He's obsessed.

Haseem starts rolling a cigarette and I am hit by relief because it reminds me that I also smoke, and thus I always have the option to go for a cigarette if times get tough. I roll one alongside Haseem. Where would we be in life if smoking didn't exist? When I meet new people, I struggle to find anything to say, but put some tobacco and a Rizla in my hands, and I'm a performing monkey. Plus there is the unwritten rule that smokers simply have more fun. If a person smokes, then—considering the whole fuck-my-physical-well-being ethos—they probably enjoy a drink too, and if they enjoy a drink, they probably enjoy a dance, and if they enjoy a dance, they are probably quite good at sex. Simple.

"So how was your trial at Grit?" I ask Haseem. I form my questions to him while hyperaware that Kit is listening to me socialize with one of his friends. I, the performing monkey, am being put to the test. Can she peel her banana and roll a cigarette while also talking in a compelling, yet laid-back, manner?

"Yeah, it was good, actually," he says.

"I've heard mixed things about the owners. How were they?" The place is co-owned by a chef wanker and his girlfriend. I am proud of my insider knowledge.

"Yeah, I'm not gonna lie, Dave's a bit of a prick and Kate seems stuck-up, but I like the food and I want to learn from them, you know?" Haseem sits down next to me at the kitchen table, as if we are both Kit's children and Kit is preparing our favorite after-school snack.

I nod solemnly, hoping I look smart. "For sure. I was saying this to Kit, even though the hours are slightly fucked at his place, it's worth sticking it out for as long as he can. Learning from someone like his Head Chef is a once-in-a-lifetime opportunity." I'm loving this. I'm right in there with his mate. I am coming across as a laid-back woman, encouraging my beau to work more hours, and I am coming across as a chef in the know.

Haseem's restaurant is a good place, but it's not the same style as mine or as Kit's restaurants. Grit is contemporary and a little hipster; it breaks the rules, whereas mine and Kit's restaurants are classic, timeless institutions that follow them. Kit and I working for these iconic, mammoth restaurants only adds to the romance for us; the hours are obscene and we both have to wear the full-on chef whites, which you are seeing less and less of in London. It binds us together.

Haseem keeps talking. He has a funny, goofy energy and is very self-doubting, so we get on well. I can only relax into it so much, though, as I know I'm about to go live, center-stage ITV. *Ready Steady Cock*: Who will get totally ridiculed and dumped tonight, due to their split sauce or their tough meat?

We head out to the garden to smoke the cigarettes we rolled.

"How's your place? Kit mentioned you moved on to a new section?" Haseem asks. Kit clearly can't stop banging on about me to his friends. It's sweet, really.

"Yeah, it's good. Just started on our Hot Starters section," I say.

"What you got on the menu?" he asks, while lighting his smoke and handing me a little green lighter with a weed leaf on it. He catches me looking down and giggles.

"Well, I do Hot Starters and Fish Mains now. My favorite dish is probably the hake with romesco. Or the steamed clams with fennel and tarragon, actually. It's fun doing clams in service if I'm not too down," I say. Hearing myself list all the things I cook makes me realize how far I've come since returning to London. It feels good, like I'm on my way somewhere.

"Classy!" he says, and I laugh. "Sounds like a pretty busy section."

"Yeah, I'm enjoying it a lot. Although this old guy, Victor, trained me on the section and he's kind of pervy," I say, opening up to him because I feel like I can.

"Yeah, Kit mentioned. Sorry about that. You should tell your Head Chef."

"Yeah, I might do." I see that he has finished his cigarette and he is flicking his lighter about. Is he bored? I wonder. I say, "Shall we go in?"

We return to the kitchen, where Kit already has the whopping great côte de boeuf out on a plate, ready to be cooked by his artful hands. He grasps the red meat, manhandling the steak like he does me in the bedroom. Sade's "The Sweetest Taboo" is playing. This would all be very romantic if Haseem wasn't here.

I start unraveling my worldly possessions and ingredients from the plastic bag. I feel like a sad orphan, so out of place in someone else's home kitchen. In my kitchen, I am the cocky landlord. I swan around in my pants with my hair frantically clipped up like Helena Bonham

Carter. I dance, I sing, and I cook. But here I feel like a fly aimlessly buzzing around. The restaurant kitchen is our common ground, but we've stepped outside that world; we're real lovers now, not just chef lovers.

"You good?" Kit comes up behind me and holds on to my hips in front of Haseem. I feel pure, unadulterated ecstasy. I love it when he touches me, and I love having Haseem see it now, like there is someone there to stand testament to this whole affair being real.

"Yeah, all good. Where's all your stuff? I need a blender and a knife." He smirks at me. The bastard knows I'm feeling nervous, but he also knows I'm taking this seriously.

"You can use that fancy blender by the hob. I don't know how to work it, though. And you can use my knives." My competitor is relaxed. Of course he is, he just needs to cook a big slab of meat, like all men have been doing since the beginning of time. Cavemen make the fire while the women actually source and prep the intricate ingredients; dads in the summer cook sausages while the mums make delightful, herby, salady things; and young male chefs advance to Hot Mains while we get stuck on the Pastry section because only we can pull off the masterful act of cooking a crème caramel so that its wobble resembles a jiggling plump arse, not a bouncing pair of tits.

I begin setting myself up. Now that Kit is acting so relaxed, I can relax into this. It is like being in a restaurant kitchen: you'd rather have a Head Chef who takes the piss out of you than a Head Chef who breathes down your neck, watching your every move, asking, "Are you sure you're alright with that?"

Haseem and Kit chat aimlessly about work; it becomes background noise as I focus on my sauce. I need to get everything chopped and sweating in a pan with a lot of butter. This is the first time I've cooked for other chefs outside of work. I don't know if it's normal to follow the same practices that we would in the kitchen, in real life. When I chop my ingredients, do I organize things like I would my mise? Do I compartmentalize my chopped chervil and chopped parsley, or do I chill the fuck out and stop being such a loser?

I take a big sip of my wine, conscious that Kit bought it to go with the beef so I can't just knock it back like I would if it was one of the second-cheapest bottles on a wine list.

Kit passes me a chopping board and I get cracking. I use the knife that he bought today to start slicing lemons. Immediately Kit interrupts my focus.

"Sorry, don't want to be a dick, but can you not use that knife to slice lemons? It's just that the guy in Kitchen Provisions mentioned that acid can react with carbon steel." Jesus Christ. What a cheffy cunt.

"Okay, Chef. Give me another one then, Chef." I smirk. He pretends to hate it when I call him Chef, but I know he likes it, because the corner of his mouth turns up. Now I reconsider the situation: Is this my worst nightmare, or could this be the start of the most thrilling foreplay ever?

Initially I was self-conscious about my knife skills but I no longer give a fuck. The whole lemon-on-knife debacle has pissed me off. I have switched from insecurity to contained fury. This happens to me a lot at work; if someone patronizes me or mansplains, I will flip my whole demeanor and hustle hard until I have proved that I don't need them watching me over my shoulder. When my former Sous Chef, Omar, tried to patronize me, I turned bitter in a way I would never be with the nice guys. It's all fun and games.

Once everything is chopped, I move over to the heat and start sweating the shallots in a big lump of butter. Kit is watching me but not making it obvious. He brushes past me and strokes my arse; I ignore the fanny flutter and focus on the task at hand—the bastard is trying to distract me.

When the shallots are soft, I remove the pan from the heat, add more butter, and let it melt with the residual heat. In one quick swoop I slide the chopped herbs, anchovies, walnuts, and garlic off the blade of Kit's bastard knife, the one he cares about more than me. The cooking is all me tonight, he's just standing there with his dick in his hands. He'll dine on my sauce.

I pour the butter mix in the blender. A blender is one of the most intimidating bits of kitchen equipment, it is dying to trip you up. The lids are always snapping, the buttons are confusing, they're always making a mess, and if you break any part of it, especially a fancy one like this, it is expensive to fix. Kit comes over to help me set it up.

Blitz, blitz, blitz. My green, greasy, lumpy mess has become a brown, homogenous, legit-looking liquid. Now, the final challenge, the one that will separate the cooking queen from the meat king: the emulsification. Emulsion is a classic chef term, like reduction. Both these terms are overused in cooking media all the time; they're like the writer's token words to create realism in a kitchen scene. To emulsify something is simply to combine two liquids that do not usually mix, such as oil and water. Just think of it as Kit and me when we fuck, two unlikely ingredients (fat and oil, or hardy boy from the gray city and posh girl from the green suburbs) mixing together, swirling around one another until, *bam!* we are one homogenized unit. We are smooth, we are fucking with conviction, and we aren't going to split. I keep telling myself that.

I crack my egg yolk into a glass bowl and add a squeeze of lemon, some mustard, and a pinch of salt—not too much as I have anchovy in the mix, and that's salty on its own. Over on the stove, I set the bowl on top of a saucepan holding an inch or two of simmering water. I slowly pour the herby, fishy butter mixture into the egg yolk and stir, desperately awaiting the signal—when the waves of oil suddenly disappear and there is a smooth, thickening effect. We are looking for a brown mayonnaise (but with not such a firm wobble as Heinz).

Everything comes together nicely. Of course it does. As the last bit of butter disappears into the sauce, I add a splash of water to avoid any risk of splitting. I dip the tip of my pinkie in to try it; it's fucking excellent. In fact, this sauce is a goddamn marvel. I knew it. I knew I was better than these smelly, limp-wristed boys.

I pour the sauce back into the pan and leave it over the warm hob with no flame. Kit has, in the meantime, cooked the meat; he is now carving it with his new knife. I saunter over to the table and rest my arse on the chair, sitting comfortably for the first time all evening. My gut is filled with pride; I cooked for two chefs and the product of my work will make them *both* fall in love with me.

Kit brings the côte de boeuf to the kitchen counter, and it looks pink and plump; it's cooked very well. His eyes flash toward mine for approval and I smile, we're both equal parts arrogant and insecure.

"Want me to just pour your sauce over?" He must really trust me if he's willing to completely ruin a sixty-quid bit of meat with a potentially disgusting mess.

"Go for it," I reply.

What happens next is too cheffy for words.

We stand around the counter and pick at the meat and sauce with our fingers. I'm finding this whole seating experience deeply absurd. Are we actually not going to sit down? There are no plates; we are just three lowly cooks picking at a very expensive cut of meat and dunking it into a rich sauce. I suspect the experience might have been quite erotic if Haseem wasn't standing right there too.

"That sauce is really, really nice," Haseem says with his mouth full.

"Really good," Kit agrees.

"It's a little too salty, sorry," I say before I can stop myself. Here she comes! A woman in full force! Accept a compliment from two men without shitting on myself? Impossible!

We mull over the last two slices. It's undecided who they belong to. Haseem, the good boy, takes the hint and leaves so Kit and I can indulge in our joint efforts before we indulge in one another. We do not clean up, we stand in the kitchen and fiddle with one another's hands wordlessly.

I look up at him in my most woman-in-desire way and he says, "I am so attracted to you, it's almost frustrating." Cor blimey. Hairs standing on end. Both arm and pussy. Up the stairs we go. Lily the cat attempts to follow; I turn around and give her a fierce glare, one feline to another.

Kit's room is small and messy but I don't care, it

already feels like the mess is my own, or that I could contribute to it if I'd like.

Kit strips down naked and I do the same. We have a routine now. He turns to face me and pulls me in at the waist. He pushes my hair away from my shoulders and burrows his face in my neck. I can feel the comfort he gets from being close to me. His shoulders drop and he hugs me tighter, letting out a little hum. I pull away and lift the duvet on his bed. I bend over at the hips, no longer aware of my naked body in front of this man, and crawl beneath the sheets. He slides in next to me and holds me. He can't let me go. He looks at me for a moment then kisses me, his lips parting mine so our tongues can meet. My pussy sizzles but my heart beats louder.

These days our sex is more romantic than when we first started dating; there is less porny performance, there is less "good girl" and less "open your mouth." Today there are no words at all, actually, just slow, meaningful, wordless sex. I do like it when we have exciting sex; it feels new and thrilling to me, and I feel cocky about it when I am with my friends who tell me about their mundane sex with the boyfriends whom they can't be bothered to fuck. I always get to tell them the latest new thing Kit and I have done. Just last week I texted them saying I put a finger in his bum. I hadn't done it before; I hadn't really felt inclined, perhaps because I didn't feel close enough with a lover to try. With Kit I feel I can do anything; we are wild and free and a bit disgusting. But I've got to say, the romantic sex is nice too. He is so delicate with the wisps of hair near my face, there is no hair pulling; he is so gentle with moving his body to fit into mine, there is no rough thrusting; he is so totally committed to kissing me, there is no rushed pecking. His sole focus is to please me, and he does.

After, we lay for an hour or so, legs flopped over each other, fingertips touching and enjoying totally mindless chat. I am so happy I feel woozy. I have found a lover. I skipped the queue and I've got myself a nice chef, and all the wine girls are going to hate me for it. His hand is in mine, and I am drifting in and out of sleep on his chest. He strokes my hair without me having to plead him to carry on.

I am thinking about our next meal, we have so many to come. We might do a pop-up together; we've discussed it already.

"What's the time?" I ask. We both have double shifts the next day, but I no longer worry about sleep; the thrill of being in love gives me enough adrenaline for a full week of kitchen work.

"I don't know actually," he says. I rotate my body so I can grab my phone to check while keeping my hand on his; it's 1 a.m. Five hours until we have to leave for work.

"Do you have a phone charger I can borrow?"

"Yeah, just under my bed."

I stretch my body over the edge of the bed to plug my phone in, momentarily losing skin-to-skin contact with him. I miss him in those seconds. My body falls back into his. I am totally relaxed and trusting: I am with someone who loves and cares for me; he puts my comfort above his own.

He turns his whole body to face mine, and I find another way to nestle back into his chest and its magical forest of hair. I rest for a moment but decide I want more of his time before I go to sleep so I stir up conversation.

"We need to stop spending so much money on food," I say. "Eighteen days till payday and we're dining out like Pierre Koffmann every day."

He laughs and brings me in tighter. "Yeah, fuck, I actually do need to save some money as well."

"What for? Are we going to the Ritz for Christmas cocktails?" My voice is muffled in his chest.

He laughs but sounds off-key. "Ah, nah." His grip on me loosens slightly and his body becomes tense. I feel his deeper inhales.

"What for then?" I'm confused. Maybe he wants to buy me something nice and regrets mentioning it, not wanting to spoil the surprise.

He clears his throat, and then, sounding even more uncertain, says, "Do you really want to know?"

I'm unnerved now. I pull back from his embrace with wide eyes, prop myself up on one elbow, and pull up the duvet to cover my braless tits. His eyes have gone dark and soulless, and they're notably avoiding mine.

My heartbeat speeds up and I dive headfirst back into the fear zone. I can't believe I allowed myself to get complacent with a fucking chef. "What do you mean, do I really want to know? Yes, tell me," I say.

He pauses, flops onto his back, and looks directly up at the ceiling in resignation. His voice cracks but he tells me with conviction, "I need to save money because my ex-girlfriend is having my baby in a month."

Of course. Of course she is.

9

ACHY BREAKY ARTICHOKE HEARTS

MARCH

I wake up in my own bed. As I sit up, I remember that I have been a victim of life's most sadistic prank: love.

After Kit told me his news last night, I ended things with him and got the night bus home. As much as I would like to continue seeing him, my heart can't quite take it. We hugged goodbye, I cried a little. He was quiet, although he did say he was deeply sorry he hadn't told me sooner. But he didn't fight for me to stick around.

I don't have time to bask in my pain this morning, it's 6:30 a.m. and I have to be at work with dry eyes by 8 a.m. The prospect of a double shift—all those hours in the kitchen—when I feel this miserable seems like unjust punishment for trying to have a meaningful relationship when I have already committed to our customers. I hope Commis Chef Maggie's working today; the thought of being around only men all day when it is a man who has caused me this pain feels like a sick joke. I don't want to be near them, I want my women friends with their open arms, soft chests, and pillowy shoulders; it is only their love for me that knows no limits.

I slog my sorrowful body over to the shower and let the water rain on me before getting dressed. March can sometimes be sunny, but today it is decidedly gray, like my mood. I mount my bike, my reliable stallion who carries me through the darkness and escorts me into the light; as if he can feel my energy, he takes off steadily but slowly, patient with me, allowing me my moment of sadness. I set off toward Dalston, and my bike is no longer a gallant horse but a broomstick; I pass through winding empty roads like a witch, with my hair blowing in the breeze and my pale face scaring the bouncy, fluorescent joggers. There is only one man I can fathom being around right now: Smokey Robinson. I click Play on Spotify and let my misery flood the streets of London.

My cycle to work flies by and I don't have time to finish the end of "Ooo Baby Baby," so I have to click Pause on the part where Smokey is still clinging to hope; it's good I cut it off before then. I don't have much hope in this case, I think as I lock up my bike.

I see my restaurant down the road. There is always a moment before a double shift when I stop and I brace myself; I am about to hand over my body to this kitchen for the whole day. It's a big enough feat on a normal day, but today it's even more daunting because my mind isn't strong enough to tell my body to start moving again. I approach the stairs and look up toward where the kitchen is. There are men up there, I think: chefs, KPs, and probably a delivery guy or two. I will have to talk to a man in the next sixty seconds whether I like it or not.

I approach the changing room as if I'm walking the plank. My heart was feeble in bed, but now it's practically deflated. I feel close to crying but my body takes the lead; it knows better than my mind that getting absorbed in my craft will help me pass the time; it knows I have to endure this pain, I have to breathe it in and squash it into my lungs, then at the end of my shift I can leave, smoke ten million cigarettes, and set the pain on fire.

It's 8 a.m. and I'm starting the countdown. My dad's in my head: "This too shall pass," he often says when I'm depressed. I give myself a little slap on the cheek and walk through the changing-room door.

There's a chef in the changing room. It's lovely Senior Sous Chef George, thank fuck; despite him being one of *them,* he is probably one of the nicest men I've ever met. He walks around the changing room clueless, unaware that the Dark Witch of Self-Pity has entered the room. He must feel my wave of black mist as he turns to greet me though.

"Heya!" he says.

I respond with meager enthusiasm, "Hey, how's it going?"

He notes my disinterest and responds with an appropriately brief: "Yeah, all good, man." Luckily, it's 8 a.m., so he will translate the lack of conversation as a sign of tiredness, not heartbreak.

George marches out of the changing room, knife-wrap in one hand, phone and water bottle in the other, with a towel neatly folded into his apron strings. I follow him with my melted heart; I am ready to fry an egg, but not flip it—that would be too much. It's 8:05 a.m., hopefully I'll forget to look at the clock when I'm cooking.

I am relieved to see the rest of the team are preoccupied unloading orders, and that Head Chef Lenny and

Sous Chef Finn aren't here; I generally enjoy their cutting sense of humor, but today it would push me over the edge. I can see Commis Jayden and, wait, is that titleless Victor too? For fuck's sake.

"Morning, guys," I mutter as I walk over to a mound of fresh produce. It's a team effort; we all have to get the food packed away as quickly and as efficiently as possible so we can start our mise.

"Who's on Pastry? Is Maggie not here?" I ask Jayden quietly. I'm confused by the team today, and why Victor is here—he never does Pastry, but if George is on Hot Mains and I'm on Hot Starters . . .

"Maggie's sick, so Victor offered to cover her on Pastry," Jayden says.

"Right," I say, while making brief eye contact with Victor, who is smirking as if we're in the throes of a secret love affair. Victor has done time in many of London's best restaurants, as well as a few of the iconic hotels. He likes to remind me that he knows more than anyone else in the kitchen, including Lenny, but only in a pervy whisper, he's not brave enough to speak it out loud. The other men might hear him and mention that being a weirdo isn't standard practice.

Initially I was thrilled to be getting trained by someone with so much experience, whom I could learn *so* much from. But then he started flirting with me. I'm completely proficient at prepping and cooking all my dishes now, yet he still finds reasons to monitor me, to creep up behind me and show off his authority like it's his penis.

I head over to the tallest stack of boxed vegetables and hide behind it. I want to avoid the usual chatter so I move fast as I unwrap some thyme, sage, and rosemary and get them in plastic containers.

George walks over to join us; good, more people. People in groups is a good thing, even if they're men, as it means I can fade into the background. That will help me escape Victor's notice, I think. And everyone else's. I really don't want anyone to realize I'm sad, because it makes me feel that I have to explain why, which feels indulgent, especially in the kitchen, where there is no time for trivial love stories. When we have to get through a long list of prep, cook for a whole restaurant, and endure each other's company for fifteen to sixteen hours, starting the day by spreading my sadness doesn't feel fair.

As George unloads the meat, Victor turns to the fish and Jayden unpacks the dairy. I move across to the veg: first, the fennel. The big, bulbous bastards fill my hands, there is no softness, no give. I must maintain my hard, fennel-like exterior. I dump them into an empty plastic container, where they tumble on top of one another.

I am interrupted: "Wait, there's already a box of fennel in the fridge," Jayden points out. Which means that I don't need to use a whole new box to unload the fresh fennel into. I should consolidate the boxes and use less fridge space.

There are times in the kitchen when chefs allow themselves small acts of laziness; every now and again we take the easier road because we are sad, or angry, or in a rush, or hungover, or coming down. For example, we might pack produce into a new box, despite knowing that we could combine it with an existing box—thus freeing up precious space in the walk-in fridge for new produce—but we can't be bothered. It is bad practice but everyone does it sometimes. I justify these small acts of laziness by telling myself I am just a chef skipping due diligence, not a surgeon skipping due diligence—doing a sloppy job of stitching up human skin after performing a lackluster operation on someone's heart. I wonder if I can get my broken heart operated on.

Jayden lets it go. "What did you get up to last night?" he asks.

Well, Jayden, I got my heart torn out of my chest by the first person I have liked in years. He told me that he is having a baby with someone else, so I left. Kit hasn't even texted, and I doubt he will; maybe if he reached out with an onslaught of romantic gestures, I would consider making it work. But no, there is nothing he can say.

I believe he is a nice guy, but I don't understand how he couldn't have told me sooner. Though I know myself, and I am too needy to compete with a baby. I want my man to love me and only me. I want to feel like enough, or more than enough.

I reply to Jayden, "Not much, really."

I can't help but feel that if I was surrounded by women, by Sophie, Raquel, and Ruby, they would immediately know something was wrong; they would notice my silence and investigate with a sympathetic head tilt, but there is so much that some men don't seem to notice. Maybe that's a good thing while I get through this shift; to be allowed to ignore the sadness for now, to just get to work.

I head over to my section, my cozy corner, my safe place. It's time to cook. Though I am still overwhelmed by the idea of flipping an egg, I have no choice but to suck it up; I have greater tasks to take on. I am on my new section and I need to work hard and fast: I need to prep artichokes for the Tuscan bean salad, make cauliflower soup, butterfly the sardines, prep fennel and tarragon for the steamed clams, make a salsa verde sauce, and prep the hake. I look through my mise list and number the sequence of events. I decide to start easy with the nice jobs and get the soup on.

I lift a big brown chopping board and rest it atop my workbench. As I go to fetch onions and cauliflower from the fridge I glance upward, toward the clock. It's 8:21 a.m. If we finish at midnight, that's fifteen hours and thirty-nine minutes to go; no escape, no hour-long lunch break where I can sulk in Pret, no working from home where I can hide behind the screen. Fuck it. I plan a ciggy break for 10 a.m.; it's the small things that count.

On my return to my section, George asks me, "How was Andrew Edmunds with Kit that time you guys went? I'm thinking of taking the missus." Only George would remember people's romantic dinner plans from ages ago.

"Yeah, really good," I say, not able to expand as I am too busy bludgeoning the pain in my chest. Plus, I don't want to tell him about Kit. He doesn't know him *that* well, but they are friends, and I don't want to make him uncomfortable. I have just realized that Andrew Edmunds was the height of our love affair and now I can't go back there because it's strictly a couples place, and I'm not a couple anymore. I never was, apparently.

It isn't the big romantic moments I will miss, nor the epic fucks or the steamy shower snogs; it is the small trivial moments when he showed he cared, like when he let me have the comfy booth after he was exhausted from three back-to-back doubles.

I chop my cauliflower into chunks, drizzle with olive oil, and season and chuck them in the oven. I can't be bothered to set a timer. I'll just remember to check them in fifteen. Now I must face peeling this mound of onions. George and Jayden are chatting away, throwing their heads back in laughter and swinging their arms about in delight. I listen to every word they say, judging them. Why aren't all men repenting the sins of their brothers, lamenting the ways they fuck us up? I feel betrayed by them as I make my soup.

The way you experience a double shift can vary massively. It can fly by as you learn more things: you fillet a new fish or try a new sauce, you are challenged by new sections, and you feel lucky to be in a job that gives *you* something valuable—a skill that brings happiness to everyone. You might have a day where you're rota'd on with your favorite people, and that means you're just hanging out with your friends. And you get to handle beautiful produce and learn how to turn it into something even more beautiful. On days like that it feels like nursery school; making playdough for the first time. We all freak out over silly things: Look at the size of this fucking courgette!

The hours slide by. Especially if you're working on a special project throughout the day. You might be making rillettes; first thing in the morning, you pull from the oven a big tray of confit duck and pork that's been submerged in a pool of fat, cooking slowly overnight. The smell of warm, salty, herby, savory meat wafts into the kitchen, and you and your favorite people stand there, breathing it in. It's a delight. While others are queuing on the Underground for a space on the Tube, you spend your morning pulling apart pieces of warm, tender meat, sneaking little bits into your cheeks as you go. Then you press the rillettes into a container and pour melted fat over the top to seal it. At the end of the day, you gaze down with pride on your rillettes as if it's a macaroni-covered photo frame; you take a picture and send it to your mum. And then you realize, this whole time you haven't been at nursery, you've been working and getting paid to be there.

But other times, like today, a double shift can be a slog. Perhaps you are counting down the hours, dying to make it on time to a best friend's birthday, or you could be tired from back-to-back double shifts, or you could just be not in the mood to work in this thankless job. Everybody has bad days, but hospitality doesn't really cater to people's bad days; your customers pay for a good experience, and you have to deliver that. At times like this, I feel bad for managers and waiters, who are the ones who actually have to face the customers with a smile. I couldn't do that, not today, when time passes so slowly it's as if it's going backward, and I just want to lie down. Today I want to not talk and not move, but my job makes me do the direct opposite. That kick up the arse is hard but it's what I need, and being in this kitchen means I get to do the thing that distracts me from pain: cooking.

"You okay, mate?" George asks me in hushed tones. I suspect he has picked up on the fact that I have not made my allotted contribution to the light-hearted bollocks. I meet his eyes and realize it's the first time this morning that I've made eye contact with someone; it feels invasive. I wonder if he can tell what's going on.

I wait a split second to swallow that sharp apple segment of sadness. "Yeah, I'm all good," I say. I think he knows I'm not; he looks dissatisfied with my answer.

"You sure?" I note at this point that if I ever get pregnant, I want him or someone exactly like him to be the father. He is so incredibly kind; he should be a kids' TV presenter or something, spending his days kneeling down and soothing the souls of kids with learning difficulties or dead mums.

I glance over at him. Now I can tell he sees I'm lying; my black mist is falling. I admit defeat. "No, to be honest, I feel like shit, but I can't talk about it because I'll cry." He leans his head to the side in sympathy.

"Ah, shit, man. Well, if you change your mind and want to chat, please let me know."

Some men do talk, of course; they do share feelings, even in a kitchen; but I am worried my matters of the heart don't meet the criteria; it's not like anyone's died. George quickly busies himself to give me an exit out of the conversation, letting me flee from my own vulnerability, escaping that brief moment when everything could come crumbling down; he knows I don't want that. I won't cry, not here. It's 8:32, Jesus Christ. I just need to get to 10 a.m., then I'm going for a ciggy.

I distract myself and enter the lovely monotony cooking requires. The onions are in a bowl, ready to be chopped; they will build the base of my cauliflower soup. Chop onion in half, roll onion onto side so it sits upright; slice off the tip of onion, pull back the skin of onion, dice onion, and repeat. The brown skin on the first onion tears as I pull it back. I could get my act together and use a knife to scrape away the broken bits, but I choose not to. I feel no motivation right now, and I don't care if I go down in service; at least then I'll be distracted from my heartache. As the air of onion invades my eyes, tears—the thing I was so desperately trying to avoid—leak from my lower lids.

I have this weird obsession with not crying in the kitchen. Maybe it's because I'm a woman and I'm trying to prove something to myself and others, that I'm as tough as the men and can be trusted with whatever comes my way. Or maybe because I know that in the kitchen you can't go and sit in a quiet space in the office; you just have to stay there, in that exact spot, and endure your pain. I have seen people grumpy or sad before: Lenny gets in bad moods and Finn gets sulky, but they throw themselves into the work and, as the hours pass, their mood usually lifts, just like it usually does for me. Maybe cooking acts as solace for the boys, too.

I sniff and wipe my onion eyes with the back of my hand. I rebalance myself. My body stands tall with my legs slightly ajar so that my back doesn't ache while I chop stuff for the next 928 minutes. I send a signal to my melted heart: it's one day, one day of pain, and you just have to get through it, you just have to cook, that's all. Heartbreak does not suffice a sick day in the kitchen.

As I chop my final few onions, I busy my mind with thoughts of him; it allows me to live in a state of limbo, to mute the heartbreak for just a minute. In my mind, we are not together but we aren't apart either, it's just a never-ending cycle of nice stories, my own private screening of our cinematic love affair.

Before I pull apart the red curtains and start the movie, I wonder if it's normal to think about someone this much. I feel grateful that no one else can see the obsessive thoughts inside my head. And then the movie starts:

it's mine and Kit's rom-com before the tragic sequel. I remember the time when we both had an afternoon shift, but we wanted to schedule in sex or a KFC before work; we couldn't choose which one so we decided to do both. As we arrived at my flat he ordered the KFC on his phone, and we went upstairs and started fucking. The sex was moving at a great pace but the Deliveroo driver was even faster; he took seven and a half minutes to arrive—I mean, come on, man, the one time you are speedy is the one time when My Chef and I are trying to factor in some serious lovemaking. We had to pause so I could run down and get the KFC from the entrance of my building. I donned the nearest pair of trousers, which just so happened to be his massive, baggy Service Works trousers. With every step I took, the trousers edged further down my bare arse. As I galloped down the stairs, I used one arm to secure my tits and the other to cinch the trouser waistband above my hips. I carried my phone under my armpit, the thing containing the proof that I was the rightful owner of the fried chicken. When I climbed back up the stairs and into my flat, Kit was standing on the landing, naked with a boner, laughing at me as I tripped back up the stairs. I laughed at myself, and then at his out-of-context boner. We were intoxicated by comfort and giddy thrill, fried chicken and gravy. Then I hurriedly stepped out of his trousers. The movie is nearly over now. I put the KFC bag to the side and we finished what we started in bed. I'm savoring the last scene. Ten minutes left to enjoy the thighs.

This part of cooking, where my body grounds me so my thoughts can wander, and I can become totally absorbed in daydreams, is part of why I love it; it is the practice that rescues me from my own thoughts.

When I am on the verge of a panic attack or tears, or maybe just enduring a hefty depressive episode, cooking is the most effective form of therapy. It is the one thing that removes me from everything, taking my hot frantic mind and placing it in a bucket of cooling ice water. So while it isn't appealing for me to be in a windowless kitchen when I feel this sad, I know that if I'm cooking, I'll be fine. Being a chef is a better alternative for me than wallowing at weekends, hiding under my duvet; or back in my old job, sitting at a desk, staring out the window at smug St. Paul's. Having something to watch, something to touch, something to smell, something to hear, and something to taste is the fundamental way to ground me. Cooking keeps me on earth.

Some say cooking in a professional kitchen is damaging to your mental health due to the lack of sleep and the stress, but I like the stress of feeling that something is urgent and then fixing it; and I like being tired, it helps me sleep. Sometimes I don't think I actually like this job, it's more that I *need* it.

My onions are nearly finished, so now the KFC sex story must come to an end. I scrape my mountain of chopped onions into a pan of hot oil and listen to it sweat. I make a bouquet garni, a little bunch of rosemary, bay, and thyme, and chuck it into the pan of sweating onions. Kit never bought me flowers, but one time he picked a yellow flower from a bush and put it in my hair. I sigh. Silence for a second before I turn around to face my next task; I must prepare the globe artichokes and unveil their hearts, which I will serve sliced and grilled in a warm salad of Tropea onions, cannellini beans, Parmesan, winter tomatoes, and bitter leaves. It is the simplest dish in my section, though the artichokes take a long time to pluck and peel. But I am pleased to have a hefty, mindless task up next, so I can really delve into a longer movie. I'll add a nice happy ending where I don't have to leave him. I take my first artichoke and begin to snap at the petals, scrolling through the memories in my mind as if I'm sifting through Netflix's New Releases.

"Why are you so sad, gorgeous?" I hear Victor's voice.

I turn around and look at him. He has small beady eyes. He comes so close that I can feel his breath on my neck. He always stands too close to me and I'm fucking sick of it. Now that we share the Hot Starter section, we are a duo act, and so we support one another to ensure our mise is in abundance, our fridges are clean, and our prep for the following day is well underway. But usually we aren't on shift at the same time so I don't have to see him much, apart from fifteen minutes or so when I pass the section over to him in between lunch and dinner, or vice versa.

I don't speak to Maggie about Victor because it might taint her own experience. And she's new and she's good and I don't want to curb her ambition. But I do often talk to Raquel about it at home or at the pub. We were complaining about it just last week over pints. We all know about how this happens in our industry, but we love our jobs. Raquel thinks I should say something to Lenny, but she understands that I don't want to. As a woman in professional kitchens dominated by men, you want to prove something to the team, that you're strong and unaffected. She's had similar experiences, and also not said anything.

And I can't exactly tell Victor to stop, because I'm scared he'll get angry or start fucking up our section.

And anyway, sometimes I worry that I'm just making it all up, and he's not doing anything wrong. Should I talk to Lenny? I don't even know how I would bring it up with him. But I'm going to quit if this guy doesn't leave me alone.

"I'm not sad, just tired," I respond. I hope he'll get the message and fuck off. What I really want to say is this: "After fifty-odd years on this planet, have you still not learned the signs for when a woman does not want to fuck you?"

He frowns dramatically and then stands next to me while I work, smirking at his phone. He pulls up a photo and shows it to me; it says *The person reading this is the most beautiful girl in the world.*

My stomach turns. I laugh uncomfortably because it's the only way I can think of to make him leave me alone. He locks his phone and smiles smugly; he has completed his quest by breaking me down and forcing me to take part in a pathetic fantasy whereby I, the young woman he works with, want him. He struts off like an evil villain's comically ugly accomplice; he is not tall or smart enough to be the actual villain.

I take a breath and get back to my cooking. I grasp one of the globe artichokes and begin methodically peeling back the petals, one by one, snapping them at the base and exposing the heart underneath. I discard the petals in a big bowl and then trim down and shave the heart so that it's smooth. I plop the heart into a bowl of lemon water to stop it from discoloring.

Just as I'm about to press Play on my next movie, Victor walks behind me again and I feel his hand stroke my left arse cheek. The gap between my body and the hobs behind me is at least a meter; there was no reason for him to come that close to my body, let alone touch it. I turn around. Victor looks back at me, grinning.

Fuck this. I stare down at my artichokes; my beautiful, floral, feminine artichokes. They look so happy and the water looks so purifying. I wish I could take a dip in there, to cleanse myself of the greasy mark that he just left on my body.

I usually don't notice the gender of my team; until Maggie joined, I was the only girl and I didn't really care. It is only today that I do, I think, because it's a man who has broken my heart. To work in a kitchen with men when you are a woman can be totally fine. I've got on well with most of the men I have worked with, even Zack in the end. But not Victor. It is not working with men in kitchens that is bad, it's working with bad men in kitchens that is bad.

Victor's actions are not chef-specific; they are cunt-specific. And being in a kitchen with cunts is harder than other workplaces, especially on a double shift. For all those hours there is nowhere to hide. The hours are long and the space is tight. You bend over to pick things up and your arse is in the air; you reach across people to grab things and your tits brush past their arm; you undress in a changing room and show your bra. You are in close proximity to men all the fucking time, even on the worst day of your period, even when your heart is broken. There is nowhere to escape, and if you are working with a bad man, it feels like you're avoiding traps all day; whether you take the longer route to the walk-in fridge to avoid them, or use a different pan because you don't want to ask to switch pans. I know it's wrong but I don't want to complain because a fucked-up part of me thinks I signed up for this when I became a chef. The job is about endurance. When we signed up to this job, we signed a contract that says we agree to work more hours than normal people in normal jobs, and we accept that this job will come with physical ailments like burns on your arms or cuts on your fingers. So when it comes to Victor's behavior, my brain is wired to think it is just something that comes along with the territory and I need to accept it.

As Victor walks away, there is a split moment where I attempt to continue prepping my artichokes but I can't. My throat is pleading with me to let the lump rise, but if I cry now, I won't stop.

I'm going for a cigarette. It's not 10 a.m. yet but I need to get out of here. I take my cauliflower, which I forgot to check, out of the oven, and luckily, they're on just the right side of roasted brown.

Outside, I take my time with my cigarette, to help smother the lump in my throat. It's time to change gears. I'm not letting Victor shit on me when I'm down. I think about my mise list. What's next? I'll finish the artichokes and the soup and prepare the veg for the clams. Then another ciggy. I head back to the kitchen to finish what I started.

After coming back, I race through the artichokes. I carve the little hearts into slices. I fry them on the plancha while I finish my soup. The onions for my cauliflower have been sweating away and they smell sweet and aromatic. I chuck them in and pour enough water in the pan to just cover everything. I leave the vegetables to bathe together for a while.

Artichokes, done. Soup, done. On to prepping the fennel for the clams. I am in mechanical mode; there is nothing exciting happening here. I take a couple of bulbs from the fridge, slice off the fronds, and chuck them in my soup for a little extra flavor. Then I use a mandoline to thinly slice the bulb; I go hard and fast, not too bothered about slicing a finger off.

Before I know it, I'm absorbed.

Soon it's 11 a.m. and I realize I have forgotten to look at the clock for a while. I've blitzed and strained my soup, added cream, and chilled it. I've made the salsa verde, which is a vibrant green and nicely seasoned. I've finished frying off the artichokes, and I've prepped the clam veg. I feel a little better, so I keep moving fast, realizing that's the trick to not letting the sadness settle. I race through the rest of my mise; shaving Parmesan, filleting hake, scaling and butterflying sardines. Then it's 12 p.m. and I'm ready for service. Victor is preoccupied with Pastry, as he wasted too much time tormenting me.

It's 12:03 p.m. and the check monster makes his entrance.

Zzzz ZZZ zzzzz.

George is patient with me and he calls checks gently, checking up on others, but not me.

I toss the fried artichokes in Parmesan, onion, tomatoes, and leaves. I am keeping up with the checks but there's no passion in my plating; it looks fine, just fine.

ZZZ zzzz.

Another artichoke salad. My hands feel lazy and my head isn't in it. Hot Starters is starting to feel boring. Perhaps I've learned all I can here. I snap the check and release a massive sigh as I tuck the check in my rail.

"Let me know if you need a hand, yeah?" George says. I only have three checks on and he knows I don't need a hand but that's his way of saying, if you need to take a break, just do it.

I look up at the clock. I need to stretch out my breaks a little more. I've already had three fags and it's only 1:30 p.m. I still have ten hours left. Fuck.

Usually when lunch service ends, we have a little chinwag as a team and saunter around the kitchen for a couple of minutes, especially when it's quiet like this. However, today I count myself out of any small talk. When lunch service ends and I spike my last check, I clean down quickly and begin prepping more Tropea onions for dinner service straight away. This shift is like riding my bike; I just need to keep moving forward.

When I finish the onions, I pick some tarragon and then wash more clams. I'm basically at the bottom of my prep list and it's only 4:30 p.m. I've filleted all the hake, I've made enough soup to last me through dinner service, I've butterflied the sardines, I've washed the clams, and I've grated too much Parmesan.

I have an hour until dinner service. Perhaps I'll just allow myself one more fag.

"Just going for a smoke," I tell George.

I grab my coat and climb down the stairs. I sit on the pavement by the bins and start rolling my cigarette. I think of Kit and how he never smoked. When I asked him why he just said he didn't like it. He was happy with who he was and yet absent of any slimy male ego. I found that combination so attractive.

I hear the kitchen door creak open three floors up the spiral staircase. It's Victor, poking his head down.

I wish Kit was here. He wouldn't hurt anyone, but

he'd make Victor feel so small, just from how big a man he was. I sit alone, with my perverted colleague, and I sink to the bottom of my sea of sadness. Victor leaves me alone; maybe he sees I'm underwater and he doesn't want to be responsible for my drowning, that would bring too much attention to him. I'm pretty sure none of the guys know he acts weird with me; if they did, they'd get him fired.

Victor heads in but I stay out. I wander down to the bins. It's a bleak, gray day. I wonder what Kit's doing. I can't believe he hasn't messaged me. I check my phone; it's 4:55 p.m. Time to go back and finish dinner service, then clean down, then go home. I'm so nearly there.

Zzzz Zzzz ZZ.

"Alright, guys, check on," George says. "One artichoke, one sardine. To follow, clams and lamb with chips and green salad."

"Yep," I say, a little louder than I did at lunch. With every check that we send, I'm that much closer to leaving.

ZZ zzz ZZZZ.

Today I like it when the check monster yells; it means I can no longer hear my own thoughts.

"Check on. Soup. Oysters. To follow, onglet and hake. Chips and green salad," George says.

"Yep," I say.

"Yes, Chef!" Jayden jokes. We don't say Chef here.

I get lost in the checks. While the boys chat, I listen to my hake sizzle when I fry it; my chips bubble when I drop them into the oil. I hear the hot pan hiss when I chuck in the cold clams and a dash of wine to steam them. By now the team has understood that something is going on with me, even Victor, so they are leaving me alone, which I am thankful for. I thought my mood would lift, but it hasn't. But I don't feel any pressure to be sprightly or peppy, or to take part. I've done enough of that in recent years.

And then at 10:23 p.m., the check monster sends us a miracle. *Zzzz Zzzz ZZ*: a check arrives with a red note on top from the waiters upstairs—"LAST TABLE."

My chest floods with relief as George calls it out. "Alright, guys," he says, "if we clean down quickly, we can get out of here before eleven p.m." It's nearly over. I find some residual fuel and my body shifts gears; I move fast. I dunk a sponge in blue bubbles. I soak up masses of water and I squeeze it out over the sticky stainless steel. I am cleaning away the shit day. I throw my whole body's weight into wiping the sponge back and forth and around the corner of my station to rid the surfaces of the spits of fat and specks of herbs. I am so close.

"Long fucking day," George says as everyone retires to the changing room. "I think we all need a beer." He is trying to rally the troops. Not today, mate, I think.

Victor looks over to me to see if I'll be staying for a beer. I avoid his eyes.

I love the after-work beer ritual more than most. I always stay until the last person leaves and I am usually the one who suggests we have another beer because I don't want that moment to end. But today I can't do it. I need to be by myself so I can let the sadness out.

I change quickly, swinging my coat under my armpit and zipping my rucksack as I go. "Right. I'm off. See you guys," I say. I close the changing-room door behind me.

———

As I reach the bottom of the stairs, the same ones I climbed to start the shift fifteen hours ago, the wind blows and lifts all the hair on my body. It's over.

I march down the street and inhale London: fresh garbage, pissed-on pavements, cigarettes, cigars, perfume, and deep-fat fryers. I feel the wind slide under my sweaty T-shirt. It is ice-cold and it feels amazing; it is cleansing me after this dark day; finally I'm with the artichoke hearts, swimming in the lemon water.

I turn the corner and see him waiting for me: my bike. He's not going anywhere without me; he's not having a baby with his ex. I feel real excitement to get on the road, to feel the wind once more in my hair and cry. As I mount my bike, I feel pride for enduring it—last night, this morning, the whole double shift. I feel emotional when I remember the broken skeleton of a woman who sat atop it earlier. I am different now; somehow tougher, more gristly, meatier. The shift was bleak, but now I can rest easy knowing I won, nothing can break me, not Victor or Kit.

I pull my phone out of my pocket and click Play on Spotify. Smokey Robinson automatically resumes his hopeful melody from this morning; the sound sickens me. It feels too loving, too optimistic, too romantic. I'm done with that shit. Sadness has been leaking out of me all day. I'm parched and in need of female power. I click Play on Ann Peebles, "I'm Gonna Tear Your Playhouse Down," slide my phone into my pocket, giddy-up my stallion, and let the tears stream down my face. Today was a challenge but I overcame it; sometimes it feels like that's all working in kitchens is.

Soon I am gliding down the open road, nothing in

front, nothing behind. I am cycling along the white road markings, balancing on a very blurred line: one of great sadness and great joy.

I arrive in my neighborhood but I pass by my flat and keep going. I don't want to go home yet. Right now, on my bike, I feel beautiful and strong. I drag the song back to the start and listen to it again and again and again. I can't budge from this line, from this desire to lean into the chaos, the up, but also the down.

I turn down backstreets and get lost among the houses. From afar, I can see an elegant silhouette of a man with long, slim limbs. I can see smoke escaping his mouth as he brings a cigarette up to his mouth. As I cycle closer, I recognize his face. It's this guy I met briefly the other week; Raquel introduced me to him at the pub just as he was leaving. He's a chef too. Raquel has known him for years; she used to work with him and says he's funny, but also a massive arsehole.

He is standing outside the front door of a terrace house, I guess his house, because he's wearing shorts and sliders and it's nearly midnight.

As I pass by him on my bike, we lock eyes.

Holy fuck, he is *so* hot. What was his name? Something beginning with L.

A message pops up on my phone a minute later.

Hey. It's Luca. Raquel gave me your number when I told her how much I fancied you. Was that you who just cycled past me?

Yeah, I send quickly.

I knew it was you, just as beautiful as I remembered

I smirk while reading his message.

Lol I'm just cycling back from a double
  You could've said hi
So could you
  Next time, wys next week?

This is just what I need. A tall, handsome distraction. How did I not realize how hot he was when I met him in the pub? I suppose I was in the throes of love with Kit. I'm still sad about Kit and pissed off about Victor. But this man and his chiseled face just did something to my body. My fickle heart is fluttering and butterflies are floating in my chest. It amazes me, the power men have in my life; they can piss rain all over me, but they can also part the clouds and make the sun shine. But fuck it, I'm not going to think about the weather now, I'm going to enjoy this cycle. I get another text.

You want to come back and hang out? I have beer at mine

I'm working tomorrow, I reply.

Yeah so am I

Haha. Nah. I'm tired, I say.

My music stops and my phone vibrates: Incoming Call—Unknown Number.

10

HOT SOAPY DAYDREAMS

APRIL

Spring is in the air. There are cocks everywhere: the forced rhubarb unveils its great erection from beneath the covers; courgettes showcase their bendy phallic form with pride; and girthy, hardened leeks pull back their skin.

And all I can think about is sex.

It's April now, a month since things ended with Kit, and a month since I cycled past that strange hot man smoking in the dark. It was Luca. And it was him who called me, trying to get me round for a booty call, no less. I picked up while I was cycling, but I politely declined and explained to him I'd just ended things with a guy. I'd also just worked a double shift and I didn't feel all that sexy, with deep-fryer hair, a sweaty body, and puffy tear-stained cheeks. But I didn't mention that to him; even in a state of wretched sadness I still think about impressing boys.

Since that night, Luca has been persistent in helping me move past my heartbreak, not with sympathy and kindness, or a shoulder to cry on, but with straight-up *sexting*.

We texted the day after and have done every day since. He is a menace, and I fancy him a lot. He is everything Kit is not: he's audacious and cocky, a little sleazy and a little sly, but my God, is he hot. And after my recent failed attempt at real love, I fancy myself some short-lived lust.

During the last month, he's hit me up for many a booty call, but it was only yesterday when I finally conceded. Although, I suppose a booty call is usually at night, whereas this was in broad daylight.

Twenty-four hours later and I'm back in the kitchen, but all I can think about is yesterday morning's sex.

Sex flashbacks can be better than the real thing. They are like the Hollywood-produced trailer of your feature-length fornication; the mediocre, clunky, bumpy bits are forgotten and the artful, intentional, glamorous bits come to the forefront: the climax, the tit grab, the cock clasp, the tongue twirl, the clawing at the back, and the burrowing in the pillow. Sex flashbacks are brief but impactful; they send shock waves straight to your groin. They have no consideration for where you are or what you are doing, even if you're at work. Unlike the PG-13 film about Kit, the one I am now fully engrossed by is high-art porn.

"You've got a bit of a spring in your step today, don't you?" Senior Sous Chef George says to me.

It's been a grueling month getting over Kit, despite having Luca's sexts to keep me entertained, but as of yesterday, I have an incredibly effective distraction: Luca, in the flesh, the handsome gazelle. All day I've been thinking about him, and me, naked.

"Of course I'm happy," I respond. "I'm making staff food an hour after I was supposed to go home after my morning shift; that's just how much I *love* being here." I'm making mac and cheese for the chefs, my silly boys. I lob a chunk of butter and a sprinkling of flour into a pan to make the roux for béchamel. Once it sizzles and starts smelling of biscuits, I pour in a little milk. I take a big spoon and use my motherly arms to stir my sauce, so the mix doesn't stick to the bottom of the pan. As I add more, it gets a little sleepier and starts moving slower. The boys don't realize their mother's glowing because she got laid last night, not because she loves them.

"What are you making for staff food? I've got loads of leftover roast lamb we could use from the menu tasting yesterday," George says.

On the days when we haven't planned a staff meal while doing our orders the day before, we raid our service fridges for leftover food and cobble something together to feed the team after lunch service. We look at our mise and see what we have excess amounts of, or we scan the big walk-in fridge to check if there's anything past its best which we could use. I'm making mac and cheese because we always have pasta to hand, and we've got a load of leftover Cheddar cheese from a private event last week.

"Nice. I'm just doing mac and cheese, I'm like twenty minutes off. I'll get Jayden to make some sort of salad, so if you heat the lamb up for four p.m. that would be great."

"Cool," George says.

Today was menu-change day, which happens monthly. It means we serve completely new dishes, which Head Chef Lenny and George have been working on over the last week. Now that it's April and we're in proper springtime, we have a whole new array of seasonal produce to use, which they've incorporated into the menu. It's not always brand-new dishes; sometimes it's just modifications to existing dishes. George has on a new dish of roast lamb and spring veg. But my favorite dish is the new steamed hake with rainbow chard, chili and anchovy, and some punchy rouille.

Menu-change day reminds me of the first day back at school: the new, vibrant produce in the kitchen and the different array of tools feels like having a new pencil case on the first day of term; there is a surge of motivation before the novelty wears off and you realize the hard work still has to be done.

The novelty has worn off for me. With each passing day, the sun lasts longer and I think less of love and Kit and more of sex and Luca. I don't want to be in the kitchen all day, I want to run wild and frolic about. I think of Luca constantly—I am in the throes of a love affair. The change to my menu of lovers is far more exciting than the menu change at work; Luca is my favorite dish; I can barely remember what Kit tastes like.

"What do you think of the new menu?" George asks me, pulling me away from my thoughts.

"Yeah, it's fine, but podding peas is a bit of a piss-take. I'm going to train Jayden up on this, right, Jayden?" I enjoy provoking our grumpy teenager. He laughs.

"God, what happened to you? You've been so grumpy recently, now you're acting all happy again," Jayden says.

Maybe I was acting grumpy. I was feeling a little bored of my job, and of my section, and I still am; my heartbreak made the work more difficult, and I suppose that as I fell out of love with Kit, I fell out of love with the kitchen. I don't feel that much desire to learn new things. Although I'm happier, it's not because of the new menu.

It's not just me who is happier right now, everyone is. George, Finn, Jayden, and Maggie are all here. Lenny left after service to write up the details of the new menu and Victor is on holiday, much to my delight. Now that it's spring we get to see more of the sun, which is a monumental moment for us chefs, who have seen very little daylight the last few months. And the sun reminds us of the upcoming summer, and of being naked. I remember naked Luca, panting from the sex; we'd barely even got going at that point, and it was as if he'd been thirsty for me for longer than I knew.

I want to do it all again, but first I need to finish the damn mac and cheese.

My saucepan for the béchamel, which is slowly bubbling away, is massive; we're not only feeding the chefs, but also the KPs, the bartenders, the managers, the wine girls, and the maintenance man. I head to the fridge to find the sack of pre-grated leftover Cheddar cheese. I open it up on my walk back to my pan and then dump it into the béchamel. Suddenly a sex flashback pops up in my mind: the weight of Luca's body falling on mine as he lunged to kiss me for the first time. It was ecstasy; after a month's wait, I melted into him. I never wanted it to end. I want more now. Then I'm back in the kitchen as quick as the flashback appeared: the Cheddar is initially frigid and hesitant, but soon it loses its inhibitions and stretches its legs to spread itself across the white sheet of butter, flour, and milk. Go on, girl.

"What time are you finishing?" George asks me. "Shall we get a pint?"

I momentarily consider what Luca's plans might be

for the evening and whether he might want to see me again; I'm already addicted to him. But then I actively stop myself from wondering: it is imperative for me to not get attached to this man; it is just sex. Plus, it is quite likely I'll never see him again, now that he's had his way with me. From what Raquel's told me, he isn't the type of guy to stick around.

"Yeah, let's do it," I say, decidedly. A life of booze and sex is better for me than romantic dinners and love.

"Are you on an early shift tomorrow?" George asks, as he piles the chunks of lamb into a dish and slides it into his oven.

"Nope, I'm on a late. You?" I wipe down my section while my béchamel waits for me.

"Same! A few pints then, at least," he says cheekily, clearly excited to hang out with this version of me, the one he hasn't seen in a while.

"Finn?" I call out to lovely Finn, who is filleting fish at the back of the kitchen. "Can you come for a few pints with me and George?"

"Yes, mate!" He is as enthusiastic as we are, and begins to work faster so the pint can come sooner.

My shift hasn't been too arduous because it has been fueled by the type of endorphins that only sex can give you. That feeling of being desired by someone in your private life, it carries over into your work life. Right now, I'm happy, so I have momentum running through my veins; I mix harder and beat faster.

I beat the lumps of gooey matter clogging up the béchamel and stare down at my sauce, fixated on achieving total smoothness. I'm going to add the little tubes of pasta to my sauce and then grill it with more cheese and panko breadcrumbs too. A week ago, I wouldn't have bothered with panko breadcrumbs—in fact I wouldn't have even grilled the mac and cheese, I would have served it as boring wet pasta so I could get the hell out of there and go home. But now I'm putting in a little extra effort; I remember how nice it feels when you make other people happy with small things, like melting their cheese and toasting their panko breadcrumbs, or playing with their balls. I take a metal spoon and dip the back of it into my cheese sauce to taste it. The sauce coats the back of the spoon and it reminds me of something; I get hit by another flashback. "I'm going to cum," he said, and then cum pooled on my abdomen before he collapsed on top of me. Afterward he turned to look down at his mess and laughed. His smile was demonic and hot.

No one in the kitchen knows what's inside my head; it's all kinds of bad things.

I stir the sauce thoroughly, leaving none of it untouched; it's like yesterday, Luca wanted to touch all of me, all at once. The béchamel thickens and begins to erupt slowly, like a volcano; a speck of cream spits at my face and lands by the corner of my mouth. Another flashback: Luca is on top of me and a bit of his spit lands on the corner of my mouth in that same place. I come to and wipe the béchamel from my lip, though my mouth remains slightly ajar as I take a sharp inhale. Fuck. I cannot get this guy out of my head.

I dump the cooked macaroni into the sauce and do a big final mix. There she is; that squelching noise that sounds just like wet pussy. I scoop it into a tray, scatter panko breadcrumbs on top, and put it in the oven.

"Alright, shall we leave in ten minutes?" George asks, interrupting my filthy thoughts. None of us want the staff food, the mac and cheese or the lamb; we'd prefer the pints. He and Finn have their knife-wraps out on their workbench and are wiping soapy bubbles off their knives. I should wipe my dirty thoughts away with soapy bubbles.

My phone vibrates in my pocket. I wonder if it's a text from Luca. From the get-go, it felt easy to talk to him. His texts didn't make me cringe like messages from other guys in the past; they were salacious and shameless, and it thrilled me. He never cared that we were practically strangers; he never held back.

Come to my restaurant tonight and I'll fuck you in the bathroom
Tell me what your pussy tastes like
Think my cock will fit inside you? (1 attached image)
I had never engaged in such filth without properly knowing someone. But I have to say, it's turned out to be a total lark. Before I met Luca, my style of messaging men was similar to that of an automated chatbot. I gave the facts and commentary in an incredibly monotone way with zero flair, very little evidence of flirting, and lots of *haha ok*. When Luca and I first started texting, he'd message me things like *I want to eat you* or *Put a finger in your ass and show me*. I'd giggle and chuck my phone to the other side of the room while biting my cheeks with excitable angst. But I've gotten better now; soon I'll be brave and tell him *I'm thinking about you in bed. Call me.*

Sometimes he FaceTimes me and we wank together on the phone. Then we talk for a bit after we cum. We talk about our jobs and our sadness. He struggles like I do with getting out of bed some days. We speak about past stories of lost love, although the thing that differs in our stories is he is always the bad guy, whereas I am the martyred victim. Aside from Topknot Barman, that is generally my role. (Topknot Barman is now forced out of my mind forever and ever.) I know that's how it will play out this time already; sometimes I imagine how many people Luca has fucked but then I stop myself because I like to imagine I'm special.

Luca is the Head Chef of a little restaurant in East London called Foil. It's trendy and refined, and his food is celebrated by lots of chefs. He worked hard to get here. He grew up in Naples and moved to London by himself when he was twenty. He's spent more than fifteen years tirelessly learning a craft, researching, cooking, getting burned, and persisting. The thing that comes with all this commitment and passion is simple: severe, *severe* sex appeal. And he knows it.

He tells me it's a waste for me, a posh girl, to give my life away to kitchens, and I argue with him spitefully. When we are not being rude to one another, or talking about feeling low, we have one common goal: to fuck well. This goal is rapidly becoming more important to me than my goals at work for progressing further and becoming a Sous Chef.

A phone begins to ring.

"Someone's phone is ringing!" George shouts.

"Ah, yeah it's mine," I say. I check it; it's Raquel. We're not really allowed to take calls in the kitchen but fuck it, none of the adults are here. I crouch down by my service fridge and pick up.

"Hey, what's up?" I say.

"Yo, where are you?" she says. "Just sent you a message."

"At work. I'm done in like thirty mins."

"Cool. I want to hear about Luca. Did you fuck?"

"Is that why you called me? Fuck's sake. I'm at work!"

"Haha, sorry, I'm just dying to hear about it. Was it good?"

"Fucking excellent," I say, quietly so the boys don't hear me.

"Wait, did you just fuck in like the middle of the day?" she asks.

"Yeah. I'll tell you about it later. Bye!" I hang up the phone.

I so badly want to be with Raquel right now, or any female friend, so that I can engage in a very detailed post-sex debrief. I think about the story, and how I'll tell her; I don't forget any of the details.

Luca had texted me a stream of wallowing messages about feeling low yesterday morning. I replied that it always helps me to get out of the house when I'm feeling that way. He responded with whimpering excuses and a picture of his cock. Fuck this. I was bored of being his digital therapist and bored of fucking through the phone; I wanted to meet.

Me: *Let's just meet and we can talk*

Him: *Argh I don't feel like getting out of bed, but I do want to see you. I feel gross*

Me: *Just get up then. We'll just have a coffee, no funny business, no sex*

Him: *Ok ok*

I suggested we meet for a coffee in a café between our flats. Despite my earnest intentions for the meet-up, I still shaved my whole body just in case.

I cycled to the park in the spring sunshine. I saw him before he saw me. He was sitting outside the café, leaning back, legs crossed, and scrolling on his phone. He was wearing a hoodie, loose cotton trousers, and Birkenstock Bostons. He looked effortlessly amazing, whereas I'd visibly made an effort; I wore bronzer *and* mascara.

I locked my bike up and nervously approached the pathway toward the café. As I walked self-consciously, feeling every muscle in my legs working, every breath into my lungs and every breath out, I questioned my decision to meet him. Is it going to be awkward in real life? A bit of me wants to get back on my bike and pretend that I never sent him a picture of my pussy. But I did, and more than once. The drunken post-shift adrenaline causes you to make weird choices.

I don't usually meet lovers in the sober light of day, especially not at such a civilized establishment, but if he felt comfortable among sensible society, then I wanted to as well. He spotted me walking toward him and grinned. I hate this bit. The first real-life hello after all the smutty digital chat. It was the first time we were properly meeting—it felt like ages since I had seen him in the pub with Raquel. I was worried I wasn't as alluring as the girl who glided past him on her bike a month ago.

"Hello," I said.

I don't feel much shame about my personality anymore. I spent so many years trying to undo my awkward bumbling, my shyness, my nervous laughter, but now I think: fuck it. Plus, I already knew he was speaking to me with the sole purpose of fucking me, so wasn't my personality kind of irrelevant? I wondered, for a moment, if that was liberating or highly demeaning. But I didn't want to think about this man being a dick, because it would have put me off him, and I wanted this to work. I needed the distraction of him in my life so I didn't miss Kit.

"Hello, you." His eyes traveled up and down my body like I was a shop window of baklava on Green Lanes. "You're not going to give me a hug?"

"We can hug," I said.

We embraced and every inch of my body fizzed.

"You smell nice," he said. I'd sprayed perfume on my wrists before I left my flat, a thing I only remember to do when I am seeing a boy. He gripped me around the waist and pressed his head into my neck and said in my ear, "You're pretty too." And then he laughed. There was a tension that I'd never felt before; I don't know if I felt comfortable in it, but I wanted more of whatever it was.

He went to get us two coffees. A few minutes later, he handed me mine and sat down. After a moment of awkward silence passed, I decided I was bored of being uncomfortable, so I asked him outright: "How come you're feeling depressed?" That was the whole reason we were meeting after all, to talk about his feelings.

"Oh, you know, the usual stuff. I keep thinking about my ex. And about how I fucked her over so bad. I just feel like I'm not where I want to be in life," he said. It doesn't bother me when he talks about his ex; I still think about Kit too. Plus, I know our thing is meaningless sex, and I'm okay with that, or at least I am right now. We spoke for a while about his career aspirations as a chef, about his desire to go back home to Naples and start a restaurant where he grew up and where his family still lived. He reminded me that I should quit restaurants before I give too many years to the kitchen and regret it like he does, but he didn't give me an opportunity to respond before continuing to talk about himself. He kept talking about himself. He asked no questions about my life, and I noticed; but I kept the conversation going with tons about his, to stay clear of any awkward silences.

"Why are you sitting so far away from me?" he said. I guess he did ask questions if it led to his body getting closer to mine. Before I could respond, he pulled his chair closer to me. He was so close that his legs were on either side of mine. I looked away at first, and then I built up the courage to meet his eyes. The way he held eye contact unnerved me. He was so comfortable in the presence of a stranger. But it made me excited for what was to come.

I looked past his shoulder; a glamorous lady, about sixty years old with gray hair and red glasses, sat behind us reading a magazine. I could see she was reading an article about the revolution of tinned fish; there was a big illustration of a sardine poking out of the top of a tote bag. She kept turning around to look at us: tall handsome tired chef with young pale shy girl. I don't blame her for staring. She saw I'd seen her looking at us, so I gave her a smile; she looked at me, woman to woman, and winked. Perhaps she could see right through us, or perhaps she too liked meeting up with complicated men in civilized cafés.

"You're very shy," Luca said. "Do you not know you're very beautiful?" He tucked a piece of hair behind my right ear. Was he trying to say all ugly people should be shy?

He stared at me. His eyes were jet-black and evil. He kept finding ways to touch me; I could tell he had conquered the art of fucking women a long time ago. I knew it would not be the same as what I had with Kit, but I convinced myself this was better, it was easier to be with someone whom I wouldn't develop feelings for, because it would never be an option with this guy. I wanted sex, validation, attention, and fun. He could give it to me, and so what if he was a bit of a cunt?

I laughed at his remark about my shyness. I liked that he was impolite. First, it made me feel irritated, then competitive; I wanted to disarm him too. It reminded me of being in a kitchen and working with a chef who is so arrogant that it's almost enjoyable taking them on, like it had been with my former Sous Chef, Zack; toward the end of my time at that restaurant, I enjoyed the challenge of racing him to the pass.

I decided we were going to fuck. It was 9:15 a.m. and we had met about seven minutes ago, but I didn't see how else this whole thing was going to play out.

"Where do you live?" I asked the demon.

"Just opposite," he said. "You see over there?" he pointed to a house across the road.

"Can I see inside?" I asked.

"My flat?" He raised both hands and said, "But you said we weren't going to fuck so I didn't clean my room."

I looked at the thirty-five-year-old man. "So, you only clean your bedroom if you know you are going to fuck a woman in there?" I asked. He jokingly pushed me away. I laughed at him, not with him. I relished in that moment; I had disarmed him.

He took one last sip of his coffee. "Okay, let's go," he said.

We said very little more as we headed to his flat together. There were blossoms on the trees and the sky was so blue it looked artificial. We walked past school-girls bunking off class and a group of young boys on bikes. I felt smug thinking about how boring their day was compared to mine.

We arrived at Luca's front door. He opened it, then turned around and said, "Come on." He laughed at me as I looked back at him: I was ignorant as to what was to come but, whatever it was, he knew and I wanted to find out. He laughed at me an awful lot for someone who was supposed to be seducing me, but I guess he knew he didn't need to seduce me; he knew I was up for it.

We took off our shoes and I walked up the stairs ahead of him; I guessed his flat was the top floor of the house. He smacked my right arse cheek and my body lit on fire. It was a random Tuesday morning and I was in the flat of a stranger who was ten years older than me and fucking hot.

The flat was nice but messy. He shared it with two other people, he explained, but they weren't there because they have normal jobs. As he bobbed about putting his keys away, I stood awkwardly and asked him, "Where is your room?" I saw his eyes flick toward the door on the right. "In here?" I smiled, and I touched the doorknob. His eyes widened and he leaped across me to hold the door shut. "No, no, no. It's too messy, we're not going in there." I was dying to know what was on the other side. I thought he might have some woman in there.

He took my hand and led me to the sitting room, where sunshine was streaming through bay windows and shining on the beige wallpaper. I looked down to the street below and spotted the café where we once sat. The woman reading about sardines being trendy was still there.

"Do you want anything?" he asked me in a noncommittal way, not knowing just how vague his question was.

"No, I'm all good, thanks," I said, slightly reverting back to shyness after the brief moment of confidence. What now? I wondered.

I sat down on the big leather sofa and almost instantaneously Luca leaned over and planted his lips on mine. They were warm and soft. All the playfulness left his body and a wave of focus replaced it. He slid his tongue into my mouth, and I could taste the coffee we had both drunk moments ago; I could smell the sleep on him, the sleep he had woken up from just before we met up. I noted how quickly everything was happening. I'd never done anything like this before.

He wasted no time. He linked his hands behind the small of my back and slid me down the sofa so that I was lying horizontally. His right hand clasped at my neck and his left arm held himself up on the sofa so he could look down at me. His hands moved artfully as his body hovered over mine. After a month of him filling both of our heads with ideas of what he wanted to do to me, he could finally do it. His gaze was obsessive. I felt like the first woman to exist. He reached over me and clutched onto any curve he could find, my skin tingling as he did so; I was barely able to control my own limbs. It was electric—someone should have been filming it, really. I was seduced by the satisfaction of this conquest; I felt proud knowing I had enough sexual prowess to entice a man who was so well-seasoned in sex.

Still fully clothed, he pushed his tongue deeper into my mouth. He knelt over me but his eyes didn't leave mine for a moment; they were wide, never blinking, not even for a second. He was either falling in love with me or performing some weird sinister ritual on me. I would bet money on the latter. He ran his hands across my trousers and said firmly: "Take these off, I'm going to eat you."

I did as he said, feeling exhilarated by his authority over me. I hate being told what to do by men, but in sex, that changes. It's fun when they take control—there's an element of wanting to do as you're told in order to get what you want; it's a thrilling game that ends in an orgasm. I spend so much time in the kitchen being a force of nature. Using my physical strength, lifting pans, or breaking through a carcass with a cleaver is empowering, but it definitely affects my sense of femininity. Being with Luca and being treated this way by him, playing with these traditional gender roles, was really hot. I was weak for him, and that felt good because I wanted him to fix that by fucking me.

He assisted me with my black M&S thong. I have never been able to achieve great heights of sexy with my choice of underwear; there's no color or lace, which I hadn't really thought about much until this point. I wanted to be all the things he expected from me. He pulled it past my thighs and then over my knees, until it was bundled up by my ankles. He used one hand to lift my legs up, then with his other hand he snapped the thong off and it went flying, hitting the TV screen and falling to the floor.

He opened my legs. He rested his face on the inside of my left thigh and looked up at me. He used his thumb to gently circle my clit. He still had his eyes on mine when he dipped his thumb inside me and then brought it up to my clit again. I wanted more, I wanted him to bury his face in me, to have all that pleasure at once, but he made me wait. He teased me with his tongue, gently flicking back and forth while he continued to hold my gaze. Jesus Christ. Call the police, I thought. It's Tuesday morning and this random chef has his face in my pussy.

I abandoned my inner commentary and leaned into the moment. I rested my head back on the arm of the sofa and closed my eyes while he ate me. A soft breeze blew into the room from the windows; it smelled like spring. The fresh air gently blew across my face, cooling my pink cheeks; what a fantastic way to spend a Tuesday morning.

Before long—men like him never properly commit to oral sex—he stood up and rushed to take off his trousers, tripping over them. He continued to hold my gaze with his demonic but intoxicating stare. I noted zero insecurity, vulnerability, or consideration in his movement. This man lives to fuck. I glanced at his dick; it was as arrogant as he was.

Before I knew it, he was inside me and we were fucking, my bare arse sticking to a stranger's sofa. My top was still on and in between his daggering stares, he'd glance down at my tits. Like a good attentive woman, I understood what he wanted and took my top off. He grasped hold of my tits and his eyes rolled to the back of his head. I almost laughed—it was a truly sensational performance. There were big thrusts and quick thrusts, fast and furious. There was nothing slow or steady; no initial trotting, just straight to a full-fledged gallop; he was a bucking thoroughbred and I was an untrained jockey, nearly falling off at every jump but maintaining a strong commitment to stay on the damn horse.

I was having an excellent time, but unsure of whether I was enjoying the sex or enjoying him enjoying the sex. His groans became louder; at that moment I started mourning the sex, because I knew it was about to be over. He said, "Fuck, I'm going to cum." He pulled out and came on my stomach. Then he collapsed on top of me.

"Jesus," he said. He glanced toward me subtly; it was the first time he showed any sense of vulnerability. I sat there, sweaty and naked, taking a deep breath. I steadied my body, which had just been fucked in every which way, and I sat up next to him on the sofa. I stayed there, dizzy and feeble, and laughed. He didn't give me an orgasm in the end. I didn't mind much because the sex was so dazzling, but I was left wanting more.

Moments passed. There was zero affection, no attempt at aftercare. I didn't feel sad, but it felt alien to me. Even if the guys I'd slept with in the past had ended up being cunts, there was usually an initial period where they pretended to care.

I stood up to get changed because I knew this is how it would be with him. I bent down to pick up my thong. I looked to see if he was watching me but he was looking at his phone. Already I was nothing to him; my body, the thing he desired the most just moments ago, was now blending into his beige wallpaper. I walked toward the window while doing up the clasp on my bra. It was still sunny outside. I looked down on the café and the glamorous lady was still there. It looked like she was reading that same article. In the time it took her to read a double-page spread, I had had sex. Maybe she read it twice. I felt this sense of achievement, of doing something valuable with my day off work. Kit can go and have a baby with his ex for all I care; I am an independent force, a liberated woman, a grown-up lady with no need to settle for less than I deserve.

I remember that feeling of his cool face resting on my warm left thigh as I lean against the oven door, watching my mac and cheese.

"Is the mac and cheese ready?" I hear George ask me, bringing me back into reality.

"Yep," I say. "And your lamb?"

"Yes," he replies.

I open the oven and waft away the steam with a towel. Much like the sex with Luca yesterday, the fun is over; the thrill of cooking, of waiting for it to be ready, the bubbling béchamel tension, is a thing of the past. I heave the tray of golden pasta and cheese from the oven and put it on the pass under the hot lights. There is a sound of delight from the queue of the front-of-house staff. They are always hungry, always ready to scarf all the scraps before any of the chefs can eat.

It's okay, though. Today I don't feel that hungry. My body is satiated from the sex; I don't need much else. I'm full up on fantasies about my next encounter with Luca.

George brings over a tray of hot lamb with a dark crust from the grill. He pours an old, slightly brown salsa verde on top; it is made up of parsley, garlic, anchovy, and lemon and does a good job at disguising the overcooked meat. Another collective sigh from the front of house: "Woowwww." They're like kids in a magic show. They don't realize the tricks behind putting things in the oven.

Ten minutes later, after I've cleaned down, George and Finn have eaten after all, and we've all changed, we march down the street in our home clothes and head to our local pub. We haven't gone for after-work drinks in a while, perhaps because it's been winter and, while we can handle the cold, standing in the never-ending darkness is a little too depressing. Plus, George and Finn have lovely partners to go home to.

George gets the first round, and then we sit on the pavement with our plastic pints. We never drink inside the pub after work, as we've been in a kitchen all day without seeing the sky. There are always the first few minutes when we sit in silence and say nothing, reflecting on all that has happened since 8 a.m. After a few glugs of lager and a couple of tokes on a cigarette, the nonsense chat begins.

I sit with my pint to the right of me on the pavement, with the evening sun on my face. It warms my cheeks and makes me smile. It reminds me of when the breeze blew through Luca's window and onto my naked body. I want to see him again, but I'm not in a rush, for now I want to savor the memories. I am romanticizing it a little perhaps, looking back on the morning with rose-tinted glasses. I feel beautiful. Luca didn't make me feel like this; I did. I had a nice time with him but it was me who made it happen, who set everything in motion.

"Did you get laid last night or something?" Finn asks me, grinning.

"What? Are you crazy!" I say, embarrassed at how readable I am. "No, I did not!"

He looks back at me and grins.

"Okay, yeah, fine, I did. It was excellent."

George giggles and Finn grabs me around the shoulders and shakes me in a celebratory way. I guess they know I have been hurt by Kit recently, and now they know I'm doing better. I love them for it; it's like they were watching me all along, cheering from the sidelines, and now they're happy for me in my moment of victory.

We drink beer like we drink water; we knock pints back in a couple of fell swoops. A busy day in the kitchen means dehydration and adrenaline; I feel giddy. I thought I loved life in the kitchen, but maybe it's the part right when you leave that I love more.

"Do you want a bit of ket?" Finn asks.

"Absolutely." I love ket too.

The four walls of the kitchen keep me focused, but when I step outside I feel like a kid who just got off a roller coaster in a fairground. I want to go on the ride again! But not the kitchen ride, the Luca ride. I want more of him and I want it tonight. It's been twenty-four hours and I'm withdrawing from his attention, from his desire for me.

Hours pass and pints sink in our stomachs. I reach levels of drunkenness where I feel comfortable talking to men about my feelings.

"The thing is, yeah," I slur, "I am either up or down. I am all or nothing."

"Yeah, but that's it!" Finn yells back at me, just as drunk as me. "We work in kitchens because it's never boring. You love it then you hate it then you love it again. It's like a proper good romance."

"Yeah. I guess you never know what makes you truly happy. Do you think cooking food is enough? Forever?" I say.

"Dunno. I don't know what else I would do," Finn says.

"Yeah, I don't know. I think I could be a good dog walker," I say, naming the first job I can think of.

"Hundred percent. You'd whip any dog into shape." George hiccups.

"You and George wouldn't be there though. I love you boys. I think I'd quit if you did," I say. Maybe I'm drunk or maybe I'm foolish or maybe it's true.

"You know what, I love working with you a lot. A good team makes all the difference," Finn says.

"The kitchen is my home. You are my family," I say. I'm definitely drunk now, because the shit I'm spouting sounds like profound poetry.

Then I remember the sex! The thing that is of far more importance to me than all this silly chef talk.

It's time to gloat. "Finn. Wait. You need to see the guy I had sex with yesterday. Oh my God, let me get you a picture, he's so hot."

I pull up Luca's Instagram page and let Finn peruse his curated life.

"Oh, shit, it's that guy. Isn't he the Head Chef of Foil?" he asks. I can tell he is shocked at the caliber of men I fuck.

"Yeah," I say, like a proud chef WAG.

"Yeah, he's hot. But be careful—apparently he's an astronomical cunt." I stare at Finn's lips moving, amazed at how his mouth produced the word "astronomical."

I wonder if I can say "astronomical." I squint my eyes and slur "Astroturf."

"What?" Finn looks back at me, confused. My brain feels like it's spilling out of my head. I don't know how to explain I was trying to say the word "astronomical." I laugh. He laughs. George laughs too. We can't stop laughing.

Finn passes my phone back and while his eyes are occupied by his lighting a cigarette at the wrong end, I subtly click Message on Luca's profile.

Want to fukc?

11

Empty Tables

JULY

I am plating the last table for lunch service. We've had many menu changes since that Tuesday morning in spring, and much to my surprise, I have slept with Luca many more times.

"You up?" Sous Chef Finn shouts over to me as he slides his pan-fried venison loin under the pass.

"Up on the gnocchi, hake is coming in thirty seconds," I say. The hake I am cooking looks white and plain; I am growing bored of these dishes, of this kitchen. In fact, a few months ago I was growing bored; now there is bitterness brewing.

I slide my spatula beneath the firm fillet of hake. I allow the fillet to lean back into the corner of the spatula. I use my thumb and the tip of my middle finger to keep the fillet in place as I bring it over to a shallow bowl of foaming, pale-gold cream sauce, made with chicken stock and sparkling white wine. In one single movement, using conviction—the most vital ingredient in cooking—I push the fish off my spatula with my thumb. It lands in the center of the bowl, so gently that it does not splash. I squeeze a few drops of olive oil onto the skin of the fish and I watch it shine for a second. I keep the bowl close to me, like it is my child; I see its beauty more than others, it is the fruit of my womb. I wipe down the sides of the plate, not wanting to hand it over to a young runner who won't protect it like I have; he'll probably allow the sauce to splash all over the edges of the dish, ruining my artful work. My bitterness is beginning to bubble.

"So where's next on your list, then?" Finn asks me. We're talking about the restaurants we want to eat at.

"I'm going to Fava tonight, actually. You know, that new space in Marylebone that does different chef residencies in the evenings? My friend knows the chef who's cooking there this month and it's opening night."

"Bet the friend is Luca, isn't it?" he says.

"Yeah, okay, fine; it is." I told Finn about how I'm still seeing Luca, because he's very into talking about sex; he's gay and very fun to talk to about hot men at work. I suppose I could also talk to Maggie about it, but I kind of feel like she sees me as her older sister, and I don't want her to know I'm susceptible to the charms of men.

"How's it going with him?" he asks, genuinely interested.

"Yeah, it's fine. It's the first time we're going out to dinner though. I don't think I've ever seen him outside of East London. I'm a bit nervous, to be honest."

"Well, it sounds like he likes you." Finn playfully thumps me on the arm. "You'll be grand," he says.

I busy myself wiping down the fridges for a moment and ponder what Finn said. Does Luca like me? Do I like Luca? I think I do. I definitely have grown to care about him, in some way or another, and I know I'd be hurt if he was fucking someone else.

"Right," I say to Finn, "I'm going to head off. Tell Victor the fridges are all stocked up. He doesn't need to do anything for service."

I try to avoid handing over to Victor properly. It means I can avoid getting my arse groped. I just make sure I've left the section bulked up and clean, and get out of there.

"See you, babes!" Finn calls to me as I'm already out the door.

I think I am looking forward to dinner with Luca tonight.

After we slept together, Luca and I started talking more and more.

Our relationship now goes beyond sex. Make no mistake, he will never turn down my *Want to fukc?* messages; it's just recently that we meet up for other reasons too. We chat regularly and he tells me about his day and I tell him about mine. Sure, most of it is him complaining or moaning about his kitchen, but I tell myself it means he values my opinion. Sometimes we meet and we don't even have sex, we just go for Turkish tea or a walk in the park. I think he might be the person I have most in common with in the world, as we both have this secret venom running through our veins, spewing criticism toward restaurants; the pompous people and the fake PR, the bad overpriced menus and the tacky aesthetics, the influencer shams and the industry gossip; we act like martyrs, forgetting it was our decision to be bound to it all by ball and chain. And we're venomous toward each other: we are always contradicting ourselves and disagreeing with each other for the sake of it; he criticizes a restaurant I went to, just to prove his superior knowledge, and I disagree for the sake of it, even though I know he's right. And then we give up and laugh it off. We have the energy to take the piss, but we don't look too deeply, because that means we might need to look at ourselves too. It's easy to blame our workplace for our struggles when we're each as deluded as the other.

But I also know that Luca has been the main reason my thoughts about being a chef have become tainted. Spending time with him makes me see what my life could look like if these thoughts stay with me and I do this kitchen bollocks forever. Luca is dragging me down.

The talking is one thing; the sex is another. It's not like any sex I've had before. It's like he takes all his darkness and focuses it on my body. He is aggressive and forceful but I like it. It floods me with adrenaline. There are some times when it gets too much and I tell him to stop; he is reluctant, but does.

Despite his darkness, I have started to care for him. I think he cares for me too. When he asked me to go to Fava to eat his friend's food, I was elated. Not necessarily about the food itself, but more the idea of going on a proper date with him. Deep down I know I'll never get the Andrew Edmunds moment with Luca, but it's nice to pretend.

I was surprised when he invited *me* to go with him, because the restaurant we're going to is sceney as fuck; I would've thought he'd want to take one of his famous, handsome chef friends. Fava is one of these trendy restaurant models where there is no regular team of chefs; it is an expensive sourdough café in the day that becomes an empty kitchen at night; a blank canvas for the nomadic culinary overlords to come in and explode their inspired, vacuum-packed spunk over the pristine white walls. Like rock stars, they take over the kitchen and gig there for a brief period before they move on to the next stage of their tour. They collect groupies in the form of Instagram followers who follow them around, buying tickets for every pop-up. Sometimes the chefs are excellent and it's a wonderful experience to try food that you might not get a chance to otherwise, but sometimes it's just rich home cooks from Notting Hill who have family connections with the founder of Fava, so they have wangled themselves a residency only to put three Ortiz anchovies on a plate and charge forty-eight quid for it. The dining room is painfully modern and pretentious; there are always too many people wearing hats, and the napkins smell of Diptyque perfume.

Luca is seduced by this world, and so am I; it is impossible not to be. But I could never work in a place like that, and now I worry I should want to. My aspirations have been wavering recently. I know that part of the reason that Luca and I criticize the London restaurant scene is because we're jealous, because we want in and we're not. Luca is halfway there; he knows a lot of people in the London restaurant scene and his cooking is celebrated by famous chefs. But he wasn't born into it with connections and wealth, and the opportunities that both those things bring. I'm a newbie, a keen observer, hanging around the outskirts, hoping to slide in; maybe that's why I'm with Luca, to use him. I didn't see this side of restaurants before he showed me, and now I've become poisoned by it all.

The socialite chef circles are small and selective, like the art world or the fashion world. It's elitist, exclusive, and often—with people prioritizing style over substance—more about *who* you know, not *what* you cook. Luca and I pretend that if we were in this world, we'd reject it, but I don't know if we would. The men who succeed seem scary and the few women who thrive are all loud and gregarious, or mysterious and beautiful. But unlike me, Luca has real reasons to feel bitter about the London restaurant scene. He has worked his arse off and has sacrificed his life and his sanity to get to the top, yet he is watching middle-class young men who have a couple of years' experience of working for a mate get opportunities he has never been given: a well-paid residency at a high-end place, agents to manage big brand deals, collaboration opportunities with iconic restaurant chains, or even a shot at starting a whole new restaurant. It seems so unfair, but I suppose you could also argue that Luca being such a massive cunt also serves as a disadvantage.

In the changing rooms I sit on the bench momentarily, with a big sigh. I check my phone and Ruby's name pops up.

I open her message.

Babes, I'm right by your work, are you about for a drink? Dying to see you!

I slide my phone back in my pocket and wonder if I should see Ruby for a drink. I haven't seen her since Kit and I ended, when of course she came running to my side to support me. Since then I've been completely absorbed by Luca, and getting fucked up with the chefs after work. I haven't made time for her and I feel awful. There's so much to catch up on.

I start to convince myself I don't have time to see her, but realistically I do; I just don't want to because I know I'll bring up Luca and she'll tell me that I should end things with him. She'll make me realize how stupid it is to spend time on wankers instead of my lovely friends. But for some reason—perhaps because I *do* have feelings for the bastard—I don't want to give him up. So I let her down with a little lie.

I say: *Sorry, babes, gonna be at work a little longer. Hope you're good and let's definitely do something soon.*

She replies: *Okay, but please let's make it soon. Haven't seen you in ridiculously long.*

I swallow a lump of guilt, slide my phone back into my pocket, and rip open the cheap poppers on my chef whites. I get changed into a pair of comfy tracksuit bottoms and a shirt, shove my feet into my Asics, and store my keys and phone in my sports bra. I feel bad about blowing off Ruby, knowing she's just around the corner, but I don't want to burst my bubble of make-believe.

As I leave the restaurant to find my bike, I am relieved that the shift is over. These days my job feels monotonous and the hard labor thankless. All the while, Luca has been telling me that life in kitchens is not for everyone, and I know he's talking about me.

My phone vibrates. I fish it out of my bra and I see his name calling me. Fuck. I bet he's going to cancel.

I pick up.

"What's good, G?" He calls me names like G or Mate or Dude to try to reinforce the fact that I am not his girlfriend and we are not dating. I ignore his limp signaling. Tonight is a date; he just doesn't want to admit it.

"Yeah, what's up? Are you still on for tonight?" I ask.

"Yeah, of course. I just went to the barber for a shape-up. We're going fancy tonight. You've got to look good too, yeah?"

"Okay, okay. I always look good, but yeah," I say, awaiting his confirmation that this is indeed true. Nothing, of course. Well tonight, he'll see, I'll look so beautiful that it will be impossible for him to ignore.

We agree to meet at a pub at 7 p.m. and I hang up. I am relieved he didn't cancel in a way I never felt with Kit, because Kit never did cancel.

I unlock my bike, loop the lock around the middle bar, put my headphones on, and push my pedals forward with power. I listen to the type of music where the man laments the hardship of walking away from bachelor independence to secure his girl, then she chimes in with romantic sentiment in her beautiful voice. I arrive home, kick off my shoes, and lie back on my bed. I do a round-robin stalk on Instagram: first Luca's ex whom he *always* brings up, then the restaurant we're going to, then the Head Chef of the restaurant, then I see if the Head Chef follows Luca—of course he does. What a great big cheffy cockfest.

I urge my body to get moving and I undress for a shower where I will remove all hair on my body, bar my vagina; no man is worth getting rid of those luscious locks for. As I wash away all the kitchen grime, I dream up what tonight could look like. I try to condense all the nice things Luca has said to me and turn it into this narrative where tonight he is going to say sorry for all the times he's been a knob. I will reluctantly accept his heartfelt apology and we will then have a deeply romantic evening where he introduces me to all these chefs, telling them all the same nice things, and playing with my hair as if I'm his pet.

I get out of the shower and I scamper across the flat, as my nervous energy doesn't allow me to move around at a normal pace. I am bouncing around like a wild rabbit trapped indoors, emptying all drawers and cupboards, and treading mud into the carpet while trying on different shoes. What do I wear for a man who is unsure if he likes me?

I look through everything I own and realize that I never wear normal clothes anymore so I don't really have anything nice. I spend sixty hours of my week in chef whites and Birkenstock Bostons; the remaining time I'm in black Uniqlo trousers, dossing around from pub to pub with chef friends. I have not felt the urge to dress like a feminine, pretty woman in a long time.

After a deep analytic thought, I decide on wearing a skirt. Straight men are simple; if they're asked whether they like big tits or small tits, they will always say big tits. When asked if they like long hair or short hair, they will always say long hair. So with this logic, I presume that if Luca was to be asked: do you prefer a woman in androgynous straight-legged trousers from Uniqlo or a small black skirt, I conclude he would pick the skirt. So I go for the skirt, even though it makes me feel like I'm sixteen years old and about to get drunk in a bush.

My outfit makes me feel unlike myself, but I ignore the feeling. I paint sharp wings of eyeliner onto my eyelids for a man who, for the most part of four months, has never seen me with proper makeup on.

I believe all this beauty malarkey is the answer to transforming a sex affair into something a little more substantial. And I want that, I think.

I cycle to the pub where we have planned to meet and see him leaning back against the exterior wall, his tall frame standing out among the short, swotty East

London beanie-hat baldies. He is wearing a very nice dark jacket, with a pale seam on the outside, and a hat as always; he has a receding hairline he thinks I don't know about.

As I get off my bike, I feel uncomfortable in my clothes, and alien in my body. As I hike my tights up to my crotch, I immediately regret my outfit. I'm wearing a too-tight jacket with a slippery shine that doesn't allow my shoulder bag to sit there without falling off my fucking shoulder. My shoes are uncomfortable and too small. My eyeliner feels over the top, and my T-shirt is hanging down so I have to tuck it under my jumper every two minutes. I don't feel comfortable in any of it. Not even my hair feels like my own. I got it cut yesterday and it feels too swishy and clean. My hair is usually the thing that never lets me down, but today it hangs in all the wrong places on my face, clumping together at the back and sticking to my face at the front. It's as if my own body is trying to tell me something is not right. I want tonight to be special for us, and easy, but the fact that my body is wrecked with angst at the sight of him suggests it's not all that likely.

I know that I shouldn't feel like this, that it means I should walk away from this man, but I can't. He has this power over me; he makes me tap into these dark feelings, and it's addictive.

"Hey, what time do you call this, dude?" he calls out to me as I walk toward him; he barely even looks at me. I hate this guy.

I lead the way into the pub. I need a drink. I can't believe he didn't even acknowledge my special effort. I think back to Kit, and how he'd always say I looked nice. A bit of me longs for him to turn up right now, to walk over to Luca, slam a powerful uppercut into his angular chin, and whisk me out of here by the hand, our love story reinstated. Best not to think about that or I might cry.

"What do you want?" I say flatly.

"Guinness, please. Why are you grumpy?" He slides his phone into his pocket and finally looks at me. Still nothing. Not even any commentary on my perfume.

He finally says, "I like this bag, actually."

"Don't comment on my bag, comment on my face."

He laughs. "Your face is always nice, and you know it." Here we go! I get a big thrill from this deeply impersonal line. I collect them all; fragments of a real compliment, then when I get home, when I'm by myself, I patch all the broken bits together to make a mosaic of all the nice things he's ever said. I give in to him and smile. Sometimes I do the same with the kitchen as I do with Luca, I romanticize things. I focus only on the fun services, the big laughs, the beautiful moments of camaraderie, and I ignore the stress, the destruction, the exhaustion.

We talk for a while about his day, then he orders us an Uber to the restaurant.

The Uber ride is brief. I am outside my head and my body, and anxiety is creeping in. I can see myself from above, acting weird and looking uncomfortable in my clothes. When we arrive at the restaurant I snap out of it: I come back to myself, and back to earth. I can feel the heat of summer on my skin; I can see big red buses, I can smell my perfume, and I can taste the Guinness on my tongue. I'm out of the car now, and there is safety in the loudness of London; beeping horns and laughing people. It reminds me to pay attention to my senses; the familiar sounds and scenes ground me.

We walk through the doors and there are recognizable chefs dotted all over the dining space: young chefs who've recently been awarded a Michelin star, older chefs who are famous for breaking rules, the social-media chefs who are famous for breaking rules before they've learned how to cook, and then a few obsessive "foodies" who have been invited to "share the love on social," i.e., promote the evening to their 500K followers. The larger tables are occupied by people who evidently work in hospitality. You can tell because the tables are often left empty, their diners waltzing to and from the bathroom while performatively sniffing their nostril. Luca is in heaven. He swaggers through the dining space, leaving me behind as he goes to the kitchen to embrace his chef friends. I don't bother going over to say hello; I know Luca is unlikely to introduce me to them and I'm not the type to butt into a conversation.

Instead, I go to the loo. I stand in front of the mirror and reapply lipstick. I look good, I think; not myself, but good.

When I leave the bathroom, I spot her.

Luca's ex-girlfriend is sitting at the most lively table in the restaurant, laughing loudly and surrounded by friends; she's the one I stalked on Instagram earlier, the one whose Netflix account Luca is still logged in to, the one who makes him smile when he reminisces about their relationship. He is regretful about losing her in a way he could never be regretful about losing me. He truly loved her but she left him because he cheated; she walked away from him with her head held high and now she's here, enjoying life, free from his poisonous bollocks. She is beautiful, with long glossy brunette hair and a big smile beneath her plump, red-wine-stained lips.

My heart sinks, but I walk through the restaurant as if I don't recognize her. My mind works a mile a minute as I approach our table, where Luca is now sitting, back from the kitchen. Did that bastard invite me tonight just to make his ex jealous? Could he be that callous? I walk right past her table. She looks so free; I suppose that must be the liberation that comes from eradicating Luca from your life. Luca looks at me looking at her. I look back at him and he turns away, the pussy. Fuck this.

"I'm going for a cigarette," I say to him as soon as I arrive at our table.

"What? We literally just arrived; you can't do that, it's rude," he says, acting as if decorum is something he possesses.

"Fuck you and your obsession with being seen by people—by all the wankers in here and by your ex-girlfriend." His jaw drops and he watches as I walk out of the restaurant; me calling him out for what he is, that's the only way this guy notices my presence.

I find a bench just down the road and sit on it with my knees up against my chest. I light my cigarette. How can he use me so overtly? This is where I have to draw the line. He swaggers out of the restaurant and walks over to me.

"Okay, I know what you're thinking, but honestly, I didn't know she was going to be here. I swear," he says. I almost believe him.

"Bullshit. You're deeply troubled, mate." I mate him before he can mate me.

"Hey, hey, hey," he says, while he brushes my hair behind my ears, and I let him, not wanting to cause a scene by batting him away in public.

"Look, I like you, whatever it is we're doing. I like

talking to you and spending time with you. Just come inside and we'll have a nice time," he says in a limp attempt to sweeten me, no longer bothering to deny his satanic plan of using me to make his ex jealous.

I smoke my cigarette, enjoying this moment where I feel like I hold some sort of power over him. I think hard about my next move. Maybe it's fine if I go back in with him? I mean, we are just two people having casual sex; I shouldn't have expected anything more from this guy. This is what I'm supposed to be doing in my twenties: messing around with stupid men, making mistakes and making memories, working in a job that takes all of me.

That's how I evolve, right, and learn all the lessons? And I don't want to settle, I don't want a boring boyfriend or a plain-sailing career. I want to feel excited about everything, all the time. I wonder for a moment if it is worth it. To go through the grueling lows just for the briefly ecstatic highs. It's exhausting, but at least it's never dull.

I know I should probably leave, but I feel myself getting weaker, my thoughts and feelings are scrambled, and I'm losing any sense of perspective; is he actually that bad?

"Hey!" he says, trying to get my attention. "Don't let me go back inside this sceney hellhole by myself."

He knows this sort of place is where I don't feel like I fit in. I don't like the socialites in there, or the stupid clothes they wear, but having him with me, a slightly well-known, very sexy London chef, makes me feel important too; it's intoxicating. I look back at him. His eyes are pleading with me.

"Fine," I say.

I lead the way back to the restaurant and he pats my arse from behind.

We sit at a high table next to the window on uncomfortable barstools. The menu is set, with seven or eight dishes that are basically unrecognizable. I haven't eaten most of the things listed on the bespoke menu card.

Each dish that arrives at our table is totally, utterly delicious. First there is an oyster with sourberry granita. We tap our oysters together, like they are drinks; he says cheers and winks at me. Shards of red ice lie atop the oyster and when I knock it back, they're sharp and acidic, but the oyster is sweet and salty. The ice runs down my throat, cold and mean, but delicious all the same. Next, a small plate of brown squiggles arrives and we are told by the beautiful waitress, whom Luca watches as she walks away, that they are crispy duck intestines. They are tangled and bitter, but the sweet sauce makes it nice. My insides are tangled too, and it's his fault.

There is raw scallop with goat cheese; the flesh of the scallop shines with such pearlescence that it's almost hard to look at. As I bite into the scallop, I can taste the exclusivity, knowing I am one of the few people in London who are allowed to be eating this tonight. It isn't open to the public yet, just "friends and family," also known as PR and chefs who have status—which Luca does. A small plate of octopus carpaccio arrives, trimmed so only the white flesh is on display; then there are razor clams, golden and gratinated. Luca and I discuss how fresh and clever the food is. The flavors excite my tongue but I can't enjoy it, knowing I am a puppet in his master plan. Despite this being some of the best food I have ever eaten, it is one of the least enjoyable meals of my life.

During the later courses, and after a few glasses of wine, we finally talk about something other than food. Luca asks me about what I want from life. I lie to him and tell him I want to work at better restaurants, but really I think I want a break from restaurants altogether. I'm a phony in food and love. He waits for me to speak; he listens and nods and holds my hands like he values my opinion. For a moment his attention is on me alone, but just as our pudding arrives he throws it all away.

"So I've been dating this girl I met in Paris," Luca tells me out of nowhere.

My heart drops.

"I really like her," he continues.

"Are you joking?" I say.

"What?" he says back to me, smiling smugly, like he is enjoying my reaction.

"Why are you telling me about other women you are seeing?" I say, suddenly stone-cold sober.

"Oh, come on, what do you mean? Don't be a child. You know how things are with us."

"Bro." I bro him—a sign of true rage. "Are you joking? Firstly, you bring me to a restaurant where you know your ex-girlfriend is going to be. Then you speak to almost everyone here, yet you haven't introduced me to anyone. And now you're telling me about another woman you're fucking, out of nowhere? Were you dropped on your head as a child? What exactly is wrong with you?"

He puts his hand on my knee to calm me.

"No, get your hand off me," I say, throwing his hand back at him. I am in no mood to deal with any more of this demonic creature's bullshit. "Try to listen to what I'm saying for once. You are deeply arrogant. We've been seeing each other for months, sharing personal stuff with each other, supporting each other, or at least I have been supporting you, and now you think it's okay to tell me out of nowhere about other women? How the fuck do you even have time to see another girl when you spend so much of your time with your head so severely lodged up your own arse? I feel so sorry for this new girl, and I feel sorry for your ex having to sit in the same place as you while you gallivant around with me, a girl ten years younger than you."

I feel powerful suddenly, in a way I have never felt in this man's presence. It feels good but dangerous, like my authentic self might be taking over, squashing the self-destructive, nihilistic me who seems to fancy this man for whatever reason. I won't dismiss my feelings anymore; I don't care if I'm being melodramatic or immature. I'm tired of acting like I'm okay with him treating me like a second option; that's not who I am. I'm the first option. I'm the prize. He's the piss on the pavement. I don't really care what happens next. Luca has shown me just how low he can go, and shown me just how shittily I am willing to be treated. I rotate my body on my uncomfortable barstool, lean my elbow on the table, pick up my fork, eat a big mouthful of lemon tart, take a sip of my wine, and look out the window, finally at peace. I have never been fully myself when I'm around him—I worried that if I was, I'd lose him. I was never clear on what I felt, or confident in what I said; I made myself smaller, thinking it would make him feel bigger. But fuck that. I'm ready to walk away now.

I look out the window at the people in London and wish I'd seen Ruby instead of him. There's a lesson.

"Wow, you are so rude," he says, with a fatherly look

of disapproval on his face. I ignore this so he gives up and says nothing more.

I finish my tart and, while rolling a cigarette, I say to him, "Right, I'm ready to get the fuck out of here."

"Okay, I'll get the bill. This one's on me. You get the next one," he says.

"Next one?" I question him; is he deluded? "You're actually funny sometimes," I say, laughing at the idea of ever doing this again.

"There she is. You're so beautiful when you smile," he says.

I shake my head in disbelief.

I leave him to pay the bill and walk out to smoke my cigarette. I sit on the bench outside the restaurant and light up. Luca comes to join me.

"Look at me," he says with his stern voice, the one he uses in sex, and the one I find completely intoxicating. I don't think, I just turn to face him.

"I love the way you look up at me," he says.

"We're not having sex tonight," I say.

"Of course we are. I'm going to eat you in the Uber home." A pang of desire hits me. For fuck's sake.

I follow him and leave behind my dignity.

On the Uber ride home, he holds on to my neck and speaks frankly. "I'm sorry, yeah. I won't speak about other women. I didn't think it would upset you. You know I care about you," he says.

"Yeah, I'm fine," I say. I'm not. I feel lonely. Going home alone right now would be worse than staying with him. It would mean me sitting in my bed, dressed up, looking at myself in the mirror and admitting how little respect I have shown myself for the past four months. I've heard the lesson but am not ready to learn it. I can't be bothered to consider what's best for me. I still don't know, should I have not left my first restaurant? Or decided to be a chef in the first place? Should I have stayed in Cornwall? Should I have stayed with Kit? How are we supposed to know any of these things? I dream up ways that could make this night worthwhile; I've come too far, I don't want to give up on him. That's how my mind works; in my first restaurant I wanted to leave but I couldn't until it got bad enough. I tell myself I need to spend substantial time in the shit before I am allowed to leave. I mistake self-destruction for noble suffering, and pride for power. I'm too tired after the dinner; I want to stay in my bubble of denial for a bit longer, where it's warm and not so lonely.

He keeps his hand firmly on me as the Uber pulls up outside his house.

"You coming?" he says, as he edges to the door to step out of the car. I look up at him with big, sad eyes. For a split second I imagine how empowering it would be to say no, drive away, and never see him again. But I know I'm not doing that, and so does he.

I follow him up the stairs and head straight to his bedroom. The sex is intense, probably the most intense it's ever been with him. He's angry with me for seeing him for exactly who he is, and I'm angry with him for not seeing me for who I am. I am better than him and I know it. He is rough with me, pinning my arms back and telling me bad things about myself. He disregards my pleasure at all times. He cums and I don't.

"You know women are supposed to cum too?" I say. My chest hurts and a lump arises in my throat. This man has never prioritized anything or anyone above his own pleasure.

"Heyyy," he says.

I roll my body over, turning away from him, and he spoons me. His hug feels nice on the surface of my skin, warm and sensitive, but beneath my skin, I am hollow. Tears slip down my cheek and soak the pillow beneath my face.

I think about Ruby and how I should've seen her, how that would've been the better thing to do.

I should've spoken to her about her nine-to-five job and her boyfriend, and I should've taken notes on how she does it. She's probably in bed with her boyfriend right now, and they're probably wearing pajamas and lying facing one another, talking about nothing and giggling about how they're turning into a married couple.

I want her life, where she surrounds herself with good people, where she wakes up when it's light and goes to bed when it's dark; where people don't touch her arse at work and she doesn't get burn marks across her arms from opening an industrial-sized oven fifty times a day.

There are things I like about working in a kitchen and there are things I like about spending time with Luca, but I don't know if I am cut out for either. In the kitchen I love learning and I love service; I love the camaraderie and I love feeling like my job is worthwhile. Around Luca, I love how he is unafraid of being authentic, even if his authentic self is a cunt. I love how he has worked solidly at something he is passionate about for so long, even if he's not where he wanted to be when he came to London. I love his commitment to cooking; it almost impresses me how he puts it above all else, even the people in his life, his friends and family. But both these things, the kitchen and Luca, have taken over my life. I'm tired from work and I miss my family and friends; I miss myself.

I need to leave this house.

I remove his hand from my waist and start climbing out of his bed slowly; he's half asleep and I don't want to wake him. I gather my things and catch myself in his mirror, I look like I haven't smiled in months.

"Where are you going? Just sleep here, it's so late." He makes a limp attempt to get me to stay and then when I tell him I am leaving he says to me, "Be good."

I leave his house and walk to the pub we met at earlier, where my lovely chivalrous bike is parked. It will take me where I want to go: home. I unlock it and get on, I have no headphones but my mind is filled with too much melancholy to hear any music. On the saddle, I feel sensitive and sore from the sex. I cycle through my town in the pitch-black and the freezing cold with my tights in my hand and my face wet with tears.

I shower him off me as soon as I get home and decide that was the last time. I get into bed and think about work tomorrow. I wonder if cooking will make me feel better; it hasn't made all that much difference recently. I used to feel safe in my baggy chef whites and my trousers; it was a costume that made me feel strong. But something has changed. I know now that I *can* deal with the job and I can deal with these men, but do I want to? When I quit my old office job and fled to the world of hospitality, I thought it would solve things and fix my feelings of discontentment; and it did for a while, but I'm bored again, and I've found new reasons why life still doesn't feel right.

I get to sleep at 2:52 a.m. and wake up three hours and eight minutes later to go to work.

12

TART

AUGUST

"So how long have you been on them?" Ruby asks me. She is sitting with a martini in one hand and a Marlboro Gold in the other; the London skyline is her backdrop. The ugly Walkie Talkie building is eavesdropping on our conversation and the August sunshine is beaming down on our bare legs.

"I don't know, I started taking them the week after I quit the restaurant at the end of July, so about a month," I say.

"Oh, that's fine, I'm sure it will come back. You're probably just adjusting," she says.

"Are you sure? I feel absolutely nothing; no desire for anyone or anything," I say.

"It just takes a bit of time. I remember I didn't want to have sex with James for like a month after I started taking antidepressants. I didn't want to masturbate either." That reassures me; Ruby is the queen of sex, so if she can get past the broken vagina then so can I.

"Don't you hate the word 'masturbate'? I looked it up the other day. It comes from the Latin word *manus*, which means hand, and the word *turbare*, which is to disturb, so then came the word *masturbare*. How unpleasant," I say.

"I'm so glad you now have the time on your hands to indulge in etymology," she says.

It is so nice to be with my old friend. And I welcome her gentle piss-taking, after she welcomed me back with open arms. Friendship, once again, has got me through another heartache. I learned that lesson, after seeing Luca for the last time. I learned a lot of things.

I ponder my new life for a moment, how in just a few weeks out of the kitchen my life is so different, the days are so spacious and slow.

"I don't research loads of words, just the ones I don't like, like 'masturbate,'" I say.

"So, what would you prefer I say?" Ruby asks.

"I don't know. Not 'wank'; I feel like that's been tainted by penises. When I use that word I feel like a teenage boy hiding soggy socks from my mum," I say.

"Yeah, there aren't really any good terms for woman-wanking," she says reflectively.

"Hang on. Let me google it," I say.

I get my phone and type into Google, reading the results out loud to Ruby.

"Sophisticated words for vagina wanking." I scroll down the page. "*Ménage à moi*?" I say.

"A bit too French," she says.

"Okay, buttering your muffin?" I ask her.

"A bit too English," she says and I laugh.

"Playing the piano? I quite like that, it's subtle," I say.

"Yeah, classy."

"Engaging in safe sex? Hah."

"Nice but a bit clunky, and too political."

"Making soup? Softening your peach? Poaching your egg?" I say, thinking of cooking.

"Hmm, softening your peach is quite chic," she says, stubbing out her cigarette and taking a sip of her martini.

"Okay. I think I've got it. How about polishing your jewel?" I ask.

"Oh yes, incredibly regal, incredibly sophisticated. Let's use that."

"So when did you last polish your jewel?" I say.

"Yesterday James called me from his work trip and we wanked on FaceTime. Sorry, we polished our jewels on FaceTime," she says.

I feel jealous that she has someone to polish with. Luca and I are over. I ended things the day after our dinner at Fava. I say "ended things," but really, I just never spoke to him again. He didn't make a single attempt to reach out, proving I was never anything important to him. And I'm not sure if he was actually all that important to me. He just gave me a thrill. Our sex was wild, and it felt good sleeping with another chef when I was in that world. It's like when you're a kid and you go on an all-inclusive holiday and you start fancying a boy from another family. It feels more exciting because you are trapped in this space, sharing the same experiences.

I fell into a depression. I stopped enjoying work, stopped laughing with Finn and George, and stopped showing up to my shift on time. The dread came back. The things that used to ground me no longer worked. I had learned so much, and worked with great people, but it still wasn't enough to make me stay. I handed in my notice and left in the last week of July. I didn't want to put anything on my parents at that point; I felt like they'd had their fair share, so I spoke to Ruby and she encouraged me to make an appointment with a psychiatrist. I went and they gave me medication, and I reluctantly started taking it. I feel better now; I probably should've given meds a go before quitting, because I'm starting to miss it again. But a bit of me misses all my restaurants—like they are my bastard exes, and now that I have gone beyond the point of upset, I just long to relive some of the memories for sentiment's sake.

The chefs gave me a good send-off and I told them I was going to work at a restaurant closer to my flat, but it's been three weeks and I haven't got a new job.

"What about you? When did you last polish your jewel?" Ruby asks me.

"Not since the meds," I say defeatedly.

"Alright, well give it another month and see how you feel. Talk to your doctor before stopping them, yeah?" she says, in her motherly way. "You do feel a bit better though, right?" she asks.

"Yeah, I do, definitely. I mean a few weeks ago I couldn't get out of bed, or shower, or speak. So yes, things have improved, I suppose," I say. "But they have messed up my appetite, so I'm not really enjoying food either."

"For fuck's sake," Ruby says, in sympathy. I'm trying not to be too self-pitying and tedious, but I know Ruby will never judge me; she allows me to indulge in all problems, no matter how self-involved they are.

"It's like fucking *Sophie's Choice*," I say. "Be depressed but have good sex and good food, or be happy and have shit sex and shit food." I continue my rant while lighting a cigarette. "It's the two best things in the world: food and sex."

"It won't be like that forever. At least we always have cigarettes," Ruby says.

"Until we quit next year, right? We have said that for too many years, we need to stick to it," I say.

"I know, it's rolling around fucking fast though. Time is going too quick." We both look out into the distance, mournfully imagining a life with no blems.

Ruby and I are sitting on the rooftop of Soho House, the one at 180 Strand.

It's nauseating. The whole idea of Soho House is grotesque. Most of the members are self-important toffs who think they're better than everyone else. Soho House has this phony criteria where supposedly they only let in creatives, yet all I can see around me is a bunch of bankers. At least the old, established member clubs aren't in denial of who they are; they are proud to cater to middle-aged white blokes with sausage-fingers and gout. You know what to expect at those clubs; perhaps a nonconsensual grope here and there, a subtle yet substantial racist remark, a laugh that turns into a chesty cigar-cough. But Soho House is different. It's tense; everyone, in equal parts, totally loves themselves and totally hates themselves. They are conflicted. It's interesting to watch, and I have a morbid curiosity that's like not being able to look away from a car crash on the M4, but I am now left in a state of anticlimax, like when you're driving past Stonehenge: What the fuck's all the fuss about?

I am looking to see who is sitting in our vicinity but, Ruby tells me, there's no need! There is an app which allows you to see who has signed in to the club. We glance around, giddy like we're playing a game. I spy with my little eye something beginning with C. Give me a clue? It ends in T. Despite the space reeking of entitlement and Paco Rabanne perfume, I'm having a fucking excellent time if I'm honest. Sue me. On this sunny day, with my oldest friend, who is a reluctant member, I am drinking a martini on a rooftop in the middle of the day like a true lady of leisure. I am gracefully holding my cocktail while sitting in the sun and gazing down on the laymen on the streets below; perhaps I should chuck some of the eight quid peanuts down to them; maybe then I'll feel less elitist. I get it—I get why people are here: it's a comfortable place to hide, to pretend to be someone you're not.

I am cosplaying as a cosmopolitan woman-about-town. I am leaning into my new life as a woman who was once a chef but now is a, um, I don't know, actually. I'll come back to you on that one.

My old days of sweaty tits, tarte Tatins, and tin-opening tomfoolery are gone! I am a former kitchen scallywag, a gastro-gremlin coming back to haunt the civilians. I had a membership to the underbelly of society, but it expired; now I'm back in the land of the civilized, where the sun going down means it's time for bed. And what's more shocking, I am dating a normal man. It's Declan, the tall copywriter with delicate hands from my old office job. Ruby was as shocked as I was at first, but she's used to it now. She loved the stories of the old days when we used to fuck, so I know she looks forward to the updates.

Only there is one small issue: he won't fuck me.

"How's it going with Declan? Have you had sex yet?" Ruby asks.

"No! We haven't! And it's not because of my broken vagina, it's him! I don't think he wants to have sex with *me*," I say. "It's so boring. Dating with no sex. What's the point?" I am frustrated by the slow pace of my new life.

When Declan and I first dated, before I worked in kitchens, we slept together with regularity, and with a great level of satisfaction. It was heated and forbidden; he was senior and I was basically an intern. It went on for a year; he was the man who introduced me to good sex and *agedashi* tofu. We hadn't made contact in five years, but in July, just before I quit my kitchen, I bumped into him on a yummy-mummy high street. He had a Planet Organic bag full of avocados like a healthy pervert, and I had a Kitchen Provisions bag with a new knife inside like a professional chef, or a rich murderer. We went for a drink to catch up, and the rest is history; quite nice, yet very uneventful, sexless, history.

"We used to be crazy," I continue. "To this day, it was the best sex of my life. I don't understand," I tell Ruby.

"Well, at least your minge is out of action, so it doesn't really matter," she says, trying to make me feel better.

"True. I'm seeing him tonight for dinner, so let's see if we finally fuck," I say.

"Exciting. Where are you going?" she asks.

"This new opening called Maldon. I think it's a wine bar with snacks instead of a proper restaurant," I say.

"Just a thought—maybe he likes you?" Ruby says. "Maybe he is taking this seriously?"

"Nah, surely not," I say. "It was only ever sex with us."

Ruby and I met in the early afternoon but it's already 6 p.m. We can chat for days, almost enough to warrant producing a podcast; alas, the market is already saturated with far too many middle-class white girls talking about their sex lives as if it's wildly controversial. But the best thing about being out of a professional kitchen is getting to spend time with friends again, especially her.

I don't know if I will go back. I'm putting off thinking about it. I'm hiding from the answer because I worry it won't be the answer I want. So for now, I'm living someone else's life, a person with means and manicured hands, a temporary life of luxury. I feel guilty swanning about London when I know my chefs are on the other side of town, working their arses off, especially on nice evenings like tonight.

I have left the poor sods in the gutter while I'm up here, looking at the Z-list stars. Tonight I am not rushing toward service, doing a thorough clean-down, and drinking post-shift beers; I'm not working hard like Raquel, or making mistakes like Jayden, or doing another chef proud like Maggie did me proud. Instead I am having a fancy drink in a fancy place; I will then go to a fancy restaurant and eat fancy food with a fancy man who won't fuck me. Fancy that.

Don't get me wrong—it's nice, but it feels a little unjust; like I was supposed to be running a marathon but instead of doing the full thing with my peers, I've decided to cheat my way to the finish line. If you spend half of your day yanking heads off dead birds, cleaning fish guts off your fingers, and cooking for other people, then you, for certain, have earned your plate of steaming hot madeleines straight out the oven at St. JOHN; but me, I'm not sure.

But I take one look at darling Ruby and realize she is not worrying like I am, she's just enjoying her damn drink. I mute my thoughts, and the meds help with that, along with the martinis.

"Want another?" Ruby asks me.

"Yeah, fuck it. One more," I say.

We continue to drink our martinis and soon we are slurring our words and speaking about unladylike things too loudly.

"I've just had an idea for how we can fix your broken vagina," Ruby says.

"Oh yeah?" I say. I'm optimistic, hoping for a better future for me, and all of mankind.

"The Womanizer," she says.

"What the fuck is the Womanizer?" I ask, a little scared, envisioning some sort of invasive vaginal surgery.

"It's this vibrator which is, like, scientifically proven to make you cum," Ruby says.

"Why is it called the Womanizer? Is it going to cheat on me? Is it going to go and gyrate on Raquel when I'm at Morrisons?" I ask. Ruby giggles.

"No, but seriously, it has this crazy new technology which has like a vacuum inside which you just hold over your clit," Ruby says.

"Sounds a bit fucking industrial. I quite enjoy the old-fashioned, labor-intensive experience of a cheap midrange vibrator," I say.

"Yeah, but you clearly need something new to kick-start your libido," Ruby says.

When I hear the word "libido," I feel like a divorced sixty-year-old man.

I take a large sip of my cocktail and say, "Okay, fuck it, I'm going to buy it now." We squeal like we're in Sex Education class in secondary school. But we're two women drinking martinis on the roof of Soho House.

I bring up the Womanizer website on my phone. Ruby has scooted closer to me and is looking down at my screen; my eyes widen.

"Eighty fucking quid? Are you taking the piss?" I say to her, outraged.

"It's *seriously* advanced technology," Ruby says, "and the design is very chic, like I almost want to take mine out with me as an accessory."

"Fucking hell. You'll have to get the next round, then. I'm spending five rounds on the Womanizer," I say.

I click Purchase and seconds later my banking app shames me: "Was that you? Buying this filthy piece of equipment, you total utter slag?" I click "Yes, it was me."

"Shit, actually I don't think I can have another round. I'm late. I have to go meet Declan." I'm a bit drunk but oh well. I'm sure the lack of sexual tension will sober me up.

I pack up my things and hug her goodbye.

"It was so nice to hang out," Ruby says. "Let me know how it goes with Declan. You look fucking great!"

I walk away quickly through the members' lounge. I don't feel like I look great. Being out of the kitchen has made me plain; my hair falls flat and limp because there isn't a constant onslaught of hot oil and sweat keeping it curly and full of character. I've lost the hunger in my stomach and the flutter in my fanny because of my new meds. I feel a bit like a blank sheet of paper from my diary, unmarked and without a story.

I rent a bike and while I'm cycling through town I send Declan a text.

Running fifteen minutes late. Sorry!! We're meeting at the pub opposite first, right?

He replies in moments.

Yeah. All good. See you in a bit.
A characteristically subdued text from my new old lover. Declan feels no need to use excessive emotion or exclamation in digital communications; that would be superfluous. I also check my banking app on my phone. Fuck, the Womanizer has sent me into my overdraft, fuckity fuck. Oh well, that's a problem for tomorrow. Rent's not due for two days; I still have time to win the lottery.

Soon I arrive at the pub where Declan is waiting for me at a picnic bench in the sun. His pale Irish skin is turning pink.
    I got hot as I cycled so I took off my jacket and now it's all tangled with my bag. Declan watches me manically rearrange myself and he laughs; he likes watching my messy existence. I think he likes it because he's so ordered, so contained. I sometimes wonder if it's weird, though, the way he encourages me to be myself. It's like I'm a mildly interesting animal and he is David Attenborough, observing my activity with real intrigue and an optimistic narration. Like now:
    "And here she is!" he says and I gleam. I do feel excited when I see him, because we do have fun and well, because he's damn handsome. But it's not like it was with Kit or Luca, or even Topknot Barman. Is that because they work in hospitality? Am I one of those weird people who are fiends for people who work in specific industries, like the women who use the websites that help them find a "man in uniform"? Is that still around? I hope so.
    He is the only man I have dated that all my friends, across the whole board, have confirmed they would not be opposed to fucking.

His skin may be pink, but his freckles are out on display, crowded around his sharp cheekbones.

He has a big sturdy nose, but in a hot French way, not an old-man way; the poor bastards' noses grow an inch bigger with every mile they crawl closer to death. He looks the same as he did when we worked together all those years ago, but I look older, less fresh-faced, and a little wounded.

Declan stands up to hug me. "How are you?" he says. He's always nervous when he first sees me. I don't understand why. We've known each other for five years, and in the old days we were permanently naked. Now things are formal, for some reason.

"Yeah, all good, sorry I'm late!" I say.

He tells me not to worry. He is cordial and polite; he is a gentleman. He has ordered us pints.

"So have you heard good things about this place?" I ask, doubting his restaurant intuition.

"Yeah. It's just opened," he says.

Once, we couldn't keep our hands off each other. I wonder if our passion was reliant on the power dynamic, the age gap, the pornographic tale of the photocopied arse. It was hot; the hottest sex I've ever had. Hotter than Kit. Hotter than Luca, even.

But the power dynamic has shifted. I have worked on my hands and knees. I know who I am as a woman, or more than I did. Now we are more like equals; he no longer finds me as helpless and endearing like a bird learning to fly; now he is impressed by me. It is a nice feeling, but for some reason, it doesn't translate well to my knickers. I wonder if he feels the same. I think he doesn't know how to seduce me anymore.

Declan and I finish our pints, walk across the road, and enter the wine bar. I can sense he's a little nervous because he chose the place and he knows I'm more judgmental than most. Declan is very into food, you might even call him a "foodie," if you can stomach using that God-awful word. I like eating out with him because I know more about food than he does, unlike my past chef dalliances. He asks me questions about the dishes, and their preparation, and listens to what I have to say.

This restaurant is beautiful, with a tall ceiling and great big beams that stretch from one end of it to the other. They're like his shoulders, clean and architecturally sound, a bit *too* smooth even. The General Manager is a professional; she takes our coats and leads us to a shit table. She knows it's a shit table and I know she is a professional because she flashes us a sympathetic smile before she asks, "Is this okay?" Does she know that I know? Does she know I was formerly in her world? Can you tell? Probably not.

I am about to say yes, it is okay. Because I don't want to cause a fuss; after working in restaurants I like to be as low-maintenance as possible, to give the staff an easy ride and make sure my table is an enjoyable one to serve, instead of a ball-ache. Declan, on the other hand—a man who works with computers and, again, has soft hands—has no problem with assertively asking the server, "Do you have any nicer tables?" albeit politely.

I'm embarrassed and I feel I have betrayed them all, all the chefs, the bartenders, the KPs, the barbacks, the front-of-house staff, and the wine girls. But I also like the idea of him wanting me to have a nicer table and asking for it. His authority reminds me of our old power dynamic, the one that *did* translate well to my pants.

"You might need to wait fifteen minutes. Is that okay?" she asks us with a smile so wide I worry her face might ache after her shift.

"Yes, of course. Thank you so much!" I say in a desperate plea to make her like me.

She leads us to the bar, where we sit on tall stools but they don't hurt my body to sit on, like they would have before, because I haven't been chopping all day. I look at the menu. I wonder if Declan will have wine or a cocktail. I love it when someone orders a cocktail; it gives you the go-ahead to order one too. You can't be the only one spending fifteen quid on a flamboyant little thing, nor the only one getting rat-arsed. And cocktails signal something; that this is more than dinner, this is a banquet, a quest to chase all forms of passion and pleasure and it starts before we are even seated at our table. Hopefully the passion will translate to my knickers.

"So, how are you feeling, being out of the kitchen? Do you miss it yet?" he asks me.

"Weird," I say, not expanding any further. I don't want to speak about the kitchen with Declan, it brings up all these dense feelings.

"Will you go back?" Clearly he did not get the memo.

"I'm not sure. What are you going to have to drink?" I ask in an attempt to change the conversation and get this man off my arse, ironically.

"I think a Manhattan." A cocktail. Excellent. I'll have a martini, then.

It's less than fifteen minutes before we are seated at our table, which is seemingly one of the best. It's a bloody booth! Oh, how a booth brings me joy. It's like we've been given an upgrade on a deluxe cruise and now we have a better view of the happenings below deck: the kitchen, the staff, the customers. I'm secretly glad Declan asked, even though I still never would.

I look through the menu while he asks me questions about the dishes. They are more like snacks than proper plates, so I won't be stuffed at the end of the meal like I might've been when eating with another chef. I remind myself how much I like this bit, the fact that he is happy to accept that I know more about something than he does. "I think we should order vitello tonnato," I say. I'm not even thinking about Luca and how I didn't touch a menu when we ate together, or how Kit and I would glance at the menu only in between hand-holding. Here, I am the boss of the menu.

"I've never had that before," he says, sounding a little more Irish the more he drinks.

"I'm excited for you to try it," I say. I order this among other delights. Declan orders wine. We sit and wait while my desire for food and fornication brews. I do fancy him, but the feelings are mild; I hope they will grow. There is no heated disdain, like there was with Luca, and no warmth from thighs touching underneath the table, like there was with Kit. Nonetheless, I'm in it to win it. I'm ready for the whole shebang: the wine, the food, and then the sex. There are only a few other things on the menu, and they're all predictable. I order the lot. Bread and butter, *panzanella* salad, oysters, cured meats, et cetera. Yawn.

When the vitello tonnato arrives, Declan asks me to tell him about it.

"Well, this isn't plated how I used to plate it; it's not meant to be rolled up like a spliff," I say, starting to feel a little cocky from the cocktail and the expensive wine he then ordered.

He laughs. "Go on."

"You are supposed to sprawl thin slices of veal across the plate, and then spread the tonnato, which is basically mayonnaise made with tuna, over the top like a blanket," I explain.

We take a bite. It's delicious, and I take great pleasure in seeing him enjoy something for the first time. He isn't cocky like Luca, or smart like Kit; he is a simple, nice man.

More food comes. Next up, we have cured meats and oysters.

"I think oysters would be my death-row meal," he says. How original, I think. When did I become such a cunt?

"Yeah, nice. They're an aphrodisiac. I don't know if I've ever experienced an aphrodisiac working?" I ask. I want to get him to talk about sex so I can decipher his thoughts on the situation with us. Maybe he's become a celibate, albeit wine-drinking, monk and I just didn't know.

"Well, let's see, shall we?" Nice, Declan. Don't feel afraid to go bigger and bolder, I think.

I want him the way he used to be; when he'd touch me as soon as he could, as soon as there was a break in conversation. I want him to lie me down and stare at my body like it was the finest piece of copywriting he ever worked on. He introduced me to good sex with adult men, showed me what it was to savor someone else's soul, to eat up every inch of them, to leave no crumb untouched, so he will forever hold a place in my pussy.

A panzanella salad arrives at our table. I take the chunks of crusty sourdough and swipe them across the plate; I want to soak up all the juice—the anchovy, lemon zest, and basil-flavored oil. He follows suit.

The food keeps coming, he keeps asking me questions, and I'm a little bored, I must admit. I've got an idea for you, matey: Why don't you ask me what color my pants are? Or which of all the times we had sex was my favorite? You know, the important questions.

"So when are you going to make me that tart?" he says, referring back to a tart I told him about a few weeks ago, the first time we met up. He has a sweet tooth; perhaps I am not sweet enough for him, I think. Is that why he doesn't stare at my lips like he used to?

"Haha, I'm not sure," I say. Maybe when you fuck me?

"You have been putting it off for too long," he says. Likewise, I think.

I am bored of waiting. I just want it now. I need to test if my vagina is broken.

"How about tomorrow?" I ask. I go out on a limb because perhaps I have to book the sex in, like a table at the Ritz. "We can have a nice Sunday afternoon tea at mine. I will make the tart and you can make the tea, yes?" I hope he understands that by "make tea," I mean fuck me. He is a writer, after all. He should understand subtext.

But Declan doesn't, and he circles back to our earlier conversation about my old job.

"So why did you leave?" he asks.

"Because!" I say obtusely, like a teenager.

"Because what?" he asks.

I sigh. I'm a little drunk, thus more in touch with my emotions, so I tell him.

"Because I couldn't do it," I say. For fuck's sake! I don't want to think about this now. I am so very bored of thinking about my failures. My chef career clearly didn't work out for a reason, the same way it didn't work out with those guys: Luca, because he was an astronomical cunt; Topknot Barman, because he had weird hair; and Kit, because he was someone else's.

I'm tired of thinking about things. If it's going to work with Declan, he needs to allow me to ignore all the thoughts in my head. And he needs to want to fuck me.

"What? Of course you could. You did," he says, knowing fuck all about working in a kitchen.

"No. I couldn't. I'm just not cut out to be a chef."

"But you seemed to love it," he says.

"It's too many hours. I want to do normal things. I don't want my job to be my whole life. It's too hard, too tiring. I just can't do it," I say, listing all the clichéd reasons in one so he can't ask anything more.

And he can't argue with me, because I'm being honest. That is how I feel.

I loved my job, and I miss it, but it's too hard.

And that's when, finally, he stops asking.

Outside the restaurant, we kiss. We always do. At least there's that. He does all the romantic stuff, the dilly-dallying about with my hair, the holding of my hand, the "you're this and that." Blahdy blah. It is nice and it makes me feel good, and that's when my jewel starts to sparkle. She's got life in her yet! But I know he will call it quits in a second, and he does. He pulls away from my lips and takes out his phone to book an Uber. For a moment I think he might book it for both of us, but then he asks my address so he can add a separate drop off.

My heart sinks. Jesus Christ. I am bored of this. It is not that I am solely focused on sex, it's not even the act of fornication that I crave; it's the moments of intimacy that surround sex, the moments of hot humid space between two bodies that I long for. There is only so much intimacy you can achieve when your street-snogging is interrupted by a *Big Issue* guy selling his last copy of the night.

"Not tonight, man. Sorry," Declan says to him. Why not tonight? Why not give the poor bastard what he wants, and me too while you're at it?

The Uber ride is short. We kiss once more before he exits the car and then I sit in silence as the driver drops me off at my lustless flat. Declan probably had a great time. Yeah, I had a great time too, I suppose, but who reaches for *great* when you could have transcendent?

When I get home, alone, I lie on top of my bed, fully clothed. Dissatisfaction hovers over my sheets. I wanted to experience something tonight; I wanted an infusion of feeling. I have been absent of real feeling since leaving the kitchen, sweet fuck-all going on in my head. Maybe that means the meds are working.

He texts me ten minutes later: *Such a nice evening. See you tomorrow for the tart, can't wait to finally try it.*

Interesting. Maybe this whole thing was foreplay and

I was just being impatient. But I'm not sure; does anyone wait that long for sex in this day and age?

The next day, I wake up after a long and undisturbed sleep; no man stole my covers or reached for my waist in the middle of the night. I cycle to the shop. I have no ingredients in my house. I haven't cooked in a while. I buy flour, and sugar, and butter, and cream, and vanilla, and strawberries, and milk, and cornstarch, and eggs.

I get home and raid my cupboard. I have no access to fancy professional equipment anymore; no Thermomix, no Vitamix, no Magimix. The only things of use I find are a set of scales and a big bowl.

I'm going to have to make the pastry in the way I was taught at cooking school, where they liked teaching us how to make things the traditional way, like we were small Victorian chambermaids, just in case we ever did find ourselves in that situation. Alas, here I am, in that very situation: begone, my slandering of cooking school! Here I am, in my quarters, cooking a tart for my master, in the hope that he will give me a grope in return.

I weigh the flour into a bowl, then I add small chunks of butter. I get two knives from my cutlery drawer and start carving away at the chunks to incorporate the butter uniformly into the flour; I chop in a swinging motion, like a pair of scissors, moving swiftly and with a light hand so as to not melt the butter. Every now and again, I shake the bowl so the larger lumps of butter rise to the surface, and then I attack those too.

About five minutes into the process, the butter lumps are still uneven, and I think: This is ridiculous, fuck this. So I go looking for something to assist me and my limp wrists. Ah! A hand blender is buried at the bottom of the kitchen cupboard, hidden among old batteries, useless plastic, and other shit. I start blitzing the dough and it comes together quickly. The powered blades are more aggressive with the ingredients than I would like, but they do the job. I use my hands to bring the pastry together into a cylinder, wrap it in cling film, and put it in the fridge to rest.

I lie on my bed. My brain tells me nothing because the meds are working. In the past, I would have been thinking about what I had to do on my section when I got to work that afternoon. Or I would think about a guy and how I can make him fall in love with me. Or I would think about how I should move the bed around so it faces the window. Or I would think about how the fat on my stomach is softer than the fat on my thighs. I would think about anything and everything.

I suppose this not-thinking feels relaxing, but I don't know if I could live like this forever.

I return to the kitchen and take the cylinder of pastry from the fridge, it's cold enough that the butter won't melt when I roll it; that'll do. I get an empty wine bottle from the recycling box, wash it off, and dry it; this will be my rolling pin. It works well. Soon I have a flat, round circle, which I roll onto the wine bottle and then lift above a small tart tin I bought from a charity shop, big enough for one person, maybe two. I remember I wanted to practice pastry on the weekends when I first started at my new restaurant. What a nerd. What an aspiring young woman. What an inspiration. Where did she go?

I wedge the pastry into each of the tin's ridges. It behaves; it's a pretty and perfect little thing. I put a sheet of crinkled-up pre-used baking parchment on top of the pastry case and pour a bagful of rice on top to weigh it down. In the oven it goes, to blind bake.

As I clean up, I notice my body moves about the kitchen in a way it never did before working as a chef. My hands are firm, efficient, and quick. I just do things better.

The pastry starts to smell. That, I learned, is my signal to check if it's done. I got to a point where I would smell first and the timer would go off within the minute, my nose proving my cooking capabilities. I take the pastry out of the oven and carefully remove the parchment, bringing the edges together to collect the rice, moving slowly so that no grains slip out over the edge. Now the tart is naked and I can see she is no longer perfect; she has a few lumps and bumps, a few cracks, but overall, she has good character. I like the tart. I feel like I know her on a personal level.

I whisk up some eggs with a fork. Fuck. I don't have a pastry brush.

I run to my room, covered in flour, and with manic focus and erratic ideas, I prod my way through my makeup drawer. I find an old bronzer brush. This will do. I wash it thoroughly in the kitchen sink, squeezing out years' worth of the shitty makeup I wore on the best nights. I shake the sodden bronzer brush out the window, spraying drops of water all over the place. I dip the brush into the egg, and then stroke big, confident swipes across the pastry; the egg firms up as soon as I paint it onto its hot canvas, leaving behind shiny golden contours within the ridges, just like my bronzed cheekbones on a night out.

I place the tart back in the oven for five minutes and make the crème pât.

I wonder what will happen with Declan—is he coming for the sex or the tart? Perhaps he doesn't want to fuck me and he just wants a slice of damn tart. Maybe he doesn't want to fuck me because I'm no longer me; I am no longer the young woman bouncing about the office, lapping up the chaos that comes with making impulsive decisions. But surely that's better, because of all the learning, and the growing and self-discovery, and the tiresome wellness words. I'm supposed to be growing up and taking care of myself, aren't I?

Using my small saucepan to infuse the milk with vanilla feels funny; at work we had massive pans, and we'd make massive batches of everything. I feel like I'm cooking for a Sylvanian Family. Once small bubbles appear on the edges of the milk, I take it off the heat. Then slowly I pour the milk into a bowl with the flour, cornstarch, and sugar, which I previously whisked up with the egg yolk until fluffy. It folds together perfectly; firm enough to hold but still with enough wobble to have a good time—just like my thighs, actually.

I take her out of the oven. Now my tart is golden, beautiful. It's time for me and her to have a break. I climb through my kitchen window onto the neighbor's roof, and I take the tart out there with me. I want her to cool down so I can add in the crème pât without it melting. I sit in my T-shirt and pants; my legs are bare. The tart and I are glowing in the sun but the breeze is blowing around us, cooling us down.

After five minutes, when both the tart and I are ready, we go back inside.

I take big dollops of crème pât and spread it across the pastry with the back of a spoon. Then I slice the strawberries with a little fruit knife. I want the tart to look neat. I want to be organized. I place the sliced strawberries with precision, creating a pretty pattern. Gone are the days of chaos and mess; let me and my tart enter a new era of order, of dignity.

I water down some strawberry jam and put it on the heat to loosen up a bit. The texture of a glaze is important; if it is too thick it might dislodge my strawberries or, worse, it might cover up the beauty of their pretty little faces. It's like how granny pants cover up the pussy, but a delicate lace can really enhance its beauty. I take the clean bronzer brush and paint my strawberry tart with delicacy, not wanting to upset my vision of what the tart should be.

Just as I am taking a moment to admire the end product—my perfect tart—the doorbell rings.

Who the fuck is that?

It can't be Declan. We agreed to midday, and it can't be Raquel because she's on a double shift. I pull on some pajama bottoms and race downstairs. I answer the door and a man hands me a small parcel.

"Parcel for Flat 4D," he says.

"Oh, thanks!" I take it from him with much curiosity.

I race upstairs and sit on my bed to open it up. What could it be? What a thrill! How the little things in life excite me now.

I rip open the cardboard box. Inside, there is another box, but this one is wrapped in pretty, cream-colored tissue paper and tied with a strawberry-colored ribbon.

But what is it?

I unwrap the ribbon and rip away the paper. Oh my God. On the box, shiny pink letters read: The Womanizer. I completely forgot that I had ordered it. I lift the lid of the box and there it is.

It's elegant and beautiful, just like Ruby said it would

be, and it fits perfectly in the palm of my hand, as if it was measured to size.

I sit there for a moment, perching on the corner of my bed, just looking down at this thing.

Well, it would be a shame to not give it a go. And there's no time like the present. Plus, it is of the utmost urgency that I fix my vagina—you know, for my mental health.

I lie back on my bed, scooch down my pajama bottoms, click the On button, and think of England.

The orgasm is like the good old days. My pussy is perfect; it's the men that are shit.

She does her job, this Womanizer; I enter a world of acceptance as I spread my legs and quiver. My head is not filled with fantasies of chefs, or copywriters; I think only of myself and my wonderful body that works just fine, my nice mind, and my excellent hair. I'm not a melting mess; I'm a stable, proud tart.

Whenever I lose the sense of who I am or what I should do, or I spin into disassociation or fall into a depression, I feel scared and worry that I'll never be happy again. But those feelings inevitably pass, and then I remember how lucky I am to be alive and to experience the pleasurable bits of being human. There are two things in my life that are a constant reminder that pleasure exists: food and sex.

And I am learning about the different forms they may come in.

With food: I could be cooking in a professional kitchen, or eating my mum's pesto pasta, or picking mussels with my dad, or making a tart in my kitchen. I could be cycling to get a *lahmacun* late at night, or getting the train to New

Malden for Korean food, or going to Andrew Edmunds for a romantic dinner. I know that if cooking and food exist I can never be too unhappy, because food is taste, touch, smell, sight, and joy. It brings me back to earth.

With sex: the possibilities could be more varied. Sex is more than the physical act. It is all that comes with it; meeting new people, experiencing new versions of myself, falling in love, and getting my heart broken. When sex brings heartbreak, it reminds me to cherish friends and family. Sex can be one night of madness, a long affair, an afternoon delight with the Womanizer, or a boring kiss with a man who is too nice for me. But either way, anyway, I know that if sex exists I can never be too unhappy, because sex is taste, touch, smell, sight, and joy. It brings me back to earth.

I put the Womanizer back to bed in her chic little case. My stomach rumbles. I walk to the kitchen in just my T-shirt. My phone lights up; it's a text from Declan.

How is my tart coming along?

I feel protective of my tart. This isn't his tart, it's mine. And I'm not his fucking chambermaid. Fuck this guy.

I lift the tart, bring it to my lips, and I bite down. I take another bite and another. My body is swimming in endorphins from the strawberries and the orgasm. I think about all my moments of thrill in life; eating an eyeball from a fish when I was eight, having sex under the sun with my first boyfriend, falling in love, realizing my heart is no longer broken. I remember my first orgasm and my first oyster. I remember my first trial shift and my last shift just a few weeks ago. I miss it: the shiny silver containers clanging against one another as you clean down, the glee on a KP's face when you bring them a secret slab of beef, the cigarette after service.

I polish off the tart and I'm nearly full, but there is still something missing. What next?

I don't want to have too little.

I still want *too much*.

I just want too much of the right thing. Is that too much to ask?

I'm not sure, exactly, but I suppose there is no harm in having a look. I unlock my phone and type into Google: *Chef jobs near me.*

ACKNOWLEDGMENTS

First I would like to thank my incredibly clever, profoundly sensitive, miraculously funny, and overly opinionated friend Bubbles. I wouldn't have pursued writing without your encouragement; thank you for your friendship, and all the hours you spent helping me edit both my words and my life choices.

Thank you to my male agent, Ben Clark, for reading my female sex stories with the perfect amount of bumbling awkwardness. Your kindness, patience, friendship, and sense of humor was everything I needed while writing my first book. Thank you to the rest of the team at Soho Agency, especially Sarah for your damn sweet ways.

Thank you to my fantastic editing duo, Grace Paul and Emily Graff. The book would be utter shite without your involvement. Thank you for holding my hand throughout it all, and for your endless supply of fundamental and brilliant advice. Thank you for your patience and understanding when I was being either too self-conscious or too self-righteous.

ACKNOWLEDGMENTS

Thank you to the rest of my team at Bloomsbury: Fabrice Wilmann, Ellen Williams, Isobel Turton, David Bond, and Shunayna Vaghela. And also to the Marysue Rucci Books team at Simon & Schuster, who took a leap of faith in publishing my book in the US. Thank you to Kat Toolan and Abby Koons at Park Fine for your support via Zoom. Oh, and to Luke Speed for thinking about this book beyond the realm of written words! That reminds me: thank you to Working Title for your enthusiasm over those first few chapters; that really put my arse in gear.

Thank you to Hayley at *British Vogue* for editing my columns and giving me the chicest job known to man.

Thank you to Lena for holding my hand and getting excited about my stories. Your involvement with my writing, and my life, is the greatest thing to ever happen to me. Your word is my gospel.

Thank you to Dolly and Marina for your wisdom and guidance.

Thank you to Doug for your ideas.

Thank you to Freddie for your opinions.

Thank you to Lizzy for your bacon sandwiches.

Thank you to all chefs; your secret society is the best in all the city.

Thank you to both the good and the bad restaurants and pubs in London: you are the perfect setting for both infatuation and heartbreak.

Thank you to my best friends.

Thank you to my cousins.

Thank you to my therapist.

Thank you to Anthony Bourdain and Jilly Cooper.

To my chef lover, thank you for your wildly excessive knowledge of food and cooking. Your being better at

ACKNOWLEDGMENTS

cooking than me was initially a massive mental hurdle for me to overcome, but I'm better at writing than you are, so put that in your pipe and smoke it. Thank you for loving me, supporting me, and caring for me, and doing all this while I was writing about having sex with other men.

And, finally, to my family: Thank you to my brother for always taking the piss out of me. You are the best comic relief in all our lives. There isn't much about you in the book because unfortunately it wouldn't pass the legal checks.

Thank you endlessly to my mum for teaching me that kindness is the single most important quality, and for being my most committed supporter. Thank you for the arduous hours—nay, days—of your life spent dealing with my swine-like ways. You are without a doubt the best mother.

And thank you above all to my greatest friend, my dad, who picks up the phone whenever I call and tells me to simply put one foot in front of the other.

ABOUT THE AUTHOR

Slutty Cheff writes anonymously about sex, food, and being a woman in the restaurant world. She first started writing on her @sluttycheff Instagram account, where she posted stories anonymously while cooking full-time in London restaurants. She now has her own column in *British Vogue*, and has also written for *The Sunday Times* and been interviewed by the *Financial Times*, *The Evening Standard*, and *Interview* magazine.

A NOTE ON THE TYPE

The text of this book is set in Linotype Sabon, a typeface named after the type founder, Jacques Sabon. It was designed by Jan Tschichold and jointly developed by Linotype, Monotype, and Stempel in response to a need for a typeface to be available in identical form for mechanical hot metal composition and hand composition using foundry type.

Tschichold based his design for Sabon roman on a font engraved by Garamond, and Sabon italic on a font by Granjon. It was first used in 1966 and has proved an enduring modern classic.